Appropriating
Gender

WITHDRAWN FROM
THE LIBRARY

UNIVERSITY OF
WINCHESTER

KA 0257813 1

Zones of Religion
Edited by Peter van der Veer

Also published in the series:

Border Fetishisms
Patricia Spyer

Conversion to Modernities
Peter van der Veer

Sponsored by the
JOINT COMMITTEE ON SOUTH ASIA
of the
SOCIAL SCIENCE RESEARCH COUNCIL
and the
AMERICAN COUNCIL OF LEARNED SOCIETIES

Appropriating
Gender

*Women's Activism
and Politicized Religion
in South Asia*

edited by
Patricia Jeffery
and Amrita Basu

ROUTLEDGE
New York and London

KING ALFRED'S COLLEGE
WINCHESTER

02578131   305.486
            JEF

Published in 1998 by
Routledge
29 West 35th Street
New York, NY 10001

Published in Great Britain by
Routledge
11 New Fetter Lane
London EC4P 4EE

Copyright © 1998 by Routledge

Printed in the United States of America on acid-free paper.

All rights reserved. No part of this book may be reprinted or reproduced or utilized in any form or by any electronic, mechanical, or other means, now known or hereafter invented, including photocopying and recording or in any information storage or retrieval system, without permission in writing from the publishers.

Papers presented at a conference held at the Rockefeller Center in Bellagio, Italy, August 30 to September 1, 1994, sponsored by the Joint Committee on South Asia of the Social Science Research Council and the American Council of Learned Societies

Library of Congress Cataloging-in-Publication Data

Appropriating gender: women's activism and politicized religion in South Asia /
    edited by Patricia Jeffery and Amrita Basu.
        p.   cm.
Includes bibliographical references and index.
ISBN 0–415–91865–0 (hardcover) — ISBN 0–415–91866–9 (pbk.).
1. Women—South Asia—Social conditions.   2. Women in politics—South Asia.
3. Women in religion—South Asia.   4. Religion and politics—South Asia.
5. Sex role—South Asia.   6. South Asia—Social policy.   7. South Asia—Politics and government.   I. Jeffery, Patricia, 1947–   .   II. Basu, Amrita, 1953–   .
HQ1726.A67 1997
305.42'0954—dc21   97–11336
    CIP

We dedicate this book to our children,
Laura and Kirin (PJ) and Ishan and Javed (AB).

Contents

Preface and Acknowledgments

This book was born of questions that the growth of religious nationalism in India raised about Hindu women's activism. At the center of the drama was the campaign of several organizations collectively known as the Hindu Right—the Rashtriya Swayamsevak Sangh (RSS), the Bharatiya Janata Party (BJP), and the Vishwa Hindu Parishad (VHP). They wanted to destroy a sixteenth-century mosque built by the Muslim emperor Babar (the Babari Masjid) in the town of Ayodhya in North India that they claimed had been built on the ruins of the Rām Janambhūmī, the birth place of the Hindu deity Rām. After an unsuccessful attempt in October 1990, they succeeded in destroying the Babari Masjid in December 1992. The intent and effect of this campaign was to polarize Hindus and Muslims at the polls and on the streets. Riots occurred in large parts of India between 1990–1993.

The Hindu nationalist campaign made extensive use of gendered imagery and actively mobilized Hindu women. Several women, including Uma Bharati, Vijayraje Scindia, and Sādhvī Rithambara, figured among the most militant leaders of the movement. Women also played a prominent role in demonstrations, election campaigns, and, most strikingly, in so-called riots, which were actually generally attacks by Hindus on the Muslim community. Indeed the very strata of middle- and lower-middle class women who had been subject to violence by their husbands and in-laws actively supported male-dominated movements directed against the minority population.

Both of us had studied diverse facets of women's social and political lives in contemporary India, but neither of us had encountered women's complicity in violence, let alone violence against minorities. We began to puzzle over a number of questions that subsequently figured in this volume. Why had feminist protests against "dowry deaths" drawn relatively few women into activism? Why had so many women organized to support the destruction of the Babari Masjid in Ayodhya? What bearing did women's class backgrounds, religious beliefs, and gender identities have on their activism? Did the forms of women's activism that we encountered in India have parallels in other parts of South Asia?

As we began to review the scholarly literature on women, religion, and politics, we found few answers to these questions. One body of literature provided an exegesis of theological texts and analysis of religious traditions, but did not tell us much about women's lived experience. The literature on religious laws devoted little attention to how women interpreted and sought to use legislation. Feminist scholarship tended to focus on women's struggles against gender inequality but to ignore the forms of women's activism that were embedded within movements of the religious right. The literature did not illuminate the fluid and changing nature of gender identities and the complicated ways in which women's activism both reinforced and challenged their traditional gender identities. Although there have been several important additions to the literature on South Asian women in the recent past, our contribution lies in the importance we accord to women's agency and activism from a multidisciplinary, comparative South Asian perspective.

This book originated under the auspices of the Joint Committee on South Asia of the Social Science Research Council (SSRC) and the American Council of Learned Societies. Our colleagues on the committee encouraged us to formulate a conference proposal on the themes of women's activism and politicized religion in South Asia. Support from the SSRC, the John D. and Catherine T. MacArthur Foundation, and the Rockefeller Foundation enabled us to organize a conference at the Rockefeller Center in Bellagio, Italy, held on August 30–September 1, 1994. The generous and gracious hospitality that we received there inspired much lively discussion over several days. Most of the papers in the volume were presented at this conference; Farida Shaheed and Shahnaz Rouse were unable to attend but subsequently submitted their papers. Shelley Feldman's paper was written after the conference especially for this volume.

Both of us received grants that supported our research and writing for this project. Amrita gratefully acknowledges support from the John D. and Catherine T. MacArthur Foundation and the Amherst College Research Award. Patricia is grateful to the Economic and Social Research Council (London), and the Overseas Development Administration and the University of Edinburgh.

Several people contributed greatly to the production of this book. At the SSRC, Toby Volkman and Itty Abraham helped us organize, fund, and conceptualize the project. At the Bellagio conference, we were fortunate to have Rachel Rosenbloom serve as rapporteur and Shelley Feldman and Radhika Balakrishnan as session convenors. David Ludden reviewed the manuscript and made some excellent suggestions.

In the final stages of compiling the manuscript, we received assistance from Katharine Charsley, Sonali Gulati, Eryn Starun, and above all from Roger Jeffery, who spent countless hours helping to check, collate, and edit the manuscript. We were also most fortunate in our editors at Routledge and at Kali, and we both thank them immensely for their patience and help with this enterprise. We are grateful as well to Mark and Roger for their support, encouragement, and enthusiasm for this project.

Patricia Jeffery
University of Edinburgh

Amrita Basu
Amherst College

Part I
Gender, Nation, State

Chapter One
Appropriating Gender

AMRITA BASU

I N THE PAST DECADE OR SO, religion and gender have become increasingly intertwined in the political turmoil that envelops South Asia. Religion has provided a vehicle through which the state has sought legitimacy, political parties have contested the state, and social movements have organized. The forces that are most committed to politicizing gender have treated women as the repositories of religious beliefs and the keepers of the purity and integrity of the community. Women have engaged in activism within and against "communal" politics.

Until quite recently, the scholarly literature tended to treat gender, religious, and community identities as static and unchanging. A preoccupation with religious doctrine, public policy, and legal processes supplanted an interest in lived experience. Reflecting colonial, Orientalist assumptions about the privileged place of religion and of women's piety, scholars ignored the ways in which states, parties, and women themselves strategically appropriated gender to achieve social change. In the process they ignored the complicated forms of women's agency that emerged from the interplay of gendered, class, and religious identities. Women were assumed to lack political consciousness entirely or in adequate measure. Such views have been challenged by numerous, varied instances of women's activism in religious politics. Consider the militant Hindu ideologues Uma Bharati and Sādhvī Rithambara in India, or the woman from the Liberation Tigers of Tamil Eelam (LTTE) Tamil separatist movement in Sri Lanka whose suicide bomb killed the then prime minister of India, Rajiv Gandhi. Or consider female heads of state like Benazir Bhutto of Pakistan and Khaleda Zia of Bangladesh, who both fortify and defy Islamic strictures on women's freedom. By exploring diverse forms of women's agency, we investigate how women construct individual selves and collective identities.

The relationship of women to politicized religion is paradoxical and complex. Religious politics has created opportunities for women's activism while simultaneously undermining women's autonomy. Contrary to the hopes of most feminists, women have not always opposed religious nationalist appeals; contrary to the hopes of religious nationalists, religious identities have not negated women's gender, caste, class, and regional identities; contrary to the appeals of nation-states, women have often dispelled the assumption that their primary identities are as self-sacrificing mothers and wives. To appreciate the complexities of women's gendered, religious, and community identities, *Appropriating Gender* engages in comparative analysis of women in leadership positions and of ordinary women, of the local against the national state, and of textual religious traditions against everyday practice. It analyzes episodic moments of upheaval, like the destruction of the Babari Masjid in Ayodhya on 6 December 1992, the place of religion in people's daily lives, and the implications for women of the "communalization" of routine state services.

The opportunity that this volume affords, of a comparative South Asian perspective, checks tendencies toward oversimplification. We are cautioned against generalizing about—say—"the Muslim woman," when her experiences are so diverse in India, Pakistan, and Bangladesh. Through comparative analysis, we seek to discern the varied meaning of gender identity and politics through time, by location, and according to political context. Although there have been some important additions to the scholarly literature on women, religion, and politics in India over the past few years (e.g., Hasan (ed.), 1994; Sarkar and Butalia (eds.), 1995), none of these works provides the comparative perspective of *Appropriating Gender*.

We are struck by how states, movements, and parties have fallen back on religious—and often gendered—appeals when their legitimacy has foundered. Yet we are also struck by differences in the strength of religious forces in India, Pakistan, Bangladesh, and Sri Lanka, the four South Asian nations that we explore in this volume. At one end of the continuum is Pakistan, where the relationship between religion and politics has been closest. Indeed, under the Zia ul Haq regime (1977–1988) the state was the prime proponent of Islamization. At the other end of the continuum is India, where the state in theory upholds secularism but has inadvertently strengthened religious nationalism. At intermediate points on the continuum are Bangladesh and Sri Lanka, where ethnic and religious definitions of national identities have competed, and movements like the Tablīghī Jama'at have generated community identities independent of the state.

The remainder of this chapter lays out the three central themes that run through the volume. First, it explores how gender constitutes a sphere of contestation involving women, the state, parties, and organizations that employ religious appeals. Second, it asks how our understandings of community and religious identities change when viewed from the vantage point of the everyday and the local. The third and most important theme running through the volume, to which we return in the concluding chapter, concerns the implications of women's agency for their emancipation and empowerment. If one objective of the volume is to provide a full, rich account of women's agency, another is to assess the disjunctions between women's agency and activism on the one hand and their emancipation on the other.

The Organization of the Volume

The chapters in this volume are arranged in three parts. The first "Gender, Nation, State," explores the ways in which the state and religious communities influence the construction of gendered identities. The second, "The Everyday and the Local," considers the meaning of religion in women's everyday lives at the local level. The third, "Agency and Activism," analyzes women's complicated expressions of resistance within and against religious and ethnic movements.

If the delineation of sections is artificial, in that several of the chapters speak to more than one theme, it helps to identify some broad areas of convergence and divergence among the authors. For example, the chapters in Part I tend to focus on the actions of the nation state or, in one case, a national political party in order to delineate the broadest contours of the political and economic context. By contrast, the chapters in Part II argue that this vantage point is partial and sometimes misleading. Reflecting the biases of nation states and parties themselves, it neglects the more complicated reality of lived experience on the ground. The chapters in Part III suggest that national/local, everyday/episodic distinctions are much less significant than a focus on agency and activism at each of these levels, for crystallized within women's agency and activism are clues to the complex, contradictory nature of the structures of domination and the possibilities of resistance.

Gender, Nation, State

Scholars who study identity construction often focus on the social and cultural domain rather than on the state. Students of the state, on the other hand, tend to be disinterested in processes of identity formation. However, the chapters in Part I (Menon, Feldman, Rouse, Hasan, and Sarkar) show that it is impossible to understand identities without exploring the ways in which states, parties, and movements contribute to their construction.

Gender provides an extremely fruitful lens through which to interpret the actions of the state and of ethnic and religious communities. In the South Asian context, the nation is represented as a motherland and the state as father. In some cases the patriarchal state exercises control with benevolent paternalism and in others, in an authoritarian fashion. The paternalistic state offers protection to "its" women and children on the assumption that they cannot protect themselves. In return for this protection, it demands control over women's sexuality. Ritu Menon's characterization of the state as abductor during the postpartition era illuminates the paternalism of the Indian state. Women exercised unusual freedom to determine their marital partners when national boundaries were in flux, but after the rupture between India and Pakistan, the Indian state took on the role of protector and provider and insisted on determining where women and their children belonged. Although one might have predicted that Pakistan, which was formed as a Muslim homeland, would have been more anxious to reclaim Muslim women than secular India would be to reclaim Hindu women, the reverse was true. Having experienced Pakistan's creation as a loss of its territory, India was determined to recover its "moveable property."

State intervention often complements, upholds, and reinforces the interests of patriarchal communities by disregarding or denigrating women's attempts to free themselves from community sanctions. Menon's exploration of "abducted women" reveals that while the Indian state proclaimed its secular character, in practice it defined membership in the national community on religious lines.

Even when the national state acts in a benevolently paternalistic fashion, local administrators have been complicit in violence against minorities amid riots in India. Institutional communalism in patterns of health and education, as Patricia and Roger Jeffery point out, are part of the context in which violence between Hindus and Muslims took place in Bijnor. In other South Asian countries, the authoritarian face of the patriarchal state is even more pronounced than in India. In Sri Lanka, the state assumed its most authoritarian role between 1988 and 1990, when it murdered or abducted anyone whom it suspected of subversive activities. The Pakistani state assumed the role of authoritarian patriarch during the Zia ul Haq regime.

Opposition to the state often emerges when the state fails to exercise its authority in a benevolently paternalistic fashion. Shahnaz Rouse argues that some secular groups in Pakistan have tried to hold the state to its promises by demanding that it maintain women's *izzat* (honor) in the public domain. In India, Hindu nationalists have mobilized opposition to the state for upholding religious law. As Malathi de Alwis argues, the failures of the paternalistic Sri Lankan state to protect families prompted the Mothers' Front to launch a peace movement.

Religious and ethnic communities alike have also employed sexual and gendered imagery to characterize themselves and their hated "others." Paradoxically, such images have their roots in colonial ideology. British colonialism drew invidious distinctions between the so-called martial and the nonmartial races, whom it differentiated according to gender attributes. Whereas the martial races were masculine—strong, virile, and aggressive—the nonmartial races were "effeminate"—passive, weak, and impotent. Today we hear echoes of this approach in Hindu nationalists' depictions of Muslim men as violent aggressors, often rapists, and of Hindus as passive victims. The Pakistani state has upheld these very images, Rouse argues, while reversing the values that Hindu nationalists affix to them. Tanika Sarkar argues that upper-caste Hindus first turned their attention to women in the late nineteenth century, when they worried about the loss of their privileges both to other religious communities and to the lower castes and classes; they conferred on Hindu women a key role in safeguarding community identity through their roles as wives and mothers. Her depiction of Hindu nationalists' fixation on controlling women's bodies, which continued well into the twentieth century, is reminiscent of Menon's depiction of the state's anxiety to recover Hindu mothers and their children from Pakistan.

Shelley Feldman argues that the growth of Islamization in Bangladesh, and its particular concern with reprivatizing women's roles, can be explained by changes in the state's class alliances, growth strategies, and relationship to the global political economy. She suggests that General Ziaur Rahman (1975–1981) contributed to women's growing visibility by supporting nongovernmental organizations that provided women with new opportunities for education and employment. This challenged the interests of the Jama'at-i-Islami (an Islamist political party) and the military, which brought about Zia's overthrow. General Ershad (1982–1990), who succeeded him, strengthened the links between the state and religious forces. Depicting publicly visible women as symbols of Bangladesh's capitulation to modernizing, Westernizing forces, Ershad went so far as to instruct the police to tar the midriffs of middle-class women who were wearing their *sarīs* in a supposedly immodest fashion. Feldman notes that the state considered women symbolic of the newly empowered middle classes at the expense of rural elites. Like Sarkar, who presents Hindu nationalists' attempts to limit women's freedoms as a response to the strains on patriarchal control that result from the growth of capitalist markets and urban consumerism, Feldman links Bangladesh's integration into the global capitalist economy with the growth of religious fundamentalism. Similarly in Pakistan, the state has sought to make religion a paramount feature of women's identities. Rouse argues that the Pakistani state used to delegate the task of regulating women's sexuality to the family. However, in the aftermath of Zia ul Haq's martial law regime, it assumed this responsibility itself—thus the growing incidence of state-sanctioned violence against women.

Zoya Hasan explores another important instance of the state's compromise of its secular principles: the landmark Shah Bano case in India. An elderly Muslim woman's demands for maintenance from her former husband reached the Supreme Court. Rajiv Gandhi, then prime minister, overruled the Court's positive decision in order to assuage conservative Muslim opinion. By treating Muslims as a homogeneous and monolithic group and disregarding the interests of Muslim women, the state strengthened conservative Hindu and Muslim groups at the expense above all of Muslim women.

The Everyday and the Local

Our picture of South Asia would be highly distorted if we focused exclusively on parties and the state at the national level. We would be left with the sense that South Asia is in a perpetual state of crisis as a result of the growth of religious violence. We would assume that the only roles available to women are either as victims or as agents. Several chapters in this volume (those by Metcalf, Shaheed, and Jeffery and Jeffery) challenge these assumptions by focusing on the local and the everyday, and exploring the meaning of religion as lived experience. Implicit within this approach is a critique of scholarship that confines its attention to the national state and to episodic moments of violence.

Patricia and Roger Jeffery argue that a focus on the national state is misleading for two seemingly opposite reasons. On the one hand, scholars often draw upon the state's own account of its activities and thus exaggerate its commitments to secularism, democracy, and social justice. On the other hand, accounts of the state's role in crisis management tend to ignore the grinding, routine aspects of institutionalized communal, class, and gender inequality. By focusing on the formation of Hindu and Muslim identities in rural Bijnor, they explore the interplay between communalism that is fostered by the state and by everyday social relations.

Farida Shaheed argues that women at the local level in Pakistan are less preoccupied with the state and religion than feminists tend to assume. Activism that focuses exclusively on repealing Islamic law depicts the state as more powerful than it really is and neglects the forms of oppression that emanate from the family. She suggests that scholars and activists should devote more attention to women's lived experience and question their own urban-middle-class assumptions.

Barbara Metcalf draws attention to an Islamic organization that provides a refreshing contrast with fundamentalist groups. She argues that the Tablīghī

Jama'at, a proselytizing religious reform movement which is active in South Asia, has positively influenced gender relations and women's position within the community. This is not apparent from a focus on its formal pronouncements or from women's participation in its organized activities and pilgrimages. However, men's attitudes toward women and relations between men and women are extremely egalitarian, for the Tablīgh rejects many of the institutions and practices that foster gender asymmetry.

Some of the authors contend that the influence of religion, particularly of religious doctrine, on women's daily lives has been greatly exaggerated. In Katy Gardner's account, religion is less significant than class in explaining the meaning and significance of *pardā* for Muslim women in Bangladesh. Moreover, *pardā* itself is less a religious institution than a facet of the social structure. Jeffery and Jeffery argue that gender relationships among Muslims and Hindus are very similar. Shaheed notes that religious influences are so deeply interwoven in people's lives that the women she interviewed did not differentiate religion from other forces. In analyzing a religious movement, Metcalf focuses on lived experience rather than religious doctrine.

Nor do these authors find religious influences necessarily an oppressive force in women's lives. Shaheed speaks of the positive aspects of religious faith in its capacity to affirm both individual self-worth and membership in the community. This sense of belonging, which is readily available to men, is otherwise less common for women. Metcalf argues that the religious tour suspends the division between public and private spheres that normally underlies gender inequality, thereby relaxing the sexual division of labor. Although women do not participate actively in the public arena, men take on many domestic responsibilities. Gardner argues that middle-class women who don the veil thereby acquire opportunities to venture into the public domain without fear of harassment.

A few papers analyze the relationship between religious and political life. Metcalf emphatically argues that the Tablīghī movement exists outside the political domain. Shaheed, like Metcalf, sharply demarcates the spheres of public and private life and argues that most women experience control by their families and not by the state. For both Metcalf and Shaheed, religion does not undermine women's power when it is disassociated from state power. Their views partially conflict with those of Jeffery and Jeffery, who show that many aspects of social life are also influenced by state policy.

The differences between the positions of Metcalf and the Jefferys might be partially explained by the differences in the vantage points they adopt. The Tablīghī Jama'at's ability to transcend the public-private divide might be attributed to its liminality: the act of joining a religious tour entails breaking regular routines to enter a world in which social hierarchies are muted. The fact that the movement transcends national boundaries no doubt contributes to the apparent absence of the state. Those who participate in the tour do so as members of a religious community, not as national citizens.

In contrast to the liminal space of the Tablīghī movement, Bijnoris' lives are spatially delimited and subject to greater state influence. Patricia and Roger Jeffery speak of the way state decisions about the siting of schools and health clinics widen communal cleavages. Differences between Metcalf and Jeffery and Jeffery on the Tablīghī Jama'at are particularly revealing. Because they situate the Tablīghī Jama'at's activities within villages composed of Hindus and Muslims, the Jefferys fear that the Tablīghī Jama'at's efforts at purifying Islam will entail eliminating Hindu influences, which will in turn exacerbate the Hindu-Muslim divide. By contrast, in the self-enclosed space that the Tablīghīs inhabit, the possibility of heightened communal divisions does not pose a problem.

An additional source of disagreement concerns the extent to which the state impinges on women's daily lives at the local level. Whereas Shaheed argues that the impact of state reforms is largely confined to urban areas, Rouse argues that Zia "spawned a politics of gender, ethnic, and religious difference that now promises to engulf the country in outright chaos if not flames and civil war." She cites human rights reports that document an alarming increase in violence against women and ethnic minorities. In face of this violence in the name of religion, Rouse questions feminists' tendency to interpret community identity in an uncritical fashion, whereas Shaheed views community identity much more positively. Although both Rouse and Shaheed fear the implications of state actions for feminist movements, Rouse believes that feminists should confront state discourse that treats men and women as different, whereas Shaheed believes that feminists should also work with grassroots women who have some autonomy from the state.

Agency and Activism

The chapters by Basu, de Alwis, and Gardner in Part III are directly concerned with women's agency in everyday life and women's activism in political movements. The relationships between agency, activism, and empowerment are complicated and often contradictory. Women's agency may strengthen systems of gender segregation, and women's activism may heighten identification with their roles as mothers. Women's activism may also empower women from particular communities but at the cost of deepening religious and ethnic divisions among them.

One striking feature of women's activism in ethnic and religious movements is its tendency to uphold and defend the family rather than challenging it, as feminists have. The "abducted" women whom Menon studies, wanting to free themselves from the clutches of the state, sought to stay with families of their own making; the Mothers' Front in Sri Lanka that de Alwis analyzes sought to recreate shattered families amid the civil war; women of the Hindutva movement, whom Basu and Sarkar describe, seek to restore Hindu men to positions of dominance in the family and society.

Moreover, many forms of women's activism that are explored in this volume are inspired by notions of sexual asymmetry rather than sexual equality. Indeed, women often uphold the very standards of proper conduct to which they are expected to conform as a basis for criticizing other groups and institutions. Thus, for example, where feminists might question the social conventions that demand self-sacrifice from women, Hindu women activists demand self-sacrifice of Hindu men. Where feminists criticize notions of honor and shame for their habitual identification of women's proper conduct with community status, the Mothers' Front employs notions of honor and shame to question state authority. Where feminists challenge the widely held belief that women are more emotional than men, the Mothers' Front articulates protest through tears and curses.

How did the Mothers' Front shame the Sri Lankan state? It highlighted the fact that the state had not only failed to perform its paternal, protective role during the civil war but was directly responsible for thousands of "disappearances." The state inadvertently contributed to the movement's popularity by blaming mothers for having raised subversive sons whom the state had to discipline. Ultimately the Mothers' Front was morally victorious. In a nation ravaged by violence, maternal symbols of peace were much more appealing than the state's promise of restoring order through force.

In contrast to war-torn Sri Lanka, where women are galvanized around maternal symbols of peace, Hindu nationalists in India employ gendered imagery to foment violence. The image that they most often invoke is that of the raped Hindu woman. Whereas in Sri Lanka mothers appeal to motherhood imagery, in India it is primarily male nationalists and a small group of celibate women who do so (Basu, 1995b). In both cases, however, women's activism is precipitated by the sense that the state has failed to do its job and protect its citizens. It is paradoxical that women who engage in nationalist mobilization should commit themselves to a cause that is not their own. The Hindu women who have mobilized under the Bharatiya Janata Party (BJP) banner would be ill served by the creation of a Hindu state, for women's rights are better secured in a secular than a religious context. However, as Basu points out, various aspects of the Hindu nationalist agenda appear to serve women's interests and liberate their energies. She notes that the BJP has become the major champion among Indian political parties of a uniform civil code. Sarkar describes the sense of empowerment that women of the Rashtra Sevika Samiti experience as a result of physical training programs that help them fend off harassment in the home and at work.

Women's agency and activism often find expression outside formal organizations. Gardner explores the implications for women of large-scale migration from Sylhet District in Bangladesh to other regions. She emphasizes that women are not simply victims of broader social processes: middle-class women express their agency through the freedom they derive from *pardā*, and poor women express their resistance through songs and rituals that defy purist prescriptions of proper behavior. Rouse argues that men are filing numerous cases against women because of an increase in single women's choosing their marital partners and divorced women's remarrying. Metcalf argues that although women do not participate in the tours that the Tablīghī Jamaʿat organizes, they create parallel women's gatherings that encourage their identification with the movement and with one another. Although the Mothers' Front provided a vital source of energy behind the election of Chandrika Kumaratunga, it did not exercise any formal power within the Sri Lanka Freedom Party (SLFP). Similarly, although there are a few prominent female figureheads in the Hindu nationalist movement, men control the highest reaches of power in the BJP, Rashtriya Swayamsevak Sangh (RSS), and Vishwa Hindu Parishad (VHP); women's influence is mainly exercised through informal means.

Women's resistance may often assume incremental, hidden forms because of the obstacles it encounters in frontally challenging gender inequality. Hasan speaks of the frustrations that Muslim women experienced when the Indian state subverted their attempts to secure their rights within the family. Feldman speaks of the futility of activist attempts to stop violence against women. Shaheed argues that the women's movement has been so concerned with exceptional forms of state-sponsored violence that it has failed to curtail the violence that pervades women's daily lives.

The rich contrasts in the forms of women's agency and activism suggest that women do not possess unified identities or interests. Shaheed argues that feminists' excessive preoccupation with the state stems from their peculiar class backgrounds, for the state has targeted middle-class women. Gardner and Feldman identify class biases on the part of the women's movement in Bangladesh. Its most glaring failure was its silence about the plight of some thirty thousand women who were raped by Pakistani soldiers in the civil war preceding the creation of Bangladesh. Most feminists are of urban-middle-class background; most rape victims were poor rural women.

Ethnic and religious differences have also hindered women's solidarity. The Sinhalese Mothers' Front in Sri Lanka failed to develop links with a parallel organization of Tamil women. Jeffery and Jeffery note that women's contacts across the communal divide were limited and that women themselves were bearers of communal stereotypes. Basu describes instances of women's complicity in violence against Muslims in the course of riots between 1990 and 1993. However artificial and constructed national and "communal" identities may be, they create real barriers to forging solidarity among women.

Conclusion

A comparative South Asian perspective is vital to exploding certain essentialist myths about women, religion, and politics in South Asia. One of the most pervasive is the assumption that religious traditions dictate particular political outcomes. From this perspective, Hinduism and Buddhism are tolerant, pacifist religions that give rise to nonviolent movements or refrain from political intervention altogether, whereas Islam is a militant religion that finds expression in fundamentalism.

A number of chapters in this volume challenge essentialist views of Islam. Metcalf shows that the Tablīghī Jamaʿat, which is often termed fundamentalist, is in fact a religious reform movement that fosters more egalitarian relations among its adherents. In Pakistan, as Shaheed demonstrates, and in India, Muslim identity is mediated by social class. Thus, being Muslim means very different things for the urban middle classes and for the rural poor. Sharply contrasting images of Hindu identity emerge when comparing Hindus' roles as perpetrators of violence in India and as its victims in Bangladesh. Religious appeals by both Sinhalese Buddhist political leaders and the radical Janata Vimukhti Party (JVP) movement in Sri Lanka discredit the notion that Buddhist principles of nonviolent renunciation necessarily find political expression.

Several chapters note that the growth of politicized religion represents a response to broader economic and political changes. Sarkar describes Hindu nationalism as a response to the growth of class and caste struggles in the early twentieth century. Feldman depicts Islamic movements as a response to women's increased economic independence in Bangladesh. Rouse makes the same argument for Pakistan.

The papers thus invite us to rethink the concepts of communalism and fundamentalism. Basu argues that however distinctive communalism may appear to be, it shares many attributes of fundamentalism and nationalism. Behind the semblance of "fundamentalists' traditionalism" there lurks a modern political project. Conversely, behind the BJP's apparently "modern" political ambitions are some very puritanical, conservative conceptions of women's place. Feldman shows that the concept of fundamentalism masks economic conflicts within Bangladeshi society. Metcalf acknowledges the links between nationalism and fundamentalism and finds the Tablīghī to be neither fundamentalist nor nationalist. Similarly, several of the chapters question whether regime types have the significance that they are generally assumed to possess. For example, the democratic states of India and Sri Lanka have been more guilty than the authoritarian states of Bangladesh and Pakistan of "abducting" people against their will. Ironically, the Jama'at-i-Islami has grown stronger under a democratically elected government in Bangladesh. The similarities among South Asian states have always been greater than a focus on the formal attributes of regimes would acknowledge. Moreover, these similarities have increased as state legitimacy has declined.

Appropriating Gender questions assumptions of women's deference while recognizing multiple, varied, often self-defeating expressions of agency. Shaheed, Metcalf, and Gardner all show that agency need not imply activism, either because the obstacles to activism are overwhelming or because women express their discontent through other channels. Nor do women who engage in activism necessarily mobilize against patriarchal domination. They may privilege their communal identities, as Basu and Sarkar describe in the case of Hindu nationalist women, or assert their interests as women, as Hasan describes in the case of Muslim women who mobilized in support of Shah Bano.

As Patricia Jeffery suggests in the concluding chapter, women's agency may improve their lot or leave them worse off than they previously were. She explores the dilemmas that confront feminist activists amid the growth of politicized religion. As her chapter and others in the volume suggest, the challenge before feminists is to harness the energy that women expend on protecting their families, communities, and nations and direct it toward creating a kaleidoscope of liberating possibilities.

Note

I am grateful for support from the John D. and Catherine T. MacArthur Foundation and the Amherst College Faculty Research Award. The ideas contained in this chapter grew out of very rewarding discussions with Patricia Jeffery. She and Shelley Feldman made valuable comments on an earlier draft of this chapter.

Chapter Two

Reproducing the Legitimate Community

Secularity, Sexuality, and the State in Postpartition India

RITU MENON

THIS CHAPTER IS AN ATTEMPT TO UNRAVEL SOME OF THE STRANDS in the tangled skein of community identity, nationalism, and gender, as they became enmeshed in the period immediately following the partition of India in 1947. The specific focus is on the figure—or should one say, body—of the abducted woman and the strategic place she occupied in a program of recovery of abducted women undertaken jointly by India and Pakistan. She was central to this program not only as the object of an apparently humanitarian endeavor in rehabilitation but as a crucial definer of identities and demarcator of boundaries between and within communities, genders, and nations. Her sexuality, because it had been violated by abduction, transgressed by enforced conversion and marriage, and exploited by impermissible cohabitation and reproduction, formed the center of debates around national duty, honor, identity, and citizenship in a secular and democratic India. It also highlighted the role of women as reproducers of national and community boundaries and revealed how, for all of these, "the integration of women into modern nationhood epitomized by citizenship ... somehow follows a different trajectory from that of men" (Kandiyoti, 1991a: 429).

In December 1947, very soon after the partition of India and in view of the large-scale abduction of women in both countries, the governments of India and Pakistan entered into an interdominion agreement to recover and restore all such women to their respective countries and "original homes." Albeit humanitarian in intent, I would suggest that the Recovery Programme, through its covert and overt rhetoric and operations, was as much an index of how India and Pakistan constituted themselves vis-à-vis each other as it was a contest of competing claims by Hindus, Muslims, and Sikhs over one another's (and their "own") women and children. To this extent, both countries were engaged in a redefinition of each other's (and their own) national character as demonstrated by a commitment to upholding honor and restoring moral order. The proper regulation of women's sexuality was essential not only in itself but because the moral depravity and sexual chaos that mass abduction represented had to be reversed. Thus, the individual and collective sins of men who behaved without restraint or responsibility in a surge of communal "madness" had to be redeemed by nations who understood their duty in, once again, bringing about sexual discipline and, through it, the desired reinforcement of community and national identity.

Feminist and other scholars of nationalism in postcolonial societies have drawn attention to the place that the "woman question" occupied in transitions to "modernity." In India, the concern of the Social Reform movement with widow remarriage, satī (widow immolation), and the age of consent was, in fact, a concern with women's sexuality. The movement's intention was to lift it out of the domain of the traditional and insert it into the political and social agenda of modern nationhood. But as various analyses have shown, the enterprise was confounded at the outset by the clear demarcation of public (represented as male and modern) from private (represented as female and traditional), and by the need to emphasize the purity and cultural superiority of Indian womanhood (Chatterjee, 1989; Bagchi, 1996; Mani, 1989). The rhetoric of modernity, however, could hardly be abandoned by a modernizing state: it was constrained to undertake the kind of transformation that would enable it to weld a nation, build a citizenry that would recognize its fellow members as part of the same nation, sharing nationality. It would have to grant rights, assign responsibility, and guarantee equality in an undifferentiated manner to all its citizens. Nonetheless, as Kandiyoti argues, definitions of "modern" take place in a political field where certain identities are privileged—even while equality is promised—and others subordinated. Wherever women serve as boundary markers between different national, ethnic, and religious collectivities, she says, "their emergence as full-fledged citizens" with concomitant rights "will be jeopardized" (Kandiyoti, 1991a: 435).

Other analysts have noted that women have been subsumed only symbolically into the national body politic because no nationalism in the world has ever granted women and men the same privileged access to the resources of the nation-state. Moreover, as Mosse points out, "nationalism had a special affinity for male society and together with the concept of respectability, legitimized the dominance of men over women" (quoted in Parker et al. (eds.), 1992: 6). The passionate brotherhood of "deep comradeship" that Benedict Anderson talks about is an essentially male fraternity, in which women are enshrined as Mother, and the trope of nation-as-woman "further secures male-male arrangements and an all-male history" (Anderson, 1991).

Floya Anthias and Nira Yuval-Davis (1989) have pointed out how central dimensions of the roles of women are constituted around the relationships of collectivities to the state, and that equally central dimensions of the relationships between collectivities and the state are constituted around the roles of women. This particular nexus has lately come in for sustained scrutiny by researchers and activists in South Asia amid escalating ethnic tension and regional chauvinisms that have resulted in fundamentalism and communitarian violence, the crystallization of regressive cultural practice, and selective reinterpretations of tradition, especially with regard to women's "proper" role in society (Hasan (ed.), 1994; Bhasin, Menon, and Khan (eds.), 1994; Jayawardena and de Alwis (eds.), 1996). Bitter and violent conflict amongst Hindus, Muslims and Sikhs led to the division of India along communal lines. As I elaborate in this chapter, in the wake of this the reconfiguration of relationships between communities, the state, and gender in postpartition India took place around the body and being of the abducted women of all three communities. By extension, she also delineated the relationship between India and Pakistan as they typified the two principal "communities," Hindu and Muslim, eternally and irrevocably locked in battle with each other. Each was projected as an essentialized collectivity: Hindustan, land of the Hindus, and Pakistan, Muslim homeland, closed to non-Muslims (nonbelievers or *kāfirs*). In the classic transposition, hers became the body of the Motherland (Woman-as-Nation) violated by the marauding foreigner.

The establishing of difference, or distinction, is a virtual prerequisite for nationalism, even though all definitions of it remain elusive. What, asks Eve Sedgwick, distinguishes the "nation-ness" of the United States from the "nation-ness" of Canada or Mexico? Of the Philippines? And from the many nationalisms within itself? Recognizing the several differences, she concludes that there is no "normal" way for the nation to define itself: "The 'other' of the nation in a given political or historical setting may be the pre-national monarchy, the local ethnicity, the ex-colony, the diaspora, the transnational corporate, ideological, religious, or ethnic unit" (quoted in Parker et al. (eds.), 1992: 3).

Most theorists of nationalism have posited that nations are haunted by their definitional Others (Parker et al. (eds.), 1992). Implying "some element of alterity for its definition," a nation, according to Perry Anderson, is ineluctably "shaped by what it opposes." Benedict Anderson further suggests that nationalism should best be conceived "not as an ideology" but "as if it belonged with kinship or religion rather than with liberalism or fascism" (Anderson, 1991: 5).

Three significant factors in the constitution of the Indian state set it apart from—and in its perception, above—Pakistan: it was statedly secular, democratic, and socialist. Pakistan was avowedly Islamic ("theocratic" to many), basically feudal, suspiciously "un-modern." This was at the level of ideology. At the "imagined" level, however, other factors informed the self-perception of the Indian state and its male subjects. Both are important for an understanding of the uncommon zeal and commitment with which the Indian government set out to recover women. The idea of Pakistan as embodying/representing the larger collectivity of Muslims, by definition inimical to Indian national interest; the sexuality of women as transgressed by abduction and forcible conversion and cohabitation; and the question of the "legitimacy" of children born of such "wrong" unions as future members of a community are the three elements that I will examine, as forging the link between secularity, sexuality, and the state. Through this, I hope to show how ambiguous and conflictual the relationship was between gender, community, and national identities; between the "secular" state and its "communitarian" subjects; between "democratic" India and "theocratic" Pakistan. (For an account of the gendered imagery that Pakistan employed in depicting India, see Rouse in this volume.)

Bodies and Borders

Sir, our country is a secular State and it is in no way proper to compare an agreement arrived at in our country with that of the other. The other country is a theocratic state. We can have doubts with regard to our sisters there but it is not justified for anyone to entertain the suspicion that fair treatment will not be meted out to women in this secular State.

—Chaudhury Ranbir Singh (East Punjab),
Legislative Assembly Debates, 1949

You are not prepared to go to war over this matter. I do not know why. If you are prepared to do so for a few inches of land in Kashmir, why not over the honour of our women? It is more important and is likely to affect our political prestige. . . . Whenever outstanding disputes between this country and Pakistan are enumerated, they mention canal water, Kashmir and evacuee property—and such is the weakness of our government, they do not mention this question of recovery of women.

—Sardār Bhupinder Singh Man (East Punjab: Sikh)
Legislative Assembly Debates, 1949

In December 1949 the Legislative Assembly in India debated a bill—when subsequently passed, the Abducted Persons (Recovery and Restoration) Act of 1949—to facilitate the return of all Muslim women abducted during the partition disturbances to Pakistan. It was an extension of a reciprocal agreement with Pakistan, whereby both dominions pledged to locate and recover all such women with the greatest possible speed. The bill under discussion set out the terms of reference for such recovery in India. Its provisions were explicit and wide ranging in the powers given to the police for what we would today call "search and seizure"; exemption from any civil or criminal action against any officer or constable for excesses committed in the course of recovery; and virtual suspension of all democratic and fundamental rights of the women and children—"abducted persons"—in question. As we have discussed elsewhere in some detail, there was considerable disquiet expressed by members regarding all of these, but there seemed to be a general agreement on Pakistan's duplicity in the matter of recovering non-Muslim women from its territories.[1]

For the Indian government, as for many leaders, Pakistan's intentions as far as the restoration of women was concerned never quite squared with its performance. Pakistan disallowed the MEO (Military Evacuation Organisation) from conducting recoveries after July 1948; was tardy in promulgating an ordinance based upon the November 1948 agreement; appeared not to be cooperating on the speedy recovery of those whose details had been furnished by the Indian government; desisted from taking action against the government servants who were believed to have possession of two thousand women; and failed to ensure that its police and social workers honored the spirit and letter of the agreement. Members of the Assembly continually urged Minister Gopalaswami Ayyangar to impress upon the government the need to put greater pressure on Pakistan for this purpose. One, Smt. Durgabai from Madras, even went so far as to say, "Thanks to the leadership in our country, we have been able to get social workers who are not only public-spirited but non-communal in their outlook, and therefore, they are inspired by the noble example set up by the Father of the Nation, Mahatma Gandhi, and also other leaders whose support and help are available in plenty for recovery activity." Another member, Pandit Thakur Das Bhargava, declared, "So far as we are concerned, we know how to honor our moral obligations," implying that the Pakistanis did not.[2]

As the discussions in the Assembly continued, it became clear that in most members' view, Pakistan itself had become the abductor country, mimicking at a national level the behavior of its (male) subjects and guilty of the same moral turpitude. By contrast, India behaved like a responsible parent-protector, in turn reflecting what was generally the responsible behavior of its people. There were aberrations, of course—"Some of our misguided brothers also share the responsibility to a certain extent"—but in the words of one member, "Greater fault lies with the people and even with the government of Pakistan." Pakistan's duplicity regarding the return of women was consistent with its duplicity in all other matters under dispute—Kashmir, canal waters, and evacuee property—and provided proof enough (if proof were needed) of its indifference to honoring agreements in general. By proceeding *as if* Pakistan would indeed keep to its side of the bargain, India was guilty of weakness and irresolution. In the face of such provocation, it had no choice but to depart from its moderate and "civilized" course and speak Pakistan's language. Pandit Thakur Das Bhargava stated:

> The Pakistan government does not understand the language of morality, it only understands the language of force and retaliation.... If this were a matter of mere international morality, I am at one with the Honorable Minister. But all the same when we have entered into a bilateral agreement—and with all solemnity they entered into the Agreement—let us see how it has been honoured in letter and in spirit by Pakistan.

In at least two very significant instances, Pakistan had betrayed its intentions:

> We knew on the 3rd of September 1947 an agreement was signed between the two governments and the ink was not dry when the Pakistan government, along with the Azad Kashmir government, raided parts of Kashmir and took away our women.... For a government to be party to this loot, to this raid upon women and property and then to say that they were not ... and ultimately to accept that they were ... nobody on earth can justify the Pakistan government.

Nor could anybody countenance the fact that two thousand Hindu women were in the custody of Pakistani government officials and not being returned. That India should have signed a cease-fire agreement before the captured women had been returned indicated that it was neither "bold enough, good enough, sagacious enough nor honest enough." Women had been spirited away to the closed districts of Jhelum, Gujarat, Campbellpur, the Northwest Frontier, and Rawalpindi, where no Indian recovery official was allowed to enter; they were stripped and paraded in Kabul; they were passed from hand to hand and sold in *bazārs*—still India stood silently by. If retaliation was the only language Pakistan could understand, then that was what India should speak, and speak it through those same sisters whom "our country has a tradition of protecting." They would be the hostages. And if the state had cast itself in the role of father to the women, then its male citizens would safeguard them like their "brothers." "Sir," said Pandit Thakur Das Bhargava, "there is no reason why ... a country is not justified in keeping these [Muslim] girls as hostages for some time.... I don't see any harm in employing this tactic in getting our girls. As a matter of policy, of strategy, it should have been done." If India could think of cutting off relations with Pakistan on economic matters, why could it not do so to "get our sisters back?"

It could not, because then India would be no different from Pakistan. "Now I wish this to go on record," said Minister Gopalaswami Ayyangar, "that [making recoveries] is a thing which, as a civilized government we ought to continue to do. Our own policy is that whatever may be done in the other Dominion, whether recoveries ... are adequate or not, we owe a duty to the large number of Muslim women who are abducted within our own territory." As powerful was the sentiment expressed by Shibban Lal Saksena (United Provinces, General): "Sir, our country has a tradition. Even now the *Rāmāyana* and the *Mahābhārata* are revered. For the sake of one woman who was taken away by Rāvana [the demon in *Rāmāyana*] the whole nation took up arms and went to war. And here there are thousands, and the way in which they have been treated was told by the Honorable Minister himself: ... what not was done to them." Several other members concurred, reminding the House of its "moral duty" to behave honorably.

Two "traditions" were being invoked: a tradition-in-the-making of responsible government, secular principles, and democratic practice (anticipated even in these debates in the discussion on the Constitution of India due to be introduced in Parliament in January 1950, and the guarantees ensured to *all* Indian citizens); and an ancient Hindu "tradition" of chivalry toward women and fierce protection of their honor. Such an invocation was consistent with what has been called the Janus-faced quality of nationalist discourse: "It presents itself both as a modern project that melts and transforms traditional attachments in favor of new identities, and as a reaffirmation of *authentic* cultural values culled from the depths of a presumed communal past" (Kandiyoti, 1991a: 431, emphasis added). In this case, it also necessitated the complete negation of any values of a *shared* Hindu-Muslim past (or present); indeed, going by the debates, one might even say that the attempt was to distance "civilized," "secular," "Hindu" India as far as possible from irresponsible, communal, Muslim Pakistan, and to crystallize difference in such a way that no other representation of either community or country could be accommodated.

Unlike community identities, which most members assumed to be predetermined and unchanging, the identity of the Indian state was being newly forged. The debates seesawed between those who were more concerned with establishing its secular credentials and adhering to democratic principles (among them members of the Communist Party of India and some Congress

MPs, men and women) and those who were pressing for a more militant resolution as proof of the state's concern with its larger responsibility both toward
its citizens and its *territorial integrity*. In the end, it was the latter who
prevailed, and the bill was passed, virtually unchanged and with all its provisions intact.

Boundaries and Being

In the context of worsening Hindu-Muslim relations, the term "abducted"
was first used in November 1946 after the Noakhali riots, in the Indian
National Congress session at Meerut. A resolution was passed that stated: "The
Congress views with pain, horror, and anxiety, the tragedies of Calcutta, East
Bengal, Bihar, and some parts of Meerut District. . . . These new developments
in communal strife are different from any previous disturbances and have
involved . . . mass conversions, . . . abduction, violation of women, and forcible
marriage."

Communal tension and the ensuing violence escalated at such a rapid pace,
especially after March 1947, that leaders and representatives of the Indian and
Pakistani governments met in Lahore in September 1947 and resolved that
steps be taken to "recover and restore abducted persons." On 17 November
1947 the All India Congress Committee passed a resolution: "During these
disorders large numbers of women have been abducted on either side and
there have been forcible conversions on a large scale. No civilized people can
recognize such conversions and there is nothing more heinous than the abduction of women."

It is important to note here that from the very beginning the concern with
abducted women or persons went hand in hand with alarm at "forcible
conversions." This preoccupation continued throughout the debates and, in
fact, underlined another important factor in India's relationship with
Pakistan: the loss of Hindus to Islam through such conversions, in addition to
the loss of territory. Abduction and conversion were the double blow dealt to
the Hindu "community," so that the recovery of "their" women, if not of land,
became a powerful assertion of Hindu manhood, at the same time that it
demonstrated the moral high ground occupied by the Indian state. Nothing
like this concern was evident with regard to the abduction of Hindu women by
Hindu men, or Muslim women by Muslim men, presumably because here no
offense against community or religion had been committed, nor anyone's
"honor" compromised.

Although there seemed to be general consensus on both sides that large
numbers of women had indeed been "abducted," a working definition of an
"abducted" person was attempted by the Indian government only in 1949 in
the bill under discussion:

In this Act, unless there is anything repugnant in the subject or context, "abducted person" means ... *a male child* under the age of 16 years or a female of whatever age who is, or immediately before the 1st day of March 1947, was a Muslim and who, on or after that day and before the 1st day of January 1949, has become separated from his or her family and is found to be living with or under the control of any other individual or family, and in the latter case *includes a child born to any such female after the said date.* ...

If any police officer, not below the rank of an Assistant Sub-Inspector or any other police officer specially authorized ... has reason to believe that an abducted person resides or is to be found in any place he may, after recording the reasons for his belief, without warrant, enter and search the place and take into custody any person found therein, who in his opinion is an abducted person, and deliver or cause such person to be delivered to the custody of the officer in charge of the nearest camp with the least possible delay. ...

[6] Determination of question whether any person detained is an abducted person:

(1) If any question arises whether a person detained in a camp is or is not an abducted person, or whether such person should be restored to his or her relatives, or handed over to any other person, or conveyed out of India, or allowed to leave the camp, it shall be referred to, and decided by, a tribunal constituted for the purpose by the Central Government.

(2) The decision of the tribunal shall be final; provided that the Central Government may, either of its own motion or on the application of any party interested in the matter, review or revise any such decision.

The looseness ("had become separated from his or her family and is found to be living with or under the control of any other individual or family") and arbitrariness ("If any police officer ... has reason to believe that an abducted person resides or is to be found in any place") of these definitions provoked intense debate in the Assembly. Many members were justifiably disturbed by the bill's implications and by the extremely wide powers given the police to determine exactly who would fall into this category. Some demurred at the absence of judicial recourse available to either abducted persons or their families. Others drew attention to the significant departures made in this definition from the legal definition of "abduction" (to kidnap; to carry away illegally or by force or deception) and the consequent culpability of the government in a court of law.

Their misgivings were often fully borne out, not only by the actual process of recovery but also by the very impossibility of establishing, beyond reasonable doubt, that the person/woman "recovered" had in fact been "abducted." Search officers and social workers told us that they used all kinds of tactics in order to locate and "rescue" the women. They would go disguised as bangle sellers or in *burqā* (veil), and cajole, threaten, and even physically intimidate families. One liaison officer said, "The operation was a raid in every sense of the word—we did many irregular things, like dipping a police officer under water and keeping him there till he told us where the women were. . . . Sometimes I would slap the women and tell them that I would shoot them if they didn't inform us."

As we learned in the course of our interviews, the circumstances of the "abductions" varied widely. Some women were left behind as hostages for the safe passage of their families; others were separated from their group or family while escaping, or strayed and were picked up; still others were initially given protection and then incorporated into the host family; yet again, as in the case of Bhawalpur State, all the women of a single block were kept back. Some changed hands several times or were sold to the highest or lowest bidder, as the case might be (the going rate in Pakistan, we were told, was two rupees for non-Muslim girls, four *ānās* for Muslims); some became second or third wives; and very many were converted and married, and lived with considerable dignity and respect. I do not mean to suggest here that there were no cases of forcible kidnapping and abduction on both sides; merely that "abduction" as defined by the act of 1949 assumed that any and every woman located in the home or under the control of a family or individual of the other community, was eligible for recovery, regardless of any indications to the contrary.[3] Resistance to being "recovered" came not only from their "abductors" but also from the women themselves. Many escaped from the centers to which they had been brought and returned to their "captors," sometimes by the most extraordinary means. We were told by one officer, in charge of recoveries from Lyallpur in West Punjab in early 1948, of a young girl he had recovered and sent to Lahore and then Jalandar: "She escaped from the camp—her men-folk dug a tunnel beneath the camp and retrieved her. . . . If I were to do this job today, I would refuse. Why should I risk my life? But at that time, my objective was, how many girls have I recovered today?"[4]

The women often protested that their liaisons had been made freely and under no compulsion; indeed, we learned that many had taken advantage of the social turmoil to marry men of their choice from outside their community, something that would have been almost certainly disallowed in more normal times. Very many such disputed cases came up for arbitration at the special tribunal set up by India and Pakistan, as recounted by Kamlabehn Patel and the police officers in charge, and they readily admit that the resolution of these cases was beset with difficulties. Of the women who were forcibly repatriated, an appreciable number simply refused to return to their natal families or husbands; some, in protest, refused to change out of the clothes they had been wearing when they were picked up by the social workers; and at least two search officers told us that, as far as they knew, not a single woman had come to a recovery center of her own volition. "Who are you to meddle in our lives?" they shouted at the social workers when they were forced to go back. "What business is it of yours?" "If you were unable to save us then, what right have you to compel us now?"[5]

Exactly how widespread this resistance was is difficult to ascertain, especially given the coercive powers of the police. But every social worker or police officer we spoke to referred specifically to it; in fact, the act (renewed every year for six years) was allowed to lapse in 1956 when social workers and the police said they could no longer continue with Operation Recovery. As early as 1949, Rameshwari Nehru, Honorary Advisor to the government in the Ministry of Relief and Rehabilitation, resigned in protest against a policy that she believed worked against women. She recommended that recoveries be discontinued altogether because she was "convinced that we have not achieved our purpose. . . . By sending women away, we have brought about grief and dislocation of their accepted family life without in the least promoting human happiness."[6]

The untidiness of the formulations in the act found its harrowing and messy consequences in implementation throughout the eight years that the program was in operation, but nowhere was this more disturbing than in regard to children. Just as leaders were beginning to take in the enormity of the impact of delineating boundaries and dividing people and territories, so too were social workers faced with the appalling consequences of dividing women like oranges and apples and deciding fortunes on the basis of who fell into which basket. And where did the children belong? With the oranges or apples? Kamlabehn Patel, a social worker who was part of Operation Recovery till 1952 and Mridula Sarabhai's righthand woman in Lahore, told us:

We used to make a list of all the pregnant women in Lahore and send it to Jalandar together with them. There, they used to keep these women for three months or so, give them a complete medical checkup [a euphemism for abortion] and only then try and find their relatives. Because if they came to know that the woman is pregnant they would say, let her stay in the camp and have her child.

It was my experience that women in the thirty-five to forty-five-year age group felt very ashamed of themselves—they had managed to acquire a certain status in their household and family. How could they show themselves to their husbands and children in this state? They wanted to burn themselves alive, to die rather than face their people. They said they would rather go to hell. . . .

The government at this time passed an ordinance that those whose babies were born in Pakistan would have to leave them behind, and those children that were born in India would stay in India. I was in Lahore at that time. There was a special conference held to discuss the implications. I said to Mridulabehn that I will not attend this meeting because my opinions are the opposite of yours. I will say frankly what I feel about this matter at the meeting, otherwise I will not come. At that time there were a lot of very conservative people in rehabilitation work.

Mridulabehn asked me, "Kamla, what are you trying to tell me?" I said, a girl and a mother who has already been treated so cruelly is now told that only she can go across and not her child—this is like stealing her child and this I will not do. Mridulabehn was worried about the future of these girls. How to settle them? Who will marry them? Rameshwari Nehru was of the opinion that if they were Muslims themselves, then why should they leave their children in India? Our officers, Gundevia and others, also said, "What will happen to the children? Because if you are a Hindu then the children should also go." It was like a double-edged sword. There was one standard to measure against on one side, and another on the other. On the one hand the women were worried that they would lose their children, on the other, there was this question, why should these children be brought back? I said, I will not do it. If any of you want to come and do it, I will help you but I will not be a party to it myself.

Finally these people agreed that these women would take their children with them to the Jalandar camp. Then, after fifteen days we would ask them whether they wanted to take their children with them or not. If yes, they could take them, otherwise the children would be left in the Jalandar camp and suitable arrangements would be made for them. I realized that women in the age group of thirty and thirty-two were not keen to take their children with them, for they had other children earlier. But the women who became mothers for the first time did not want to leave their firstborn in the camp. When their relatives or parents came to see them, they came to the Self-Service Corporation, an all-India refugee organization, and they had to decide whether they wanted to go with their parents or continue living in the camp. But they realized that they could not stay in the camp indefinitely and finally they would agree to leave their children behind. They wept and fell at our feet to beseech us, but there was no other solution. (Menon and Bhasin, 1993: 7–8)

The two governments had agreed that neither forced conversions nor forced marriages would be recognized by either country. It followed that all children born of such unions would then be illegitimate, and for the purpose of the act were defined as "abducted persons" if they happened to be born to any able woman within the time frame set out in it. Now, those very members who had protested that no forcible recovery or return could be countenanced, and those who believed that every abductor had been guilty of a "shameful crime," was a murderer, and could not be relied upon to provide either security or dignity to the woman he had forcibly converted and married, found that there were no grounds for their children to be treated as abducted persons. "Why should they all be forced to go to Pakistan?" they asked. "You must realize," declared Pandit Thakur Das Bhargava, "that all those children born in India are the citizens of India."

> Supposing a Hindu man and a Muslim woman have married. Who should be the guardian of the offspring? . . . Now when a Muslim girl is restored, she will go to Pakistan; she may change the religion of that child. . . . The child will be considered illegitimate and is liable to be maltreated and killed. Between father and mother, who is entitled to guardianship? . . . If the father insists that he would look to the interests of the child and will see that it is properly brought up, I do not understand why, by executive action, that child should be given to Pakistan merely because we have written these words here in the ordinance.

Other members differed. "Our society is different from Muslim society," said Brajeshwar Prasad from Bihar.

> My friends made the suggestion that the children of such abducted women should be allowed to go back to Pakistan. May I know whether these children are regarded as legitimate? They are illegitimate in the eyes of the law . . . our Hindu society has no place for illegitimate children. . . . I do not know how a child born of a man and a woman can ever be illegitimate . . . but we have to take facts as they are. . . . Such children if they are to live in India, will remain as dogs.

Yet others cautioned that if the government did indeed regard such marriages as illegal and, consequently, the children as illegitimate, then according to the law, only the mother could be the legal guardian. Those who professed to speak on behalf of the abducted women admitted that the abductor had been guilty of

> highly reprehensible conduct; but let us look at the question from the point of view of the abducted woman. The children to her are a sign of her humil-

iation, are unwanted, and if she returns to Pakistan . . . I think we may feel almost certain that they will not be treated as members of their mother's family. . . . Why should they not then be retained in this country where their father, *whatever his original conduct might have been*, is prepared to claim them as his own? (Pandit Kunzru, emphasis added)

Moreover, it was the opinion of yet others that if the Pakistan ordinance had no provisions for the return of children, why then should the Indian one? "It should be left to the discretion of the authorities to decide which children should be retained and which . . . sent away."

Once again the minister assured the members that "the mere inclusion of children in the definition of abducted persons does not mean that those children are necessarily sent away to the other dominion," for he too believed that "children born after March 1, 1947 would not be welcome in the original homes of these abducted persons when they go back . . . in 90 cases out of 100" (Constituent Assembly (Legislative) Debates).

Indeed, implementation of government policy actively discouraged women from taking their children with them and pressured those who were pregnant to have abortions before they returned to their families. Of the children born to mothers in Pakistan and recovered by India, only 102 had come to India as of 21 July 1952; the total number of women recovered was 8,206.

The reason given by the minister for including children in the act was that "in the actual working of the law, our own officers felt that . . . [the children's] presence was an impediment in the way of [the women's] being taken out," that is, mothers would not leave without their children. "If the original [natal or marital] home is willing to take such children, they are sent to the other Dominion. If they . . . are not welcome there, other arrangements are made. . . . I have already taken steps to persuade the Pakistan government to introduce similar words in the definition of an abducted person in Pakistan, and I would ask that this very desirable improvement . . . be allowed to remain" (Constituent Assembly (Legislative) Debates).

The contradictions between the earlier ordinance and the present bill made for predictable confusion in understanding the scope of the legislation: Hindu fathers should be allowed to assert their right of guardianship, "for no child born of a man and woman was illegitimate," but children born of Muslim fathers could not be accommodated in "our Hindu society." The definition of an "abducted person" included not only "any female" but also any "male child below sixteen . . . before the 1st of March 1947" and "any children born after March 1947 and before 1 January 1949."

The confusing nature of the debates reveals a curious logic. For one, the concern with male children below the age of sixteen had clearly to do with forcible conversions rather than with sexual transgression. The first ordinance on children in 1948 (referred to by Kamlabehn Patel in her interview) was an initial response to the experience of social workers and others, that Hindu families demurred from taking back their daughters, wives, and daughters-in-law if the women had also had other children in the meantime. The ordinance laid down, and implicitly acknowledged, *that the child belonged with the father, Hindu or Muslim,* and should be left behind in either country. As recovery work progressed, it became clear that removing women without their children was proving intractable, and in order to wrest both from their "captors," the children had to be legislated into the definition of "abducted persons"— primarily, I would suggest, to put pressure on the Pakistani government and on those men who were unwilling to let their children go. The debates reflect the intrinsic impossibility of legislating the boundaries of identity: were the children to be considered Hindu or Muslim? Illegitimate, because the conversions and marriages were invalid? Wards of their mothers or fathers? As far as the women were concerned, the situation was even more problematic: abducted as Hindus, arrayed and converted as Muslims, recovered as Hindus but required to relinquish their children because they were born of Muslim fathers, and disowned by their own families because they were now "impure," that is, neither Hindu nor Muslim. The debates also reflect the disjunction between the letter of the law and the spirit of the legislators. While the bill called for the repatriation of all women and children who fitted the definition of abducted persons, the preoccupation of several legislators was with maintaining community "purity" and difference, with blood and belonging. More important, the disjunction underscores the deep ambivalence of the Indian state, striving to uphold its secular character vis-à-vis Pakistan but compelled to secure communitarian interests at home in the aftermath of a division of the country on communal lines.

Secularity, Sexuality, and the State

The single most important point about the Abducted Persons (Recovery and Restoration) Act was that it needed to be legislated at all, because the maximum number of recoveries had been made between 1947 and 1949, before the bill was introduced in Parliament. Why, then, was the Indian government so anxious to reclaim women, sometimes several years after their abduction? Why should the matter of national *honor* have been so closely bound up with the bodies of women, and with children born of "wrong" unions?

The experience of Pakistan suggests that recovery program was neither so charged with significance nor as zealous in its effort to restore moral order. Indeed, informal discussions with persons involved in the work there indicate that pressure from India, rather than their own social or political compulsions, were responsible for the majority of recoveries made.[7] There is also the possibility that the community stepped in and took over much of the daily work of rehabilitation, evidenced by findings that the level of destitution of women was appreciably lower in Pakistan. We were told that both the Muslim League and the All Pakistan Women's Association were active in arranging the marriages of all unattached women, so that "no woman left the camp single." Preliminary interviews conducted in Pakistan also hint at relatively less preoccupation with the question of moral sanction and "acceptability," although this must remain only a speculation at this stage.

Notwithstanding the above, some tentative hypotheses may be put forward. For India, a country that was still reeling from partition and painfully reconciling itself to its altered status, reclaiming what was by right its "own" became imperative in order to establish itself as a responsible and civilized state, one that fulfilled its duties toward its citizens, both in the matter of securing what was their due and in confirming itself as their protector. To some extent, this was mirrored in the refugees' own dependency in turning to the *sarkār* (government) as its *mā-bāp* (mother and father) at this time of acute crisis.

But the notion of recovery itself as it came to be articulated cannot really be seen as having sprung full-blown in the postpartition period as a consequence of events that had taken place during and after the violence that accompanied the exchange of populations. If we pause to look at what had been happening in the Punjab from the mid-nineteenth century onward with the inception and consolidation of the Arya Samāj and the formation of a Punjabi Hindu consciousness, we might begin to discover some elements of its anxiety regarding Muslim and Christian inroads into Hinduness and the erosion of Hindu *dharma* (religion), values, and lifestyles through steady conversions to these two faiths by Hindus (Sarkar, this volume). With the creation of Pakistan, this anxiety found a new focus, for not only had it been unable to stem conversions to Islam but it had also actually lost one part of itself to the creation of a Muslim homeland. Recovery then became a symbolically significant activity (its eerie resonance in the current frenzy to recover sacred Hindu sites from the "usurping" Muslims is chilling), just as earlier the *shuddhi* (purification) program of the Arya Samāj, even if it resulted in bringing only one convert back into the Hindu fold, served to remind the Hindu community that losing its members to Islam or Christianity was not irreversible. Recovering women who had been abducted and, moreover, forcibly converted, restoring them to both their own and the larger Hindu family, and ensuring that a generation of newly born Hindu children was not lost to Islam through their repatriation to Pakistan with their mothers can be seen as part of this concern. Because, in fact, such a recovery or return might not be voluntary, necessary legal measures had to be taken to accomplish the mission. In one sense, it seems that the only answer to forcible conversion was forcible recovery.

The key to understanding the anxiety surrounding the matter of the children of abducted women lies in the importance attributed to legitimate membership of a family, a community, and ultimately, a nation. The sanctity of all three lay in keeping the boundaries intact, in maintaining difference, and in refusing to allow sexuality to be contaminated by secularity. This was why the forced alliances resulting from abduction could be neither socially acknowledged nor legally sanctioned, and why the children born of them would forever be "illegitimate." This was also why the fake "family" had to be dismembered by physically removing the woman/wife/ mother from its offending embrace and relocating her in the "real" family, where her sexuality could be suitably supervised. The Abducted Persons Act was remarkable for the impunity with which it violated every principle of citizenship—fundamental rights and access to justice—and for contravening all earlier legislation with regard to marriage, divorce, custody and guardianship, and eventually, inheritance—not so much in regard to property but, more critically, in regard to membership of a (religious) community. The freezing of boundaries, communal and national, calls for what Kristeva (1993) terms "sexual, nationalist, and religious protectionism," reducing men and women, but especially women, to "the identification needs of their originary groups," imprisoning them in the "impregnable aloofness of a weird primal paradise: family, ethnicity, nation, race." The state cannot absent itself while these negotiations are taking place, for, Kristeva continues, "beyond the origins that have assigned to us biological identity papers and a linguistic, religious, social, political, historical place, the freedom of contemporary individuals may be gauged by their ability to choose membership, while the democratic capability of a nation and social group is revealed by the right it affords individuals to exercise that choice" (1–49). Free choice, freely exercised, is what neither nation nor social group could allow the abducted woman in postpartition India, so much so that it was legislated out. In its eagerness to restore "normalcy," and to assert itself as the "protector," the Indian state itself became an "abductor" that forcibly removed adult women from their homes and transported them out of their country. It became, in effect and in a supreme irony, its hated Other.

Notes

1. For a fuller discussion of the bill and the issues raised by it, see Menon and Bhasin (1993, 1996).
2. Constituent Assembly of India (Legislative) Debates, December 1949. Unless otherwise stated, all quotations in this section are taken from the official transcriptions of the debates.

3. See Devi, 1995, for a most poignant account of a Hindu girl sheltered by a Muslim family in Noakhali in 1946.
4. Personal interview with Shri K.L. Bindra.
5. Personal interviews with social workers.
6. Private papers of Rameshwari Nehru, Nehru Memorial Museum and Library, Delhi.
7. We owe this information to Nighat Said Khan, who is researching the Pakistan experience.

Chapter Three

(Re)presenting Islam

*Manipulating Gender, Shifting State Practices,
and Class Frustrations in Bangladesh*

SHELLEY FELDMAN

> Who am I? Am I an East Bengali? An East Pakistani?
> A Bangladeshi? Am I all of these people?
>
> —Rokeya Kabir

A *FATVĀ* (RULING) AGAINST TASLIMA NASRIN, a novelist charged with defaming Islam and acting with malicious and deliberate intent to hurt the religious sentiments of the Bangladeshi people, generated significant international attention. This briefly covered event contributes to Western constructions of Islamic fundamentalism as backward, regressive, and oppressive, especially to women. In the wake of the Rushdie affair, moreover, such events, and the subsequent harassment and murder of Bangladeshi women and destruction of Bangladeshi communities by the religious right, were seen to require no further analysis. This was because such incidents support an a priori interpretation of Islam as homogeneous and fanatic. The *fatvā*'s political significance, however, coincides with the ethnicization of global politics, the changing international role of the Islamic community, and the reframing of economic and political alliances in the post–Cold War period.[1]

Within Bangladesh, the summer of 1994 was distinguished by protests, demonstrations, *hartāls* (strikes), and pitched battles demanding the execution of Taslima Nasrin and the intellectuals, journalists, and government officials who supported her. In addition, included in the 29 July 1994 Dhaka *gherāv* (encirclement) was a call to restrict nongovernmental organizations from operating in the country (Human Rights Watch/Asia, 1994; Rashiduzzaman, 1994). Some have argued that behind these confrontations is a larger cultural divide between the religious right and liberals (Rashiduzzaman, 1994). In the context of expanding ethnic and communal strife in the region and the country, Nasrin's writing and various reactions to her by fundamentalist groups, the ruling Bangladesh Nationalist Party (BNP), and opposition parties, as well as the women's and nongovernmental communities, may be open to a different interpretation. Characterized by the economic and political transformation of Bangladesh since its creation in 1972, this interpretation emphasizes the competition between new economic and social constituencies in shaping various articulations of national identity, religious expression, and the rights of citizens. A focus on competing economic and social interests draws attention to the different constituencies that employ or support Islam and the varied ways in which they construct a symbolic politics.

Attention to changing economic and social conditions recognizes that Bangladeshis retain a strong attachment to Islam, which reverberates in the daily customs and practices of people's lives (Huque and Akhter, 1987; Osmany, 1992). However, the meaning of this attachment has changed over time and has been called upon as the idiom of mobilization in different and contradictory ways, even over the brief period between the partition of India in 1947 and 1994. A historicized reading of Islam suggests that it is impossible to frame an analysis of fundamentalism without situating Islam—as religion, belief, and cultural construction—within the country's changing economic, social, and political history. Once situated, its meaning can be understood as contingent upon specific political objectives and party organization, and its deployment as a means for antisecular mobilization can be recognized as an expression of particular vested interests. Such an understanding departs from purely culturalist and homogenized interpretations of religious revivalism and incorporates what Zartman (1992) refers to as the rise of political Islam. I argue that attention to the construction of different economic and social constituencies provides a window on the politicization of Islam and manipulations of gender relations in contemporary Bangladesh.

In this chapter I address three interlinked questions: How have changes in material circumstances and the reorganization of economic and political relations provided a space for the politicization of Islam and the rise of communal tension? How has the chronology of these processes been constituted by a changing nationalist discourse? How have women's interests and struggles constituted and been manipulated by the intersections of the cultural and political economy? I examine these questions chronologically by focusing on regime history and the interests that emerge in the policies that have framed the political landscape. I identify the expansion of Islamic political authority and show how gender relations both constitute and are products of particular interactions amongst political initiatives, popular mobilizations, and changing production relations.

I argue that the religious resurgence in the country simultaneously builds upon and reorders gender relations, class demands, and Islamic practices. Like Basu and Metcalf (in this volume), I avoid the term "fundamentalist" because of its pejorative connotation. However, I draw attention to the shift from Islam as religion to its embrace by institutional politics. Today struggles for political legitimacy and authority are made in the language of authentic readings of the Qur'an Sharif and demands for an Islamic state. I further argue that religious resurgence is part of a broader "development crisis," which frames efforts at nation-building and constructions of nationalism and identity politics. Here I draw attention to the contradictions posed by changing economic and social relations and changing expectations regarding women's behavior, particularly as they recast women as subjects who threaten extant social practices rather than as objects or victims of new economic and social opportunities. In this view, female wage workers are not envisioned as victims of the modernization project but as invokers of change who challenge particular urban and rural petty bourgeois interests. I also suggest that the struggle for political legitimacy cannot be viewed solely through the lens of parties or state ideologies—although political legitimacy's form is contingent upon specific party and state practices—but can be refined through an examination of challenges to new forms of global integration that have recentered gender contradictions within a series of national political and institutional realignments.

Setting the Stage

Zartman (1992: 182) argues that political Islam has arisen "as a political formula in reaction to the failures of modernization and secular socialism."[2] In contrast, I posit that political Islam represents the relative *success* of the modernization project and the development of an outward-looking entrepreneurial elite, and a consequent loss of various economic and political benefits for a segment of urban elite and rural petty bourgeois and agricultural interests. The political realignments that have followed situate the transition from religion as a set of practices that reproduce a belief system to religious ideology deployed as a tool of political mobilization and party politics. The dynamic among these processes recognizes Islam as an ideology embodying particular social and economic interests. The policy priority given to the development of entrepreneurial interests, represented by the shift from import substitution to export-led development, has meant that the interests of the Jama'at-i-Islami, the most prominent Islamist political party in Bangladesh, have been slowly undermined with each successive political regime since independence in 1972. This helps to explain its growing political salience as well as the need for oppositional parties to negotiate with it, given that it represents constituents ripe for mobilization.

Contradictions and contestations around these processes of negotiation transform people's lives and challenge, perhaps most dramatically, the meanings of women's lives. For instance, dramatic shifts in Bangladeshi women's employment, participation in training programs and increased education, access to and use of credit, and greater visibility in social and political life have made rural and urban lower-middle- and middle-class women more visible than ever before and have enabled them to negotiate for control of resources heretofore unavailable to them. These shifts highlight the changing space and physical presence of women as they come to share resources and places once limited to men. They also highlight women as independent subjects who make decisions and frame demands that challenge previous forms of labor control and subservience. The new areas of participation focus attention on women's bodies and their new public role as a site for contesting previous and new social relations and forms of production, power, and patronage.

Such changes reflect and respond to Bangladesh's colonial history and the need for both connections to and autonomy from the past. Engaging Kandiyoti's argument regarding women, Islam, and the state, I too recognize that "while the boundaries of Islam and the nation are interdeterminate and their juxtaposition variable, the centrality of women in guaranteeing the integrity of both is not. The . . . association between women's appropriate place and conduct, however defined, and notion of cultural authenticity is a persistent theme which deserves further exploration" (Kandiyoti, 1991b: 7). Kandiyoti suggests that the destruction of local communities and the loosening of traditional family forms can be attributed to the unintended consequences of capitalist penetration. By contrast, I stress the ways in which global interests and state practices build upon and reconstitute extant organizational structures and social relations and challenge the customs and practices deemed to impede social progress in order to expand their control over the socialization of Bangladesh's citizens.

Islamist parties, in contrast, reclaim social practices that embody the interests that are being eroded by the growth strategies endorsed by entrepreneurial elites. These "traditional" interests embody gender relations constituted on the basis of women's unpaid work in agricultural and craft production based in the domestic economy. They also embody kin relations and networks, and forms of patronage and obligation established on the basis of collective and reciprocal exchange. Kin relations are often associated with that which is defined as feminine, concerned with the private space of the home and its attendant kin networks, and build upon what Papanek refers to as the arena of women's "family status production work" (Papanek, 1979). These social relations differ from those that are established on the basis of the self-reliant individual, the wage earner, or the independent entrepreneur. Transforming collective and reciprocal relations into market exchanges frames contemporary policy priorities and, when the latter characteristics are attributed to women, mark all that is wrong with the modernist transformation of the cultural and political economy.

Crises of Difference, Crises of Legitimacy

Mobilizing broad support for the independence movement that brought Bangladesh into being in 1972 required departing from the religious nationalism that legitimated the 1947 partition of India and formation of Pakistan. It necessitated the dismantling of Muslim identity, constructed as a natural affinity between Bengalis and Pakistanis, and replacing this "imagined community" with an ethnic, linguistic, and cultural nationalism centered on Bengali identity. This symbolic shift, from religious identity to shared ethnicity and language, provided the basis for what it meant to be a Bangladeshi, as distinct from what it meant to be an East Pakistani.[3] In this shift, identity was neither forged nor was mobilization organized in anti Muslim terms, a point crucial to interpreting the struggles against secularism that followed.

But this cry for Bengali nationalism was not without its contradictions. Prepartition religious differences as well as cultural alliances between the two Bengals had continued to resonate in East Pakistan after 1947. The particular history of the region sustained a need to differentiate between a Bengal that was Hindu and Indian and one that was uniquely Bengali and Muslim. The subsequent tensions that emerged between Islamic and Bengali identity were poised to enter the debate on secularism, especially since they were easily connected to the pro-Indian politics of the Awami League. After 1971, the political alignment had particular significance up to 1975, given the abandonment of Bangladesh by the West and its support by India and the Soviet Union. These alliances indicate the issues that would form a backdrop to contestations over the constitutional defense of secularism.

Also foreshadowing contestation of secularism during the independence period were the activities of the Jama‘at-i-Islami. As a counter to the independence struggle, in 1971 Pakistan President Yahya Khan formed a ten-member East Pakistan government that consisted of members of the rightist political parties, including the Jama‘at, who had been defeated in the elections of 1970. In addition, in the pamphlet "Don't Blame Centre," the Jama‘at attacked the Awami League and other progressive forces and brought out a procession against what it called the "Secessionist Movement" (Mukhapadyay, 1971, in Sen, 1986: 279). The Jama‘at-i-Islami is also held responsible for identifying socialist, democratic, and secular intellectuals who were subsequently killed by its front organization with the help of the Pakistan army (*Far Eastern Economic Review*, 1971, in Sen, 1986: 9).

Members of the rightist opposition represented elements of the middle class and the upper stratum of the feudal *jotedār*, or landowning classes, who fought against the 1970–71 independence movement. In the early 1960s, fearing the potential militancy of this class, Pakistan President Ayub Khan had presumed that they could be contained by giving them a direct stake in the development of East Pakistan. As Sobhan (1980: 8–9) argues: "If enough Bengalis could be set up in industry and trade and introduced into the upper echelons of the bureaucracy and professions ... [t]hey would come to depend on the coercive power of the Pakistani ruling classes to secure their gains and would, in turn, serve as their surrogates in ruling East Pakistan." This opposition also included the urban-based foreign-born Islamic elite (the "Biharis"), which strongly resisted assimilation into indigenous Bengali culture and maintained its position by adhering to orthodox Islamic practices and to speaking Persian, Arabic, and Urdu (Kabeer, 1991: 118).

In addition to recognizing the creation of this comprador bourgeoisie, the struggle for sovereignty and nonalignment in terms of Bengali nationalism recognized the double colonial cloak of British and Pakistani exploitation. This made more transparent the relations of inequality across spatially distinct, linguistic boundaries that had been partially masked by Muslim unity between East and West Pakistan. Mobilizing against this Islamic connection drew attention to the contradictory ways in which Islam had been used by Pakistan: to integrate economic relations, albeit unequally, and to maintain distinctions between social and cultural practices in the east wing and the west wing of the country. This is perhaps most notably exemplified by the efforts of West Pakistan to maintain economic dominance while seeking to synthesize points of difference, as indicated by its attempt, and subsequent failure, to establish Urdu as the lingua franca.

Relations of economic exploitation were at the forefront of the movement for Bangladesh's independence, and class and nationalist politics served to center the platform of the Awami League. The interplay between the Awami League's economic and social critique, coupled with a cultural discourse used to mobilize a national constituency, is perhaps most visible in its constitutional commitments to democracy and socialism as well as nationalism and secularism. It is also suggested by the fact that despite broad support for the Awami League through the independence struggle, when it actually came to power in 1972 and created a government, it drew its leadership from urban elites and sought support from the rich peasantry, who, with sufficient state patronage, could be relied upon to contain unrest among the rural poor and to muster votes at election time (Kabeer, 1991).

The strategy was not without its costs, since addressing the concerns of university students, urban middle-class supporters, and selected rural elites, failed to generate mass-based rural support (Sobhan and Ahmed, 1981). The result was a crisis that manifested itself in middle-class factionalism, an unengaged rural population that accounted for almost 85 percent of the total population, and a highly contentious institutional sector framed by conflict and struggle for power between the Awami League and the military. The military was also factionalized and could not redefine itself from a traditionally anti-Indian force to become part of a pro-Indian ruling party. The inability of the Awami League to create a hegemonic project provided a political opening both for the military and for the slow rise of the Jama'at-i-Islami. In both cases, a politico-religious rhetoric has helped to mask the opportunism that constitutes struggles among the military and the democratic and Islamist parties.

How were contestations over secularism framed by a religious discourse and used to support a particular class politics? First, in the immediate postindependence period, both the West and the Middle East refused to recognize the sovereignty of Bangladesh or to provide aid and technical assistance to the new regime. This excluded Bangladesh from the Islamic community and disrupted the uneasy alliance between those who believed in more textual readings of Islam and those who supported a syncretic interpretation of Bangladeshi Islam. Given the fragility of this alliance, the regime of Sheikh Mujib-ur-Rahman could ill afford to ignore these disagreements if Bangladesh were to survive as an aid- and oil-dependent country. Second, the regime needed to secure its own political legitimacy and thus was dependent upon successfully mobilizing the people around Bengali as distinct from Islamic nationalism. This meant constructing an ethnic and linguistic understanding of citizenship and community membership, even as this sat awkwardly in the transition from Bengali to Pakistani and then to Bangladeshi interpretations of identity.

Because the regime could not afford to alienate potential sources of financial assistance any further, Sheikh Mujib increasingly moved to gain a wider political space in the global community, including among the Islamic countries. For example, he made efforts to have Bangladesh recognized as an independent nation in the United Nations; participated in the Islamic summit held in Lahore in 1974; took steps to rehabilitate those who collaborated with the Pakistani military forces; and recognized the creation of the Islamic Foundation of Bangladesh (Alam, 1993: 97–98). These initiatives underscored the ruling party's interest in mediating differences among possible sources of financial assistance while maintaining a commitment to secularism.[4]

Mujib's strategy should also be read as an effort to regain the momentum of the independence struggle. Seen in this light, constitutional support for secularism was a way to gain political legitimacy in the global economy, to construct hegemonic authority nationally, and to remove recognized oppositional religious parties from the political landscape. The strategy distinguishes between a secular politics and an anti-Islamic one. As stated in the Constitution:

> The principle of secularism shall be realized by the elimination of (a) communalism in all its forms; (b) the granting by the State of political status in favour of any religion; (c) the abuse of religion for political purposes; (d) any discrimination against, or persecution of, persons practising a particular religion. (Government of Bangladesh, 1972: 7)

And, as a way to distinguish further between an anti-Islamic posture and an interest in banning religion from party politics, the Constitution continues:

> Every citizen shall have the right to form associations or unions, subject to any reasonable restrictions imposed by law in the interests of morality or public order; provided that no person shall have the right to form, or be a member of, any communal or other association or union which in the name of or on the basis of any religion has for its object, or pursues, a political purpose. (Government of Bangladesh, 1972: 7)

As implied earlier, this view of secularism acknowledges the importance of Bengali religious life and tradition but constitutionally secures secularism as a way to limit particular forms of political opposition. Such a strategy was not an antireligious maneuver because the regime utilized a broad array of religious symbols in the media and, later, increased and then emphasized Islamic symbols in Sheikh Mujib's speeches and activities. But the strategy was not without its contradictions, which are perhaps most clearly expressed in the regime's position on religious education.

When viewed within the narrow debate on secularism, the removal of religious training in primary and secondary schools alienated a portion of Sheikh Mujib's broad support. Yet this decision reflected the party's commitment to the urban, modernizing middle classes who often conflate modern institutional forms with the separation of religion and the state. In their view, religious belief and practice, the private domain of individual rights, was now secured by constitutional decree. The eventual inclusion of religious education in parts of the curriculum also reveals the politicization of religion as well as the regime's ambivalence in realizing the four constitutional principles it had established when it gained control of the country.

Secularism is also an often stated value of the Mahila Parishad (Women's Council), an organization that grew out of the Awami League Women's Wing and had more than thirty thousand members by the 1980s. Embodied in the interpretation of secularism embraced by women activists, scholars, and advocacy groups are goals of empowerment and social transformation that suggest as much about the middle-class position of women in these movements and the assumptions that frame their interests in gender equity as they do about the exclusion of poor women as a voice among their membership. (See Shaheed, in this volume, for a similar argument about the women's movement in Pakistan.) For instance, despite the government's inadequate response to the approximately thirty thousand women who were raped by the Pakistan army and their local supporters during the independence struggle, there was little mobilization among women, especially those urban women who had a history of reformist activism, around this form of gender violence. The failure to respond can partially be explained by urban women's naiveté about the plight of rural women, their sense of middle-class vulnerability, and their unwillingness to challenge patriarchal traditions, which could result in a backlash against rape victims. The divide between middle-class urban and rural women is perhaps best indicated by one middle-class urban woman's diary entry, written at the beginning of the struggle in April 1971: "These days the soldiers commandeer private cars. It has become a routine affair. But they spare the cars which have lady passengers" (Imam, 1994: 185).

During the early 1970s, struggles for secularism and democracy were increasingly difficult to manage as the regime became mired in personal greed and corruption, and as relations between the Awami League and the bureaucracy grew more factionalized (Jahan, 1977; Maniruzzaman, 1982). The factionalism, coupled with clashes between the regime, the military, and the opposition parties, eventually undermined the government's authority. Contributing to its decline was its inability to restore production levels to those prior to independence, the poor productivity of the nationalized sector, the rapid growth in inflation rates, and the deteriorating standard of rural living, epitomized by the 1974 famine. These conditions were used by the opposition and the United States to undermine further the regime's control and political legitimacy, providing a ripe environment for a military coup. Interestingly, the principles of secularism and socialism came to characterize the corruption and economic failure of the regime, and provided the symbolic context that eventually crippled efforts to build democracy and nationalism.

The Period of Military Rule

With the change in government in 1975, Islam was more explicitly introduced into party manifestos and documents. Maulana Bhashani, leader of the pro-Beijing Leftists, had advocated Islamic socialism during the Mujib period, while Muzaffar Ahmed of the pro-Moscow National Awami Party (NAP) also linked religion and socialism with the slogan "Religion, hard work, and socialism" (Maniruzzaman, 1983: 208–9). Other parties, including the Democratic League, likewise invoked Islam in their desire to establish a just society, and the Islamic parties, including the Islamic Democratic League and the Muslim League, framed their political agenda on the teachings of the Qur'an Sharif and on religious practice (Huque and Akhter, 1987). As I will suggest, this challenge to secularism is linked to the dismantling of socialism and the nationalization project that also characterized the Mujib period.

The periods of military rule under both Ziaur Rahman (1975–1981) and Ershad (1982–1990) significantly altered the political stage.[5] Zia increased the defense budget from 15 to 16 percent to between 20 and 30 percent of the annual revenue budget. In the last year of Mujib's rule the defense budget was $34 million or 0.7 percent of Gross National Product; by 1978 it was $130 million or 1.8 percent of GNP (Jahangir, 1986: 80). The increase did not resolve the factional interests and generational differences that characterized the military. In fact, in 1975, the almost fifty-five thousand persons in the army were about equally divided between those who had participated in the liberation struggle and those who had been repatriated from West Pakistan. The senior repatriated officers had lost seniority and status to the younger recruits, who, because of their participation and experience in the liberation struggle, were able to rise in the military hierarchy. This generated a range of hostilities among the cadres, with repatriates representing a conservative, anti-Indian constituency with a pro-Islamic world orientation and young officers and soldiers constituting the more politicized elements of the service (Maniruzzaman, 1982: 285).

Ziaur Rahman also strengthened diplomatic and trade relations between Bangladesh and both the West and the Middle East. He dismantled the socialist orientation of Bangladesh and secured closer alliances with the oil-rich countries of the Middle East and support from the European Community and North America. He also sought the greater involvement of the World Bank and the International Monetary Fund in reorganizing the Bangladesh economy, and initiated increased trade with countries of the Pacific Rim. The regime also increased the capitalization of agriculture and rural petty commodity production, turned its commitments to the enhancement of private investment, and promoted the rapid denationalization of the industrial sector to create a new class of entrepreneurs and traders whose interests became central to the politics of the newly formed Bangladesh Nationalist Party (BNP). These initiatives coincided with tube-well and input subsidies to peasant producers, a government procurement program, and infrastructural support for roads, irrigation, and grain storage. Such resources offered new channels of patronage to rural power brokers and sustained the status of Union Council members, whose support was important in building the BNP. This meant, in short, a dramatic turn in the country's development agenda from import substitution to export-led growth and a shift in political alliances from India and the Soviet Union to the United States and Europe. The shift engaged symbolic identifications that included renaming the nationalist fervor of the war—Bangladeshi nationalism rather than Bengali nationalism—in order to distinguish between Bengali Hindus and Bangladeshi Muslims.

Building on the turn toward Islam already implicated in the symbolic politics of the Awami League, and the political space that emerged with the murder of Sheikh Mujib in August 1975, Ziaur Rahman also formally moved to alter the constitutional commitment to secularism and introduced, by presidential proclamation, the phrase "absolute trust and faith in Almighty Allah" in its place. To emphasize this shift, Zia warmly recognized those who completed the *hajj* (pilgrimage to Mecca) and also made his own visits to Saudi Arabia. Islamic banks began to operate in Dhaka and Chittagong; mosques and *madrasās* (Islamic schools) were established in and around the capital and in the provincial towns, acknowledging their support from the Saudi government; and Islamic parties were provided a larger space in political fora as a show of Islamic solidarity.

Despite these moves, Zia projected himself as a modernist, espousing a progressive version of Islam, including support for women. For instance, his modernist stance was articulated through backing a rising number of non governmental organizations (NGOs), which provided, among their explicit goals, literacy training and population planning for poor rural women. While a number of NGOs began as relief and rehabilitation efforts after the 1974 famine, their commitments broadened to include securing women's interests through consciousness-raising, a task accomplished by employing women as project personnel. Zia also supported the employment of women within governmental and semiautonomous programs in health, family planning, and cooperative organizations, slowly transforming the configuration of the rural labor force.

Additionally, and coinciding with the UN International Women's Year (1975) and the UN Decade for Women (1975–1985), Zia ably exploited the "women in development" banner to create the Bangladesh Jatiya Mahila Sanghstha (BJMS, the national women's organization) that served predominantly middle-class women, and to support a growing number of government programs that extended resources and generated employment for women. He initiated the countrywide Integrated Rural Development Programme (IRDP), in which rural women's cooperatives extended credit to women while maintaining a commitment to population control, established the Ministry of Women's Affairs, and reserved parliamentary seats and public-sector jobs for women. These efforts were class- and gender-specific, and were implemented in ways that did not undermine extant production and gender relations. For example, the IRDP provided credit for activities that did not challenge women's central place within the household, but enabled women to capitalize rural activities such as cattle raising, vegetable gardening, and home-based sewing. Such programs extended and reorganized domestic work rather than undermining the central place of women in the rural economy.

Through his support for the expansion of the NGOs to engage the poor, the landless, and women, and through expanding opportunities for middle-class rural women in the cadres of government service, Zia creatively manipulated the public discourse on Islam and its interpretation of women. Zia also ably used these opportunities to channel resources and patronage to the country-side; in this way he built a rural constituency and simultaneously legitimized a dramatic increase in the resources controlled by and public presence of women. Moreover, and unlike Sheikh Mujib, Zia cultivated a "man of the soil" image, often visited rural communities, and played on his role in the liberation struggle in order to strengthen his rural support.

Although Zia's support of these initiatives recentered Islam in the political project of constructing Bangladesh within the fold of the Islamic community, other policies enhancing women's resource access and creating opportunities for women's employment helped to sustain a syncretic interpretation of Bangladeshi Islam. This posture challenged the Jama'at-i-Islami, which argued for female seclusion and a return to earlier forms of patronage and informal exchange. The process of mediating these interests coupled with Zia's move toward civilian rule threatened relations within the military and eventually led to his downfall.

Ershad's seizure of power furthered Zia's export-led development strategy and also advanced Islam as a political doctrine. Ershad put Islam at the center of his ideological discourse, extended Zia's move toward denationalization and divestment, increased the country's dependence on foreign capital, and set the conditions enabling the creation of an industrial bourgeoisie. According to Alam (1990: 37) the shift toward denationalization was part of a state initiative to privatize some of the surplus rather than creating a means to generate it.

Moreover, agricultural and input subsidies were removed, credit was directed toward urban and industrial development, and the voices of the burgeoning urban industrial elite had the ear of Ershad and the support of the multilateral and bilateral aid community. The shift in rural and agricultural policy is exemplified by Ershad's promotion of the popular politics of decentralization, which shifted authority for resource allocation and local-level decision making to the *upa-zilā* (sub-district). This was part of a reorganized development bureaucracy that created a vehicle for his own political control in the hope of building a rural base for his new political party. This altered the patronage connections established by previous regimes and removed the benefits that had previously accrued to selected rural interests. It is not coincidental that these efforts both built upon and diverted attention from the growing number of landless households, the decreasing demands for agricultural labor, and a growing need to generate nonfarm rural employment. These processes of economic reorganization were subverting the rural domestic economy, increasing the likelihood that all family members would have to secure their own subsistence, and increasing the demand as well as opportunities for women's employment.

In this context of declining rural resources and a growing proportion of resources represented by the NGO community, it is not surprising that a space was created for the Jama'at-i-Islami, which combined proselytizing and social welfare work to extend resources to the rural poor.[6] As Kabeer (1991: 134) notes, "The outcome of Saudi munificence has been the creation of alternative networks of patronage (scholarships, vocational training, student accommodation, employment, and medical aid) which materially bolster the appeal of the Islamic constituency." Not surprisingly, the success of Jama'at-i-Islami has been most dramatic outside the Dhaka metropolitan campuses and among those who have been most frustrated in their search for employment in a limited labor market. Women who join the movement are both recruits and recruiters of a separate women's front.

Changes in the rural economy also created the political space for a rapidly expanding nongovernmental sector that initially provided resources and services to the rural poor. During this period, NGOs broadened the issues they addressed and the constituencies they served. Given the gender politics of developmentalism, women became the mark and the clientele characterizing the modernizing economy. Although government resources to rural women did not significantly rise, except in population control, NGO programs designed to generate employment and improve women's literacy and health care grew. In response to Ershad's industrialization initiatives, the demand for rural women workers in the emerging export sector generated a growing and diversified female labor force.

Support for the 1982 industrial policy concretized the government's acceptance of structural adjustment, caricatured by the development of export-processing enclaves in Dhaka and Chittagong, credit and tax holidays for an emerging entrepreneurial class, and bureaucratic support to develop and enhance the interests of this ascending class. Built upon the export-led strategy required by the World Bank, this policy advertised the competitive wages and docile labor of Bangladeshi women during a time when US and European import quotas had begun to restrict imports from Korea and the Newly

Industrialized Countries (NICs). The result was an expansion of the female labor force that made visible women who had heretofore been absent on the streets of Dhaka city and whose presence came to represent what it meant to be modern in the new urban environment of the capital. In the course of little more than a year, women were living in hostels that had previously been limited to the university campus, going to the cinema halls, shopping in the small markets that surrounded the emerging manufacturing sites, waiting for buses, and walking arm in arm on the street. This change profoundly challenged even those of us who were often the only other (Western) women on the street.

Ershad responded to a group of women who were wearing their *sārīs* in a fashion thought too risqué for the streets of Dhaka, by ordering the police to tar their midriffs. This action was quickly stopped in response to immediate demonstrations of people's outrage. The event occurred in the middle-class shopping area of New Market, at the time a favored spot for married, often professional, urban women to shop. Their expeditions usually meant being dropped off by *rikshās* or car directly in front of the market, so that few women were seen to venture unaccompanied on the road to the market. This contrasted starkly with the openness of young working "girls" walking in groups along the main road. The example highlights the innocent yet apparent challenge embodied in this shift in women's visibility and behavior and suggests why women's public behavior can be seen to embody all that is distinctive about that which is modern. It is also likely that conservative reactions to women working in the factories and utilizing the shops and cinema halls are a means to criticize, if indirectly, the emerging urban upper middle class that has benefited from the new inputs and infrastructural resources that once were controlled by selected rural elites.

Despite popular censures, Ershad took a further step toward linking the state and Islam by exempting mosques from paying their electric and water bills; instituting a *zakāt* (alms) fund under his control; requiring television broadcasts to be preceded by a call to prayer; and requiring women in the media to be appropriately modest. He also refused to ratify a number of clauses promoted by the World Plan of Action of the UN Decade for Women and part of the UN Convention on the Elimination of All Forms of Discrimination Against Women (1979), which related to inheritance, marriage, child custody, and divorce, on the grounds that they conflicted with the *Sharī'a*. He vowed, as well, "to give Islam its rightful place in the future constitution of the country" (speech by Ershad reported in *Ittefaq*, 18 February 1985, in Huque and Akhter, 1987: 224). These efforts were viewed by some as a way to engage Islam in order to promote a nationalist mass politics and new forms of solidarity and legitimacy, which were assumed to mask the class cleavages of civil society and to prevent an oppositional class politics from emerging (Alam, 1993: 102).

Ershad's inability to secure his legitimacy is perhaps best represented by the March 1988 elections, which he won but which were boycotted by the opposition parties and in which only 3 percent of the electorate participated. His fragile political status next led him to negotiate with the rightist opposition and amend the Constitution. On 7 June 1988 Parliament introduced and passed Section 2A of the Constitution: "The state religion of the Republic is Islam but other religions may be practiced in peace and harmony in the Republic" (Kamaluddin, 1988; Human Rights Watch/Asia, 1994: 7). The reaction was a mass mobilization of protest in Dhaka that included a range of women's groups that, in some cases, had never before participated in a public rally. Despite the amendment and various other negotiated compromises, Jama'at-i-Islami leader Moulana Delwar Hosain still accused the government and secular opposition political parties of "letting women in the street, which he argued was eroding Islamic values" (Kamaluddin, 1989).

The shifts and compromises represent a diversification of patronage to urban and town elites from previously more narrow alliances with the agricultural elite; a breakdown in the once-resilient family-based domestic economy; and a more public presentation of a gendered labor force. Such material changes, coupled with Ershad's unwillingness to create a civilian power base independent from the military (as had Zia), expanded the political space for right-wing Islamist parties, among which the Jama'at-i-Islami became the most powerful. In 1990 a movement for democracy removed Ershad from power and opened the way to elections.

The Democratic Space of 1990

In February 1991, Begum Khaleda Zia, the widow of former president and martial law administrator Ziaur Rahman, led the Bangladesh Nationalist Party (BNP) in what has been touted as the country's first real democratic election, winning 31 percent of the popular vote. The Awami League, under Hasina Wajid (the daughter of Sheikh Mujib), won 28 percent, and Ershad won 12. Jama'at-i-Islami, with eighteen parliamentary seats, emerged as the fourth-largest party. Early on, Khaleda Zia promoted a strategy of negotiation with the "fanatically ideological Jama'at-i-Islami party" (Maniruzzaman, 1982: 283), a strategy viewed by some as a pragmatic initiative to secure political power by limiting the effect of any alliance between the Awami League and Ershad's Jatiya party. However, the negotiations have included shared decision making on, among other things, the distribution of the thirty seats reserved for women and chosen by Parliament (Kamaluddin, 1992). Moreover, such collaboration legitimates "fundamentalist" readings of social behavior that depart from the syncretic interpretations of Islamic everyday behavior, which were an important contribution of Ziaur Rahman. By challenging progressive forces, such as the NGOs and other nonaligned interests, this collaboration undermines representation in a democratic polity and critical political opposition, whether through benign support or what might be called conscious inaction.

Collaboration with the Jama'at-i-Islami has all but transformed a democratic state into an Islamic one. For example, the secretary-general of Jama'at introduced a private member's bill in Parliament in July 1992 that sought to make acts that "defile" the Qur'an Sharif or the name of the Prophet criminal. Under this bill the Penal Code would be amended such that

> whoever willfully damages, or desecrates the Holy Qur'an or ... uses the Holy Qur'an ... in a derogatory manner shall be punished with imprisonment for life, [and] whoever by words either spoken or written, or by signs or visible representations, or by an imputation, innuendoso [sic] or insinuation, defiles, directly or indirectly, the sacred name of the Holy Prophet Muhammad (peace be upon him) shall be punished with death, or imprisonment for life and shall also be liable to a fine. (Human Rights Watch/Asia, 1994: 5)

Should this pass, anything that diverges from a textual reading of Islam could be challenged by government efforts to secure law and order.

Not surprisingly, a forum of intellectuals and professionals in Bangladesh urged the government to resist enacting such a law, anticipating that it could be used as a tool of repression. These progressive forces are often led by women and members of the NGO community, who have been the most direct targets of Jama'at attack. Yet despite their calls, the government has failed to denounce, investigate, prosecute, or punish crimes committed in the name of *fatvās* or to take action against those who issue *fatvās* that are a direct incitement to violence even though this violates the Bangladesh Constitution (Human Rights Watch/Asia, 1994: 2).

As a consequence, throughout 1994 women were stoned to death for committing adultery, presses destroyed and writers banned or executed for their "blasphemous" work, and NGOs firebombed and demolished for the programs they offered to women. These instances were neither rare nor localized. For example, the Jama'at-i-Islami organized villagers against a Sylheti family by engaging traditionally organized community relations, such as the *salish* (an informal meeting for settling disputes), to represent their interests. In one well-known case, Nurjahan, a woman who had been living with her parents when her first husband abandoned her, was remarried after her parents fulfilled the obligations of an appropriate annulment. Claiming that this behavior was inappropriate and offensive to local interests, a religious leader called a *salish*, where it was declared that Nurjahan should be placed in a waist-deep hole and pelted with 101 stones. Nurjahan survived, as did her parents, who were also publicly brutalized, only to return home to commit suicide because of the public shame and humiliation (*Daily Sangbad*, 1994, in Guhathakurta, 1994). This example and others of verbal abuse and physical attacks against women for allegedly committing adultery highlight the kinds of practices promoted by the Jama'at and how women get caught within a web of competing forms of personal and social legitimacy. The example also supports the fear identified by progressive democratic voices in Bangladesh that the alliance between the BNP and the Jama'at-i-Islami has legitimated repression, particularly against women.

What is also striking about the strategy of the Islamist parties is their effort to control information in the public press. Secular presses in Bogra and Dhaka have been set aflame because of allegations that they printed anti-Islamic articles. On 20 May 1994, for instance, in addition to setting fire to the offices of two Bengali newspapers, marchers demanded the execution of Taslima Nasrin and a ban on four newspapers: *Bhorer Kagoj, Sanghad, Janakantha,* and *Bangla Bani*. This was followed by attacks on newspaper offices, threats to their editors, and charges against or warrants for the arrest of editors whose papers were alleged to have published articles with malicious and deliberate intent of hurting the religious sentiments of the people.

Another example is offered by an incident following a nationwide call for a *hartāl (strike)* by the Islamist parties. During the *hartāl*, the Bangladesh Women's Health Coalition clinic in Zakiganj, Sylhet, was set aflame by a mob of two thousand to three thousand people led by the sons of a local *pīr* (Muslim holy man). They eventually let the medical officer, Dr. Mohammed Sultan Ahmed, escape, but the clinic was gutted and an adjoining NGO, Friends of Village Development in Bangladesh, was badly damaged. Despite charges and the identification of a number of attackers, ten people were arrested and released the next morning, reportedly following a call from the prime minister's office. The clinic, founded in the early 1980s, offered women health and family planning information and services. Its head, Sultana Kamal, has been an important voice in the struggle for women's reproductive rights, an area of intervention that was touted as a major success for Bangladesh at the 1994 World Population Conference in Egypt.

These incidents are part of a pattern of attacks that have been levied against the NGO community in Bangladesh. Two highly respected and internationally recognized organizations, the Bangladesh Rural Advancement Committee (BRAC) and the Grameen Bank, focus their program support on women and provide, among other things, training and credit to the rural poor. The NGO programs offer an alternative to existing forms of *madrasā* education and informal credit or money lending that serve as sources of legitimacy and areas of investment for members of the Islamist parties.[7] It is not surprising that NGO rural programs have been attacked, program workers harassed, and schools and buildings burned.

In Bangladesh, the struggle to survive is constant, economic divisions are increasing, and women are obvious markers of these changes—since many women seek employment because a family can no longer be sustained by one income earner or because their prior forms of work have been eroded with changes in agriculture and in small-scale, home-based craft production. In such a context, it is advantageous for Islamist parties to secure their own legitimacy by confronting women who "step outside the bounds of social norms" (Feldman, 1992; Guhathakurta, 1994: 65). The bounds, of course, are reconstructed by the Jama'at-i-Islami in terms of a romanticized past and an idyllic future, playing on the promise of a better life where women could be secure within the patriarchal household. The discourse of the good Muslim woman is, of course, contradictory because it undermines the benefits many women have come to enjoy in the past decade; divides women between those who support the interests of the Islamist parties and those who challenge the politics of Islam; and limits the opportunities women may choose to engage. All this follows, moreover, upon a long and difficult history of negotiation between syncretic and more fundamentalist readings of Islam in which women have increasingly taken the lead in struggling on behalf of women's rights and the rights of all the people of Bangladesh. The Gono Adalat (People's Tribunal), for example, led by Jahanara Imam, demanded the government try the leaders of Jama'at-i-Islami for collaborating with Pakistan and committing war crimes in 1971. The government responded only by demanding "law and order," but such an initiative draws important links between the contemporary attacks on the cultural prescriptions of daily life and the vested interests of collaborators with the Pakistani elite in their attempt to maintain a colonial status for Bangladesh.

Ironically, although Islamist forces were supported through two military regimes, under a movement for democracy, supported by a democratically elected government, the Jama'at-i-Islami has emerged stronger than ever before. Yet despite its success, the Jama'at is continually challenged by an increasingly organized opposition, which has included a more vocal and organized women's movement that has successfully mobilized rural women. One consequence of these mobilizations was that the democratically elected regime of Begum Khaleda Zia faced intensified problems of legitimacy under her increasingly ineffective leadership.

Concluding Comments

A number of important tensions situate the growth of Jama'at-i-Islami within the changing economic and political forces in the country. These competitive forces are constituted by the changing position of Bangladesh within the global economy and the alliances that have been drawn through trade and aid dependencies, as well as the shifting alliances between state bureaucrats, party politics, and the military. The forces are also shaped by declining economic and social stability among a growing proportion of the population, with the simultaneous increase in the new urban industrial elite whose members are the beneficiaries of the export-led growth strategy. Since the late 1970s there has been an expanding, dynamic, and gradually coordinated NGO sector that has provided an increasingly diversified rural community with educational and credit resources. The NGOs are envisioned to constrain, if not undermine, previously dominant informal networks of credit and education provisioning. Additionally, women have gained employment in rural family planning and health care services and other public-sector programs in both rural towns and urban centers.

In this and other ways, women's position has been among the most dramatically altered by the economic changes. With the decline in family farming, women represent a growing proportion of the beneficiaries of NGO resources and of the increasing demand for workers to support the country's largest export industry, manufactured garments and apparel. As a result, households and families have contributed to a transformation of the image and materiality of rural and urban labor markets. Patron-client networks that had previously constituted social relations have since been dominated by wage contracts and institutionalized access to credit and other resources to sustain their viability. National policy similarly has redirected resources from the once-predominant commitment to the agricultural sector to rural nonfarm production, small-scale semiurban manufacturing, and industrial growth. State subsidies and control of the networks of access to state resources are now geared toward the development of the urban private sector. This has generated a new political constituency that has had the increasing attention of each successive regime as well as the international aid and industrial community.

Notes

This chapter's epigraph is a reflection of Rokeya Kabir's. It has remained with me and perplexed me since 1979, when I first met her. Rokeya Kabir is an important figure in the institutionalization of women's nongovernmental organizations.

1. It is not surprising that the aid community has begun to focus attention on policies that foster governance and what it defines as democratic pluralism. See, for example, USAID (1991), and World Bank (1994a; 1994b).
2. I follow Zartman in distinguishing between Islam as religious and cultural

practice and political Islam, with the Jama'at-i-Islami as its key exponent, as the site of ideological and material struggles for state power. The distinction both situates and historicizes Islam as a socially constructed and constituted set of practices that embody changing and often contradictory interests. The distinction also enables us to limit our discussion to specific themes regarding Bengali or Bangladeshi nationalism and nation-state formation, even though broader questions about these issues have figured prominently in recent debates on Islam (Maniruzzaman, 1983; Ahmed (ed.), 1990; Alam, 1993). I do not discuss the question of political legitimacy and institution building in the post-Mujib period (Ahmed (ed.), 1983, 1990; Maniruzzaman, 1982; 1983; Osmany, 1992) and also exclude questions of identity politics and their salience for understanding contemporary social movements.

3. Bengali Islam is characterized by its assimilation of a pre-Islamic past as expressed in its popular beliefs and practices not necessarily drawn from Qur'anic ideals and principles. This syncretic tradition continues to characterize Islam for many Bangladeshis (Roy, 1983). See also Geertz (1968), on Indonesia.

4. For an alternative interpretation of secularism as a pragmatic idea imported by Western-educated nationalist leaders rather than a commitment to the separation of politics and religion, see Maniruzzaman (1982) and Alam (1993). Posed in this way, secularism is deployed merely as another "religious" ideology rather than as a different axis upon which to base a political practice.

5. The entry of the military into political power indicates the class factionalism of the Mujib period and Sheikh Mujib's failure to offer a hegemonic project that could mediate the varied interests that had supported independence, particularly those of the military. Seen in this way, the corruption that was inevitably to bring the downfall of Sheikh Mujib was simply the final straw in his regime's failure to address the constituents who brought him to power.

6. Preliminary discussions reveal that election results along the border areas with India gave the strongest support to the Jama'at-i-Islami. In addition, migrants returning from the Middle East also disproportionately supported Jama'at.

7. These incidents are abstracted from Tax (1993); Human Rights Watch/Asia (1994); Guhathakurta (1994); various issues of the *Far Eastern Economic Review* (1993–94); and personal conversations in Bangladesh in 1993.

Chapter Four

The Outsider(s) Within

Sovereignty and Citizenship in Pakistan

SHAHNAZ ROUSE

B OTH SOVEREIGNTY AND CITIZENSHIP have carried varied significance depending on their disciplinary location and contextual usage. Until the advent of current feminist and critical theory, the focus was on "the nation" defined in terms of its territorial opposition to other nations, or on the individual as an autonomous agent—the Cartesian subject. The assumed independence of the nation-state and/or the individual was not initially problematized. Emphasis was thus laid on the public domain, on formal, legal structures, and on the rights and responsibilities of individuals in relation to them.

Drawing upon recent reformulations, I intend to go beyond the public, macro arena, drawing into the frame issues of private and everyday life. I will discuss the shifting social production and reproduction of the twin dynamics of sovereignty and citizenship in contemporary Pakistan with a view to explicating how these categories and resulting practices position women and also religious and ethnic minorities. The chapter will proceed from an examination of nationalism and identity formation, drawing into the framework the relation of these processes/practices to family life, social organization, and gender relations. This should also enable us to understand continuities and shifts in women's location—within the hegemonic discourse—as well as ambiguities within and contestations to such hegemonies. Since this is an extremely large topic, the focus during the latter portion of the chapter will be on specific incidents that indicate the current status and construction of citizenship viewed through the prisms of identity and difference.

Ever since its creation, Pakistan has had to deal with the contradictions and problems generated by its very birth. Coming into existence as a Muslim nation, the location and position of Islam in the body politic and the social body have been hotly contested. Within Pakistan, constitutional debates, religious lobbying, and judicial and political pressuring have all sought over and over again to address the issue of whether Pakistan was intended as merely a country "of Muslims" or a country "for Muslims." Given this historical fact, it seems problematic to cast an absolute opposition between Pakistan *prior* to and *after* 1977, when Zia ul Haq came to power, emasculated his political opposition, and amended the Constitution to reflect and adhere to what he and his supporters proclaimed as "Islamization" policies designed to bring the country more in line with its historical "intent" (Rouse, 1993).

Marking Gender in the Pre-Zia Period

Rather than positing an inevitability to the current location of religion in Pakistani politics and civil society, I suggest that the changes brought about by Zia ul Haq's regime can be understood only if their antecedents are traced back to early postindependence tendencies, and perhaps even further back to the independence movement itself. From 1948 onward, there has been continuous contestation regarding the basis of Pakistani nationalism and identity. I have also suggested elsewhere (Rouse, 1993) that at least part of the logic for successive shifts toward a more rigid conceptualization of Islam must be sought in the class character of the state,[1] and in external factors, for example, Pakistan's dependence on the United States and the Gulf states, especially starting in the later part of the Zulfiqar Ali Bhutto period (1970–1977) and continuing on with Zia. An exclusive focus on these dimensions, however, remains inadequate.

The demarcation between the pre- and post-Zia periods becomes less pronounced if we introduce gender into the picture. Not only the state but women's groups have sought to deploy religion on their own behalf. Thus, women's groups themselves fought for the *Sharī'a* to be introduced so as to permit women's inheritance rights. Similarly, British law prevailed in criminal and civil courts; however, in matters of the family and personal law (marriage, divorce, child custody, etc.), religious law continued to hold. Even Ayub Khan's now-famous Family Laws Ordinance (1961) did not attempt to transform the framework within which personal laws were adjudicated; rather, the ordinance sought to minimize the worst excesses of current customary practice and to regularize marriage, child custody, and divorce practices, strengthening the hand of the state in "private" life. Last, I would argue that the law sought to reinforce middle-class morality and strengthen the nuclear family rather than undermine it. In doing so, it was following a practice common to most modernizing states—i.e., simultaneously extending its intervention in those aspects of life previously outside its aegis, and equally importantly, constructing notions of "permissible sexuality". Nowhere did the Family Laws Ordinance challenge the family as a site of oppression and violence against women. It merely sought to improve women's conditions marginally within its parameters.[2] Public interventions in the private domain, in other words, sought not to challenge or overcome the public/private split with its attendant gender implications but rather to bring the private realm under increased state supervision and control.

In those arenas where the state sought incorporation of women into public life, one instance of this being women's education, it did so on the grounds that educated women made better mothers and wives. This pattern can be traced back to the construction of a bourgeois class in the subcontinent. Indeed, from the very inception of the social reform movement in Bengal, the concerns of the reformers startlingly paralleled the conceptions of Victorian morality. Women's education was not construed necessarily as a right for women but as part of the process whereby the bourgeois class was to define itself in opposition to its others, most notably the working and producing classes, as well as so-called tribals. In the Pakistani context, modernism sought to base its appeal to the populace on universalistic grounds, but was in effect to be the privilege of the few and the means by which these newly emerging classes were to rationalize their sociopolitical domination over the remainder of the population.

Just as women's education constituted part of a larger class agenda, women's work came to be seen as necessary to realizing the developmental project of the modernizing state. Built into this particular construction was the assumption that women, up until then, did not work. Such logic was (and still is) reflective, once again, of the class character of the struggle for women's rights. Not only were women expected to work for the larger good (to argue solely on the grounds of women's own good was cast as illegitimate), but it was essentially middle-class women and men who were at the forefront of the struggle. Proponents of this viewpoint either deliberately or unconsciously failed to recognize that women from the urban lower classes and 80 percent of women in the rural areas were productive members of the labor force (Rouse, 1988). The struggle, therefore, was initially not for greater control by women over their work nor for better work conditions but for inclusion of women theretofore excluded from the work force to participate alongside men. In doing so, it was understood that women would maintain their private roles as mothers, daughters, and/or wives.

While a necessary and previously unavailable space was thereby created for women in some sectors of society, patriarchal privilege was maintained through the private domain. The earliest jobs that middle-class women entered reproduced their private roles—as charity and relief workers, or teachers. Certain other jobs became available precisely because of the segregation and seclusion of women, for example, women entered the medical profession early on because it was considered inappropriate for women to be treated by nonfamilial men. Thus, segregation created a space for some women to enter the professions.

An anecdote might be instructive here. My own mother was widowed a few years after Pakistan came into being. Rather than have her family take care of her and her children, she went to work in a bank and was the first woman to do so. In this job, she encountered incredible sexual harassment. Drawing upon her own negative encounters in the workplace, she succeeded in establishing separate women's departments in the bank. This permitted women who would be reluctant to bank to do so. Simultaneously, it reproduced their separation from other parts of the bank: women who worked in these institutions were shut out from many key aspects of banking and relegated to a subordinated, ghettoized position in the financial sector. The move did, however, allow many other women to enter banks as workers. This constitutes both an example of women's struggles and of their limitations, given the gender/sexual parameters under which women's struggles were undertaken.

The example also shows that women acting within the contingencies of their everyday lives were not passive subjects. They were clearly involved in a struggle over their position in both public and private realms. However, the articulation of their struggles within and as a response to existent social and sexual norms, often simultaneously led to confrontation and reproduction of the very structures women were challenging.

What is noteworthy in all of this is that women's status continued to be determined by their separation from men. Although women were not excluded from the public, state apparatus, they were differentially inserted within it. Their distinctiveness was emphasized and reproduced even as they entered workplaces previously closed off to them. In the arenas where women had previously been present, not much changed. Everyday and work life continued much as before except insofar as it reflected changing socioeconomic conditions that either doubled women's work or cast them out and replaced them with men. Later, I will attempt to demonstrate that it is precisely this dichotomy that has come to be stressed in the post-Zia period. Yet, while the emphasis on women's separation and distinctiveness might have been accentuated since 1977, the actual terms of the debate go much further back. The debates about equality and around education and work were always narrowly confined to the public arena. In private, women achieved minimal gains.[3]

Ambiguity and contestation over religion and secularism emerged immediately after the inception of Pakistan, but gender contestation occurred within very narrowly defined parameters. Middle-class women demanded and attained gains in the public domain, yet the gains did not radically alter the discursive construction of gender. In certain ways, they merely reproduced the same terms outside the domestic framework that existed within it. Furthermore, the nature of women's struggles over private life served to strengthen existent ideologies privileging the family, marriage, and sexual union through marriage, thereby reinforcing ideas of appropriate sexual and social locations and the attendant hegemonies resulting from them.

Another aspect of gender identity needs to be explicated here: dress. Men had taken to Western clothes early on in the colonial administration. This trend continued after independence, especially in the cities. Women, on the other hand, were expected to wear Pakistani clothes—with whatever regional distinctions prevailed. In other words, modesty in clothing, as manifested in local dress, came to be another marker of difference between men and women. It also became a marker of women's identity and belonging. Women who wore skirts were invariably outsiders or treated as such. Pakistani Christians, who had taken to Western-style clothing from the colonial period, were thus clearly demarcated from Muslims. This could be read as a form of nonproblematic "othering"; however, accompanied by the epithets used for Pakistani Christians, the distinction takes on more sinister tones.

Throughout the early period in Pakistan's history up until 1977—excepting differences of degree—there is, then, a clear homogenizing effect that produces national identity through a privileging of women's distinctiveness from men, and that of Muslims from others. There are two significant departures from this process. First, under Zulfiqar Ali Bhutto there was considerable privileging of what came to be called "the 'awāmī [people's] dress"—that is shālwār, qamīz—for men and women alike. In a sense, Pakistan during this period saw the generalization of unisex clothing for men and women. Three aspects need to be noted here. First, women were not restricted to wearing this style of clothing alone. Sārīs and ghatāras [wide-legged trousers for women] continued to be worn. The shift brought about by Bhutto was focused primarily on men and constituted part of his populist strategy and rhetoric. Second, women were expected, though not coerced, to wear the dupattā along with the shalwār qamīz. This marked them off from men and their clothing. Another marker of difference was the colors adopted by the two genders: women's clothing was bright; men's, more subdued and mostly confined to neutral shades.

Difference and National Identity under Zia ul Haq

The second and more significant shift with regard to women's clothing came during the Zia period. Previously, men's and women's dress was distinguished and Muslim women were marked off from Christian women (who occasionally wore dresses). Zia sought to tighten further the norms of socially permissible dress. The sārī was denigrated as "Indian" (meaning Hindu) and frowned upon. The number of women wearing sārīs declined dramatically. The insistence on the *chādar* (head covering) also became more pronounced, though by no means universal, and women public servants were required to wear a chadar to work. During this period sleeveless dresses, previously common enough among college students, became noticeable by their absence, even in private gatherings.

Within Pakistan, the valorization of the *shalwār qamīz* came at the expense of other clothing styles that are common in different regions of Pakistan. Distinctions were made and boundaries established—through dress— between gender, religion, and ethnicity. At the international level, women and their clothes were also markers of identity, with the attack on the *sārī* marking differences among Muslims and especially demarcating Muslims from Hindus. These moves with respect to dress were paralleled by anti-Indian— read: anti-Hindu—sentiment, as well as profound borrowing from the West economically but a denigration of everything Western in terms of dress and sexual relations. Note, too, that this point applies primarily to women. Men were free to have premarital sexual relations, to wear Western clothes and so on. Women, however, were the repositories of culture via their clothes. Should women protest and resist such strictures—and some did and continue to do so—they risk accusations of being Western and culturally deviant, and they are subject to rebuke and sanction.

Women's changing dress styles may reflect the more conservative milieu during Zia's period and the internalization of norms regarding appropriate dress by some women and/or their fear of sanction and harassment by others. The shift also points to an insistence that in order to belong, to be seen as part of an Islamic—Pakistani—community, to win their citizenship in the Pakistani state, women must dress in a certain manner and conform to cultural, social, sexual norms that permeate Pakistani society from the level of everyday life through to the highest organs of the state.

During the initial period after independence, the primary forces exerting control in these domains resided in the private sector. The state was a more distant force and intervened only when issues pertaining to marriage, divorce, child custody, and the like came up. In most instances, these matters too were dealt with at home. The state did, however, maintain a contradictory position vis-à-vis women. It encouraged them to participate in public life, but as second-class citizens insofar as men formally controlled their sexuality, and it expected them to see such participation in the public domain as additional to their prescribed and primary roles—which it continued to cast as private ones.

All this came to a head in 1977 when Zia ul Haq came to power. After Zia deposed Zulfiqar Ali Bhutto with the help of the military, he proceeded to announce his plans for establishing *Nizam-e-Mustafa*—the Islamization of the laws and social fabric of Pakistan. His regime has erroneously been represented as having begun its tenure through a direct assault on women and their previously held rights. In fact, Zia's regime began by launching an assault on all democratic institutions and practices in the country. It was only after Zia had taken care of his primary political opposition—the PPP (Pakistan People's Party)—that he turned his attention to women.

It is worth remembering in all of this that Zia replaced the populist regime of Bhutto and the PPP. When Zia came to power, he did not have any support base other than within the military. Pakistan's conservative religious groups had been struggling since the very inception of Pakistan to establish an authoritarian state bereft of any democratic rights, but had failed miserably in their efforts. Their *main* accomplishment lay in preventing the extension of women's rights. However, another development can be traced that is just as alarming: the shift of the discursive pendulum away from even the previously limited concessions on equality toward an emphasis on difference. Again, this transformation is by no means limited to women; Shias, Ahmadiyyas, Christians, ethnic minorities—all came under attack on this score. In all cases, difference was stressed over universality, but superimposed on this difference was a hegemonic ideal of the individual (read: male) Pakistani, a Sunni Muslim committed to protecting the entire geographical territory of Pakistan against encroachment from its threatening others, be they internal or external. Within the already prevalent and now reinforced notion of woman as other (i.e., intrinsically different from man), the idealized woman was one conforming to this difference. Women who either fail or refuse to live up to this ideal risk losing their right to both sovereignty and citizenship. In this sense women who are different are similarly positioned to other minorities.

There is a curious development here. The universal (we might say "sovereign") Pakistani is now emphatically defined as Muslim. Of necessity, this heightens a focus on difference and stresses its significance. Simultaneously, secularism has been criticized (by some *ulamās* and progressives alike) as denying difference. This particular configuration produces an interesting synthesis.

What I am arguing here is that boundary protection and definition—sexual, geographical, political, social, cultural, and moral—became more pronounced after 1977. During the Zia period, a powerful alliance emerged discursively and in power terms between the guardians of the state—the military—and the guardians of public and private morality—segments of the *ulamās* who collaborated with Zia's regime to use the media, the mosque pulpit, and private vigilantism to assure intimidation and harassment of any and all elements that challenged conventional wisdoms (read: hegemonic ideological formulations). It can be argued that Pakistan's role in the late seventies and eighties as a front-line state (in the Afghan war against the Soviet

Union) was a major factor in bringing conservative political and religious forces into prominence. Although this is certainly the case, and the culpability and involvement of the United States in bringing this state of affairs into being can by no means be understated, I would suggest that the internal politics of difference was also a major contributor to this situation.

Intolerance, Violence, and the State after Zia

Since Zia's death in 1988, there continues to be a rearticulation of what it means to be Pakistani, a struggle over for whom and for what the country was created, and what the conditions of belonging are. The ideological consensus that was formulated by the state during Zia's regime and continues to maintain its hold over it and segments of civil society has spawned a politics of gender, ethnic, and religious difference that now promises to engulf the country in outright chaos if not flames and civil war. This, too, can be linked to the politics of repression and militarization of Pakistani society that has been heightened since the Afghan resistance and its accompanying drug trade became based in Pakistan. For Pakistanis, however, this connection comes as little consolation as they struggle with a politics of intolerance that now pervades the culture. The eighth, ninth, and twelfth amendments still remain on the books, the *Sharī'a* law was made an issue post-Zia and remains a major legal obstacle to women's freedoms today, and new laws such as blasphemy laws are very much in force in contemporary Pakistan (ASR Publications, *Herald*, and *Newsline*).

Jehangir and Jilani (1990) detail innumerable recent cases primarily of women, but also men, charged under the new laws. They also supply information about police brutality against women in custody. Periodic reports by the Lahore-based Human Rights Commission of Pakistan, as well as WAR (Women Against Rape) newsletters, provide additional documentation of the severity and extent of violence in all sectors of society but most noticeably against women after the demise of the Zia regime. Let me cite but a few examples (Human Rights Commission of Pakistan, 1994; *Newsline*, April 1995):

- Professor Akhtar Hameed Khan, a prominent social worker, renowned and respected for his involvement in community development work in Karachi, was charged with being "anti-Islamic." Although the state eventually withdrew the charge against him, a Sahiwal judge decided as of 1993 that the case against him should continue.
- Two mentally handicapped individuals were taken into custody for "insulting the Prophet." A thirteen year old, illiterate boy, was accused of "writing blasphemy." During this same year, a Jama'at-i-Islami member was also charged under the blasphemy law. It was later discovered that he was framed because he

had refused to support a local MNA [Member of National Assembly] during a recent election. In 1993 as well, a blasphemy suit was filed against Benazir Bhutto in the Lahore High Court on the grounds that she stated that the blasphemy law and system of separate electorates violated human rights.

- Numerous charges were brought against Ahmadiyyas for using Islamic language and displays. Additionally, anti-Ahmadi demonstrations and mob action occurred in various parts of the country. In 1993, in Lahore it resulted in physical assaults against Ahmadi students (women and men); in Shabkadar (in the North West Frontier Provinces), it resulted in a mob killing of an Ahmadi male and serious injury of another. Similarly, each successive year since the passage of the blasphemy laws has seen instances of harassment and discrimination against that community and also violence against Christian women, encroachment on Christian properties, and the use of the blasphemy law against Christians.
- Also in 1993, more than five years after the demise of Zia's regime, human rights groups documented that seventy five to eighty per cent of all women in jails were held on charges of *Hudood* offenses. These groups documented police assault on women in custody.
- Women's and human rights' groups published data that a woman was raped every three hours, fifty per cent of those raped were minors, and one fourth were gang raped. Increasingly, those charged with these acts were persons in powerful positions.
- Public humiliation of women in the Punjab alone (most often through stripping) occurred at the rate of four cases each month. It is not unknown for those subjected to such abuse to commit suicide.
- Domestic violence cases grew too. Half of these resulted in death. Additionally, death by burning [stove deaths] occurred at the rate of one every other day.

The fact that there are now institutions and activist groups tracking down such abuses and practices may be one factor accounting for the alarming increase in publicly noted cases. However, anyone familiar with the Pakistani sociopolitical milieu recognizes that these incidents signify a qualitative and quantitative shift in civil society. This is visible even aside from the instances and types of violence enumerated above. The presence, for example, of private armed security guards speaks to the heightened militarization of everyday life. So too does the now-pervasive practice of firing rifles at weddings (a custom previously restricted to the tribal areas). Relatedly, increased materialism is evidenced by the number of consultancy firms (often registered as NGOs, nongovernmental organizations), the increase in traffic, restaurants, video outlets, expensive boutiques, and so on. Alongside of this is a diminishing presence of women on the streets (aside from *bazārs* and specific market concentrations).[4]

Sexual Violence and the State

I would now like to focus on one specific aspect of the shifts noted above in the post–1977 era: the realm of increased sexual violence against women. Legal entrapments here combine powerfully with public morality and misogynist ideas to capture women's bodies and curtail their freedoms. As Afiya Zia (1994: 2) argues, "The rigorous forms of controlling female sexuality in Pakistan find extreme expression in legal punishments meted out to those women who breach prescribed sexual behavior." These "were introduced in the form of *Zinā* laws, promulgated in 1979 under the Hudood Ordinances, as part of the Islamic-defined reform system of the legal and social structures."

The years since 1979 have seen issues of rape and adultery being taken out of the criminal justice system and redefined through sections of the Hudood Ordinances (which came into effect in the early eighties). Covered under these laws are crimes of rape, abduction, adultery, and fornication (Zinā Ordinance); false accusation of Zinā; and the mode of penalty for those convicted under the Zinā and Hudood Ordinance. There have also been alterations in the laws of evidence such that women can no longer testify in courts on their own behalf or on behalf of others in rape cases; four adult male witnesses are needed. Not only are these laws weighed heavily against the victims, that is, women, but because the Hudood Ordinances privilege the testimony of male Muslims over female Muslims and all non-Muslims, they also legally sanction discrimination and secondary status on the basis of gender and religion. Even at the level of legal machinery for adjudicating cases under these laws, women and non-Muslims suffer discrimination. Jehangir and Jilani (1990) point out that courts trying Hudood cases must have a Muslim (invariably a male) as their presiding judge. At the subordinate court level, where the accused is a non-Muslim, a non-Muslim judge *can* (but does not necessarily) preside. However, at the appellate court level for such cases, which is the Federal Shariat Court (established in 1980), all the judges are Muslims, appointed by the chief executive; even non-Muslim lawyers are not allowed to appear before it. Given that the Federal Shariat Court has exclusive jurisdiction with regard to appeals, and all Hudood sentences have to be confirmed by this court, the scales are heavily tipped in favor of male accusers against the defendants.

Subsequent to the promulgation of these laws, we see a sharp rise in the number of women incarcerated in Pakistani prisons, the majority serving time under the Hudood Ordinances. What is noteworthy here is not just the law that has made this possible but also the logic used by its wielders— accusers, as well as presiding judicial review officials—as a weapon against women. False charges are frequently filed by former husbands and by author- itarian fathers against their own daughters, that show that divorced women are remarrying and that young women are making choices with respect to their marriages.

Thanks to these laws, rape victims have been transformed into women accused of adultery. The differential positioning of women through these laws in comparison with their positioning under the criminal legal system inherited from the colonial period illustrates the differential construction of patriarchal systems. Under colonial rule, rape was recognized as a crime punishable for men only. Under today's Hudood laws, women too can be accused of and convicted for rape. Also, under colonial laws, only the husband could file a charge of adultery against his wife and he could also revoke it at any time. Marital rape was a recognized offense. Under contemporary laws, however, marital rape is not an admissible crime, and a male accused of rape can claim it was consensual, thereby converting the accuser into the accused (under Zinā charges), because the woman's accusation can be cited as evidence of illicit sexual intercourse and be turned against her. Thus Jehangir and Jilani (1990: 86) argue that penal laws prior to the Hudood Ordinance carved out a *protected* but *secondary* status for women, but contemporary laws have removed the protection without altering the secondary status of women. Since rape is subsumed as a subcategory of Zinā (primarily conceptualized under the Hudood laws as adultery or fornication), and raped women cannot testify in their own behalf, as Afiya Zia (1994: 17) points out, "The foremost consideration in such cases will be proving or disproving consent, rather than forceful coercion or violation; this has the effect of shifting the focus of all subsequent prosecution from the aggressor to the victim."

The details of the very laws and their misogynist nature are startling in themselves; however, equally instructive is the logic of arguments in cases brought to the courts under Hudood laws, as well as the logic of the courts' decisions (Jehangir and Jilani, 1990). In one example, a fifteen-year-old was punished for Zinā upon admission of pregnancy. The case had been brought to court by her maternal uncle, who entered a complaint of perpetration of rape by the young woman's uncle and his son. The victim was *presumed* guilty of illicit sex by the court and punished precisely because her pregnancy was seen as demonstrable proof of her guilt. In another case, the father of a woman who had married of her own will saw her husband charged by her own father and sentenced for rape. The court chose not to believe the marriage certificate. In one well-known case, a divorced woman since remarried was sentenced to death along with her new husband. Her previous husband charged that she was not divorced (even though the defense produced the divorce decree). Legally, it was the former husband's responsibility to have filed the decree. Because he had not done so, the woman's second marriage was ruled illegal and the couple were convicted of raping each other. In yet another case, a man and a woman were charged with

Zinā by the woman's husband, from whom she had been separated for more than nine years. Her husband asserted that the separation had arisen from her lack of "good character." He had remarried, but clearly the expectation was that the abandoned wife would remain celibate and loyal to him.

All court language, justifications for convictions, and linguistic currency regarding sexual violence especially rape, reveal the deeply rooted culturally subservient standing of women. Thus, terms such as "easy virtue," "loose woman," and "unchaste character" are encountered repeatedly in the cases. The Federal Shariat Court has the power to interpret what constitutes immoral conduct. If Zinā is not established, it can transform the language of accusation and charge the accused with, say, "bad character" and "obscenity." This language is invoked not only in Zinā and rape cases but cases having to do with the murder of women.

Afiya Zia points to the absence of a linguistic term for rape in the customary language(s) of Pakistan. All references to this ultimate violation of women's bodies are, as she aptly comments, through "euphemisms such as *izzat khona/izzat looti jana* (loss of virtue / theft of virtue) or *bay-izzat karna* (causing one to lose one's honor)" (A. Zia, 1994: 18). Such terms point to the crime of rape not as a crime against women but as a loss of honor to the male and/or the community, or at best her "shame." Afiya Zia argues that "this reasoning stems from the network of familial relationships within Pakistani culture, where women are 'properties' of their male relatives and thus representative of the latter's hearths and honour" (19). Although I agree with her logic, I would argue that such reasoning and justification is of a piece with patriarchal norms and structures that, through various forms and mechanisms, strive to subjugate women's subjectivities and experiences, constantly defining women, their bodies, and their social/cultural existence through references to some broader "good." The same logic applies to the justification for women's work and education that I referred to earlier. Ironically, women's groups and activists often get caught in the trap of proving a woman's "virtue" in order to question violence against her. Many media publications on violence against women written by women activists themselves initiate their discussion with a biographical narrative that cites the given woman's religiosity, morality, and virtue *before* proceeding to denounce the brutality against her.

Aside from these forms of violence against women, several new forms have emerged. These include dowry deaths, or wife immolation; public humiliations of women primarily through stripping them and parading them in public; and finally, "political" rapes, which include the rape of women connected to significant political figures and/or of women political activists. None of these types of violence had received public scrutiny until the past decade; most were unheard of until recently. Their significance resides in the manner in which, in present-day Pakistan, public morality seems to mimic private norms already in existence and to give license to underlying sentiments. This is not dissimilar to the full-blown emergence of racism during the Reagan-Bush era in the United States. One cannot argue that racism was caused by Presidents Reagan and Bush, but it was certainly encouraged by their administrations. An analogous situation prevails in Pakistan since the shift in laws and social mores during the Zia period.

Violence against women is nothing new in Pakistan; rape, forced marriage, and divorce have existed since the country's inception. What is new is the manner in which this violence now occurs: in the open, within the public domain. Women have gone from being public objects of respect, while often being privately abused, to being denigrated in public. And clearly, the state has had a visible hand in facilitating this shift.

Masculine Pakistan, Feminine India

A clear instance of this facilitation is discernible through a reading of government-sponsored school texts. Two recent studies, one by Rubina Saigol (1994) and one by K. K. Aziz (1993), look at curricular and content changes in Pakistan's recent history. Aziz highlights the radical shift in the meaning of Pakistan that has been wrought since Zia and is manifested in the texts. One text states: "This country is an overwhelmingly Muslim country and was created on the basis of an ideology, and this ideology is the Islamic religion of the Muslims. This is the generally understood meaning of the ideology of Pakistan" (Aziz, 1993: 87). Another quotation: "The change which came on 5 July 1977 in the shape of the imposition of [Zia ul Haq's] Martial Law might have been on the surface a political incident, but in reality it was the starting point of an Islamic revolution" (92).

Through this and copious other references, one can glean several transformations being wrought through state regulation. The first, is a rewriting of the history of Pakistan as a history of the formation of an Islamic state—not even, as Jinnah averred, "a state *of* Muslims," but a state *for* Muslims. Second, there is a privileging of certain elements in the Pakistan movement (primarily Urdu speakers from Uttar Pradesh and Punjabis), and a silencing of alternative voices and ethnicities. Third, there is a direct and frontal construction of India as a Hindu state through a denial in government schoolbooks of its Muslim populace by charging, as one does, that "the Hindus wanted the Urdu language to disappear from the subcontinent. But the elimination of Urdu was tantamount to the elimination of the entire [Muslim] nation, and Indian Muslims realized this very well. Therefore, one of their primary objectives was the protection of Urdu; in this way the creation of Pakistan emerged as their demand" (Aziz, 1993: 102). In one broad sweep three things are accomplished:

Hindus are constructed as an enemy, the logic for Pakistan's creation is recast in linguistic terms, and the contribution of other regional and linguistic groups to Pakistan's history is effaced. This is a poignant irony, given the history of Pakistan, the separation of Bangladesh, and current demands by its ethnic minorities for greater cultural and economic broadening.

Saigol's work is even more relevant to our purposes. Emphasizing as she does the social studies history curriculum, she depicts the discourse that Aziz also points to as a "gendered discourse."

> The period before the advent of Islam [in India] is almost always a "feminine" period. It represents unbridled desire, darkness, mystery, strangeness and uncontrolled moral laxity. After Islam conquers and subjugates the sensuous pre-oedipal/pre-Islamic society, it brings the Law of the Father and the society enters its moral and cleansed oedipal phase.... The masculine finally defeats the feminine and establishes its law. Conquest here is equivalent to purification through insemination. The society of the mother is conquered and corrected by establishing the society of the father. However, the feminine lurks underneath and rears its head in revolt frequently to overthrow the dominant father.... The terms in which the conquest of India by the British is described are strongly reminiscent of a woman who has betrayed one lover/master for another. The alleged Hindu collaboration with the British is seen as betrayal—the Hindus being feminine and the feminine seen as fickle and inconstant. (Saigol, 1994: 45)

Several themes are noticeable through Saigol's analysis: the privileging of the masculine over the feminine; the "naturalization" of gender; the subsequent need for control over the feminine because of its supposed inherent limitations and flaws; and the desire to regulate pleasure, the power of regulation perforce residing in the masculine domain. Texts are ultimately just that—texts—and thereby amenable to multiple readings, yet it nonetheless becomes apparent from a perusal of these two works that a self-conscious effort is under way to remake Pakistan into an entity that defines itself in masculine, Muslim, and exclusionary terms. Street placards in Lahore following the Indian government's actions at Charar Sharif in Kashmir were one indicator—one read *"Hindustānī bheriye Kashmir ko chor do"* ("Indian wolves, get out of Kashmir")—and point to the continuation of this policy even during Benazir Bhutto's period.

Alternative Discourses

However, as Saigol points out and as was alluded to above, alternative discourses do exist and it is to these I now turn. While public framing of gender, religion, and ethnicity proceeds along its own contradictory path, numerous groups at the level of civil society struggle to come to grips with, compromise with, and/or contest hegemonic trends. This is especially true of women's groups. As Farida Shaheed's chapter in this volume shows, since the late seventies women have been vocal and organizing in ways unparalleled in Pakistan's history.

There is a noticeable ambivalence and split within various groups as to how best to address the current problematic regarding the reconstruction of identity in Pakistan. Part of this stems from an intellectual-cum-political aversion to the current demonization of Muslims and their singular "otherization" that is so prevalent in Western media and political discourse. It is by now well recognized that Muslims and the Islamic world have been singled out as the new enemy in the aftermath of the demise of the USSR and Cold War rivalries. As Feldman points out in this volume, Muslim women, with Taslima Nasrin as the most recent example, figure in the Western media as symbols of Muslim villainy. Another strand evolves from an uncritical reading of postmodernist theorization whereby fracturing and decentering are seen as necessarily counterhegemonic, democratic moves. In the Pakistani context, this posture has lent itself, through some of its feminist and other trendy interlocutors, to privilege community over other arenas of struggle. More specifically, some spokespersons representing this tendency have expressed sympathy for the citizens of Malakand who are agitating for the Sharī'a to become the law of the area to the exclusion of other alternatives.

Related, albeit not entirely reducible to the above position, is the argument for Islam on the grounds of its cultural relevance, that is, the argument for cultural authenticity. Among those espousing this position, some hold to it on tactical grounds, and others genuinely believe that Islam contains the answers—if only we would get the "right" version/interpretation. Still others see this, as do the postmodernists, as a form of arguing that opens new spaces, as well as a way of destabilizing the hegemonic center.

Yet another tendency calls for a return to a secular state. Women's Action Forum (WAF), during the first Nawaz Sharif regime, adopted a resolution calling for a separation of religion and the state at one of its meetings. This position runs the risk of suggesting that all women's problems stem from the Zia era and that women's status and gender location is reducible to one factor, religion, in the Pakistani case, Islam. Part of the problem, of course, has been that the debate itself has often been articulated—ironically just as much by the state that introduced the laws and policies discussed in this paper—as one of secularism versus cultural authenticity. In light of Pakistani history, I argue that since there never has been a secular state, a retreat into cultural authenticity can serve as subterfuge and a means of solidifying a new and more terrifying hegemony, albeit in the name of difference. Proponents and detractors on both sides of the debate seem entrapped in the terms set by the very center they purport to oppose.

Arising from this is a desire for a return, on both sides, to an earlier, ideal-ized past. Thus, supporters of secularism keep referring to those of Jinnah's speeches in which he insisted Pakistan was to be a country for *all*, regardless of religious belief, gender, and ethnicity. Opponents, of course, draw upon those speeches in which Jinnah clearly outlined his case that the Hindus and Muslims of India constituted two separate nations.

Given the increased violence against women, we see, on the one hand, the establishment of innumerable groups agitating, educating, and providing women with services hitherto unavailable to them. On the other hand, we also see a privileging of the previous state of affairs, wherein women were suppos-edly accorded *izzat* (honor) in the public domain. Women were always, and continue to be, verbally harassed in public. However, prior to the current trans-formation, such public behavior was at least rhetorically considered unaccept-able. It is primarily in this sense, and with the increase in public assaults on women, that there is a breakdown of the public/private split regarding women. The breakdown in regard to the mistreatment of women lends itself to a call for a reprivatization of the issue and a return of *izzat* lost to women.

What I am arguing is that following the exacerbated public maltreatment of women, some intellectuals and activists began to argue that the state should restore to women the "respect" they were previously accorded in Pakistani society. Such a position runs the risk of ignoring the private abuses women suffered in the past and suggests that the problem can be resolved by a return to the prior status quo where instances of (public) violence against women were rare. It does not problematize the family and the private domain as signif-icant sites for women's oppression and link them to the current public humili-ations to which women are being subjected. This was demonstrated in the case of Veena Hayat. In the aftermath of her rape and the state's refusal to bring the culprits to task, her father took the matter out of the courts and to the tribal *jirga* (council), which tried the case according to community laws. This not only preempted any serious prosecution of the case but also meant the substi-tution of one form of patriarchal control for another. The whole rhetoric of restoring *izzat* to women represents a call for protection from either the male-dominated family and/or the state as the new patriarchs, rather than question-ing and overturning the very term and practice of *izzat* itself.

Thus on all sides, from the feminist movement to the larger body politic, the processes and mechanics of gender construction, identity formation, and citizenship in Pakistan continue to be formulated within a rhetoric of binary oppositions. Salient among these are the following: secularism/religion; universalism/difference; external/internal (the latter defined as who qualifies as an "authentic" Pakistani and is accorded full citizenship). Rather than accepting these terms as logical and necessary oppositions, these very cate-gories need to be historicized and subjected to closer scrutiny and analysis.

What do these terms mean contextually? How have they been enacted concretely? How have they served to empower women and minorities, and what have been their limitations? Going further, is such empowerment available to women individually or collectively? It seems to me that the very notion of culture itself bears close scrutiny. Whose culture are we speaking of when we use the term "cultural authenticity"? If we accept, as indeed it seems to me we must, that various cultures exist within Pakistan, how do we articulate a gender struggle that accommodates and respects difference and, at the same time, lays the groundwork for tolerance and equality? In other words, how do we theorize a noncoercive notion of universalism and difference?

I have suggested a first step is to reread Pakistani history so that we move away from simplistic notions of secular versus Islamic states. Without glossing over their differences, I have attempted to demonstrate the continuity in the manner in which the state (pre-Zia, during Zia's time, and since) has sought to control and define women in ways that permitted its agenda to move forward. In explicating the changes between the past and the present, I have argued that the domain of struggle has moved from primarily private control over women to surveillance and monitoring in both the public and private levels. Last, I have advanced the view that the narrowing of space for women must be seen in relation to an increased curtailment of political and civil rights for the populace as a whole.

Women's bodies and identities have been, and continue to be, a key site of contestation and definition of self and other in the Pakistani context. I have tried to relate this to notions of sovereignty and citizenship. Advances have been made by women's groups in undertaking concrete activities to better women's lives, but the groups' theorization remains inadequate. Discursive and related historical frameworks alike need to be (re)addressed. This is crucial not only for women but also for other minorities. Because of their positioning across boundaries, women are well placed to lead this development. The salience of history, context, and gender experience requires that issues of sovereignty, citizenship, and identity be reexamined. In the Pakistani context, such a political and theoretical move is imperative if women and all currently excluded others are to gain control over their lives.

Notes

This chapter was originally a paper written for a panel, Feminist Perspectives on the State, part of the XIII World Congress of Sociology, Bielefeld, Germany, 19 July 1994. Partial funding was provided by an NSF/ASA Travel Grant. The paper has since been amended and modified considerably for inclusion as a chapter in this volume.

1. In the above-mentioned paper and in Rouse (1993) I have argued that the struggle in Pakistan must be seen as one between democratic and anti-democratic forces, not as categories of "secular" versus "religious." Rather, we must recognize that *all* governments in Pakistan (post–Liaquat Ali Khan) have accommodated both secular and religious ideas at the state level. It is precisely the desire to suppress the democratic forces—made up of women, ethnic and religious minorities, workers, and peasants—that has brought about this collusion. There are also obviously marked differences within and across each of these groups; they cannot be consistently and homogeneously conceptualized as democratic. Structurally, however, they are inclined toward such a position. Second, the situation in Pakistan is not much different from the processes at work in India or Iran.

2. Sex outside marriage, same-sex relationships, even celibacy as a form of resistance to established norms were never considered. The focus remained on raising the marriage age (marginally), registration of marriages and divorces, and the sanctioning of polygyny only under specific conditions, to name its key clauses. Even here, the implementation machinery was not strengthened considerably, and sanctions for violation of the changes introduced were starkly absent.

3. In the early years after independence, Saadat Hasan Manto, a member of the Progressive Writers' Movement, became the target of a conservative backlash stemming from ferocious opposition to his novella *Thanda Ghosht* (Cold Meat), which spoke directly to women's sexual exploitation in the private domain. This novella (Manto, 1955), dealing with the objectification of women as sexual bodies subject to male abuse, was attacked on grounds of obscenity. After a court case against this book, very few writers (except those writing and publishing religious tracts, most notably the prepartition tome *Bihishti Zewar*) dared, until the seventies, to speak explicitly about sexual exploitation and women's bodies. In the seventies poets like Fehmida Riaz, who also experienced state and social opprobrium, returned to a virtually taboo subject.

4. When I went to high school in the sixties, young women from the middle classes frequently used public transportation to get to and from school. Today this is seldom the case. Although this may result from a decline in the public transportation sector, and/or an increase in middle-class standards of living, it also reflects a greater wariness of women's presence on the streets. This stems from the justified fear of physical abuse and violence against women and from an internalization of some of the moral values perpetuated since the late seventies.

Chapter Five

Gender Politics, Legal Reform, and the Muslim Community in India

ZOYA HASAN

SINCE THE EARLY 1980s, India has witnessed a resurgence of politicized religion in which Hindu and Muslim communal politics alike have given a central place to gender issues. Women have figured as important signifiers of differences between groups. Sometimes they have vigorously participated in various communal projects, at other times they have spoken out against communal identity. The heightened mobilization of women has become the focus of debate in analyzing the empowerment of women.

This chapter addresses recent events in India and the various ways that Muslim women's rights have been debated and refracted through contestations over secularism, community rights, and gender issues. I have chosen to steer clear of discussions about the status of women in Islam or the injustice and inequity of existing Muslim personal law in India. My concern is to contextualize and problematize the debate about legal reforms that arose from the controversy over the Muslim Women (Protection of Rights on Divorce) Bill 1986. I shall explore the arguments of the defenders of the status quo and of those who advocated changes in personal laws, and analyze the responses of Muslim women to legal reform.

The controversy over the Shah Bano issue underscores the important role played by official state discourse in perpetuating patriarchal relationships and community identity. Rather than challenging the concept of community identity as a basis for a person's relationship with the state, the Congress Party legitimized communal identities, in terms both of state policies and of strategies for political mobilization. For the Congress Party, national unity would be strengthened by accommodating minority interests, for instance, through Muslim personal law. In the realm of civil society, however, the debate was dominated by the Hindu Right, which opposed minority rights on the grounds that it would erode national unity and women's rights. For the Bharatiya Janata Party (BJP), national unity could best be achieved by curbing minority rights and introducing a uniform civil code (UCC) that would apply to all communities. These two conflicting positions set the limits on a debate in which women were simply emblematic of differing conceptions of state, nation, and minority rights. The debate about Muslim women's rights was particularly important in developing a critique of secularism, and it played a crucial role in the delegitimation of the Congress Party and its displacement from the center of Indian politics.

Personal Law and Politicized Religion

There are nearly sixty million Muslim women in India, the second-largest female Muslim population in the world, but they have made few tangible gains during five decades of economic and social development. They are conspicuous by their absence in the world of politics, in the professions, bureaucracy, universities, and public and private sectors. They rarely figure in debates on political empowerment, rural poverty, education, or health; nor does their economic vulnerability arouse much concern. The economic invisibility of Muslim women must be viewed in conjunction with their high political visibility, albeit not in their own right as women but subsumed and then made visible in the debate about minority rights versus minority appeasement, personal law versus uniform laws, secularism versus communalism, and modernity versus communitarian traditions.

Much of the debate on social reform centers on the meaning, substance, and importance of legal reforms for accelerating the processes of modernization and national integration (Parashar, 1992; Baird (ed.), 1993). The urge for greater economic and political participation by women and for the protection of their new roles leads inevitably to the quest for legal rights. Women's rights are guaranteed in the Indian Constitution but denied in actuality. Nevertheless, legal reform is imperative if women are to achieve a measure of equality. Reforms with regard to property, inheritance, and marriage in Hindu laws, combined with economic and educational advancement, have provided some support for Hindu women's active participation in society. Muslim and Christian women have not been similarly served, however. It is still extremely difficult for a Christian woman to obtain a divorce.[1] On the other hand, a Muslim woman can be divorced by her husband all too readily (or she might have to live in a polygynous household), but she cannot so easily divorce her husband. The lack of reform in family laws is an important obstacle to establishing women's equality before the law. Personal laws are, of course, only one form of discrimination, but they constitute a significant source of disadvantage for Muslim women. Women's lack of rights in law is crucial in maintaining their subordination to men, and it sanctions their limited access to property and inheritance.

Renewed interest in legal reform was stimulated and shaped by the changed context of politics in the 1980s, which was dominated by the contending agendas of secular democracy and majoritarianism or religious nationalism. Political Hinduism or Hindutva poses an enormous challenge to the governing principles and ideological perspectives of independent India. Hindutva has offered itself as a political alternative to secular democracy. Its main targets are secularism, pluralism, and cultural autonomy, which it argues are harmful for national integrity. Until the late 1980s, political Hinduism and the BJP were a weak political force. Since the early 1990s, however, the BJP has acquired unprecedented strength. It won 161 seats in the 1996 general election, which made it the largest single party. In May 1996, it was called upon to form the government. It could not assemble an overall majority, for it failed to muster support from the regional parties, and the government lasted only thirteen days.

The upsurge of support for the BJP is not a spontaneous phenomenon. It crested during a period of crisis generated by the decline of the Congress Party and the ensuing organizational and ideological vacuum in Indian politics. While professing secularism, the Congress Party leadership—especially Indira Gandhi and Rajiv Gandhi—made pragmatic compromises with communalism to refurbish their declining political legitimacy. The resurgence of communal politics was also encouraged by the failures of economic policies, which engendered widespread disillusionment with existing frameworks of economic and political development. The legitimacy of the institutions, laws, and processes of the modern state was open to question, which enabled the votaries of religious politics to lay claim to "authentic" alternatives for national regeneration. As in most other countries undergoing similar changes, the urban middle class is most receptive to such religious appeals. The mainstay of such politics are lower-middle-class, educated youth in search of employment and an identity to counter their alienation. They sometimes turn their anger against Muslims, whom they see as a "pampered lot." In other places, especially where the upward economic and political mobility of the agrarian and urban petty bourgeoisie was most marked, there was also a noticeable urge toward acquiring a broader Hindu identity. Politicized religion provided such people with a sense of identity, a link to the past, and a framework for coping with the profound socioeconomic transformations under way in Indian society.

Secularism and Cultural Pluralism

The turning point in the debate on legal reforms was the Shah Bano case. Shah Bano was an elderly divorced Muslim woman. Under a provision in the Criminal Procedure Code (CPC) originally introduced in the late nineteenth century to prevent vagrancy, she appealed for maintenance from her former husband. He contested the case, but it culminated in the Supreme Court's judgment granting Shah Bano a very modest sum in maintenance. Conservative Muslims saw this decision as an intrusion into Muslim personal law and the judgment provoked quite a furor. To soothe the ruffled feelings of the articulate and conservative Muslim leadership, Parliament passed the Muslim Women (Protection of Rights on Divorce) Bill, which prevented Muslim women from claiming maintenance under the CPC, a right still enjoyed by women from all other religious communities (Hasan, 1989). The debate surrounding these events took place in political institutions and civil society alike, and it involved not only Muslims but various political groups and parties, women's organizations, and the media.

The basic thrust of official discourse revealed assumptions about Muslims and their role and place in a secular polity and society. The Congress Party's response was unmistakably influenced by the political crisis that the party faced in the mid-1980s. A new strategy of conciliation and compromise was devised to try to stem the steady erosion of support for Congress. Compromise on Muslim personal law was part of the effort to win back Muslim voters, but this strategy neither resolved the crisis of hegemony nor generated new support among Muslims. On the contrary, the Congress Party set in motion a political process—which it then could not control—of compromises with Hindu and Muslim communal politics. As a result, unresolved questions concerning the community and its relationship with the state came to the fore in the late 1980s.

The debate on the Muslim Women (Protection of Rights on Divorce) Bill was reminiscent of similar debates on fundamental rights and minority rights in the Constituent Assembly in 1949 and on the uniform civil code during the passage of the Hindu Code Bill during the 1950s (Dhagamvar, 1993). Then as now, there was much confusion about the meaning and relevance of secularism. Supporters of the official notion of secularism were skeptical of the possibility of separating religion and politics in a country where religious loyalties often molded political and social attitudes. As in the past, the critics of secularism feared that the Congress Party's view of secularism would reinforce communalism and ultimately undermine secularism itself. Congress arguments were anchored in the party's past achievements, forever invoking the record of the preceding forty years in government. But its claims did not match the government's record in combating communalism or curbing communal violence or its shaky commitment to secularism in the 1980s. Nor did the party's proclamations of secularism and modernization match its past performance in uplifting disadvantaged sections of society, including backward classes, Muslims, and women. The arguments reveal a strong continuity in the terms of Congress Party discourse in the 1940s, 1950s, and 1980s. As in the past, the master narrative derived its inspiration from an Indian conception of secularism, distinguishable from the Western notion of complete separation of state and religion (Madan, 1987; Nandy, 1990). Far from advocating the strict neutrality of the state in its relations with religious institutions and diverse community practices, the law minister dwelt on the equality of all religions in political and private life.[2]

> Tolerance of diversity and differences should be the hallmark of governance in a multi-cultural society. Secularism demands that everybody should not be tarred with the same brush. The Constitution sets up a secular democracy not in the way of the uniformity of the grave... If we start on a fine mosaic and try to draw one single pattern all over the country then we shall be playing absolutely against the very foundation of our philosophy (Lok Sabha Debate, 1986: 313).

The core argument rested on the understanding that minority communities have the right to cultural autonomy and that their personal laws thus need protection.[3] This respect was the cornerstone of government policy.

Women's status was a very secondary consideration in government policy. The law minister stated that Muslim personal law was derived from the Sharī'at, and that the Supreme Court judgment granting maintenance to Shah Bano had transgressed the limits of Muslim personal law (Lok Sabha Debate, 1986: 318). His interpretation echoed the position of the All India Muslim Personal Law Board and showed no recognition of how Muslim leaders—many of whom helped to reinforce the Congress Party view—were manipulating issues of religious identity for their own ends. In reality, maintenance for destitute women did not amount to interference in personal law, and minor modifications did not constitute an attack on Islamic tenets. Having uncritically accepted the notion of the divine immutability of the Sharī'at, however, the Congress government, with party functionary backing, was constrained to introduce the Muslim Women (Protection of Rights on Divorce) Bill.

> We have to tread very carefully, for Muslim personal law is linked to the Muslim religion in the minds of most Muslims.... We must look at it from the point of view of Muslims ... and then try to find out what is the law

which governs the Muslims and which according to them is not merely a law of man's making but a law ordained by God. This is the belief of Muslims (Lok Sabha Debate, 1986: 319).

Thus, the justification for the new legislation was premised on the religious sanctity of personal law.[4] In this way, the Congress Party established an equation of law, scripture, and community identity as the centerpiece for the integration of minorities into national life. The hallmark of its policy was to observe neutrality in areas that were defined and accepted as being within the religious domain.

Throughout the debate in the institutional and public arenas, government spokesmen focused on the "feelings and beliefs of Muslims" and how "the government cannot ignore the voice of Muslims" because "every minority has a guarantee that it could conduct its own affairs; it could have its own way of life; preserve its own cultural identity; its own religious identity; have full freedom to practise its religion and so on" (Lok Sabha Debate, 1986: 516). The theme of the interdependence of religion and secularism threaded through the debate.

The language of official arguments articulated the assumption that discrete communities of Hindus and Muslims existed. Government claims about a distinct Muslim identity were buttressed by sharply distinguishing between Hindu and Muslim, and conceiving of them as mutually exclusive and autonomous heritages. This made for excessively narrow, and sometimes misleading, interpretations of what was actually going on in the social realm (Hasan, 1996). Yet throughout the controversy, Congress Party Members of Parliament referred to Muslims as "them and their laws" as distinct from "us and our customs and religious practices" (Lok Sabha Debate, 1986: 411). Muslims were assumed to be an indivisible community, different from others, which implied that there was no other way of dealing with them except through recognition of their religious laws (Baird (ed.), 1993). As Home Minister Arun Nehru warned, "There would [otherwise] be a law and order situation and this is one problem which no police force or paramilitary force can solve satisfactorily" (Lok Sabha Debate, 1986: 411). K. C. Pant cautioned "extreme care" in dealing with Muslim personal law and argued that the alienation of Muslims would threaten political stability and national integrity. The essence of government policy was summed up in the words of the law minister: "If the majority of Muslims feel that the Bill is in their interest we cannot impose our views on them" (Lok Sabha Debate, 1986: 317).

The debate signaled a significant shift in Congress Party thinking. Early on, Congress leaders (most notably Prime Minister Rajiv Gandhi) defended the proposed legislation on the grounds that it would enhance women's interests by giving them a better deal. By May 1986, the Muslim Women Bill was being debated in the midst of countrywide rage against it. At this point, the Congress Party jettisoned its earlier position; its defense of the bill was now conceptualized in terms of deference to the wishes of the Muslim community (Hasan, 1989). Not surprisingly, there was an outcry against minority appeasement. An increasing number of people in the intelligentsia and the media came to view secularism as an instrument for protecting Muslims.

By translating its own assumptions about Muslims into concrete legislation, the Congress government contributed to the strengthening of a Muslim identity in Indian politics. Crucially, the government was not only acknowledging an independently existing identity but recreating and shaping it. Talal Asad (1993: 34–35) has argued that it is not mere symbols that implant true religious dispositions but power, ranging from laws and other sanctions to the disciplinary activities of social institutions; in short, power creates the conditions for reinforcing religious identity. And this could have serious implications for the social and economic development of Indian Muslims. Social reform has often excluded the minorities because the dominant Muslim leadership patronized by the government is opposed to reform, and liberal Muslims argue that the impulse for reform must originate within the community itself and not the state. The Congress government readily accepted this logic. This was clear from the arguments made by Congress leaders such as K. C. Pant in the Lok Sabha:

> We cannot depend only on the law of reforms. The society has to be ready for reform. The wellsprings of that reform have to come from within and then the law and sentiment that have been aroused by a certain movement, they coincide and then society moves forward. . . . Reforms must come from within the Muslim community (Lok Sabha Debate, 1986: 390).

The Congress Party emphasized that no change in personal law could be envisaged without the consent of the Muslim community. This, the law minister repeatedly stated, was "the position accepted at the time of the adoption of the Constitution" (Lok Sabha Debate, 1986: 516).

By treating Muslims as different, Congress created a space for them to organize as a politically distinct group, which amounted to their virtual exclusion from the larger processes of social transformation and national development.[5] In effect, the state's reliance on the views of the conservative Muslim leadership resulted in a trade-off between religious identity and economic and social advancement for most Indian Muslims.[6] Furthermore, Muslims have been successfully marginalized and displaced from the legitimate agency of reform, the state. Consequently, in comparison with other countries with Muslim populations, there has been virtually no change in the civil and institutional life of Muslims in India. The contrast is apparent if the position of middle-class Muslim women in India is compared with that of their counterparts in Pakistan and Bangladesh.

Muslim Women, Appeasement, and Pseudosecularism

The lack of reform in Muslim personal law and its stout defense by the Congress Party was exploited by the organizations of the Hindu Right to build a critique of the state. In the process, they appropriated for themselves a civilizing role, claiming a mission to reform these backward laws (Mani, 1989). Symbolic of the effect of such laws was the plight of the Muslim woman, the victim of personal law that institutionalized easy divorce and polygyny.[7] Muslim women were represented as "unfortunate slaves" of the "evils of Islam." Muslim men were seen as "the most backward and aggressive" (*Organiser*, 20 October 1985), operating outside the national mainstream and sympathetic to an international conspiracy to undermine Indian/Hindu civilization and culture. Muslim men's legal right to polygyny received the greatest attention in this discourse and was linked to assertions that Muslims breed faster than Hindus. The *Organiser* spoke incessantly and obsessively about polygyny and how the population problem it creates would upset the demographic balance between Hindus and Muslims (*Organiser*, 9–16 February 1986). Linked to this was the emphasis on Muslims' purported proclivity toward violence. Together, these elements created a stereotype of Muslims as aggressive, backward, and communal. The ability to produce and reiterate these stereotypes, sometimes through sheer repetition, is the most important source of communal power (*Organiser*, 19 January 1986). The Muslim who emerges from this discourse is an undifferentiated, congenitally monstrous figure (Pandey, 1993), and this narrow construction of Muslimness comes to define all Muslims (Bacchetta, 1994). The significant difference among Muslims is their attitude toward reform, not their sect, class, language, or region. Good Muslims favor reform and bad ones oppose it because of their obscurantism (*Organiser*, 18 May 1986). Muslim women were thus turned into an ideal terrain through which to denounce personal law, the legal inequality between Muslim men and women, and the inequity of Muslim society.

For the protagonists of Hindutva, their mission was to rescue Muslim women from the clutches of these oppressive religious laws. Unlike Muslim women, Hindu women had gained their rights as a result of the reform of Hindu society. Hindu reformers prepared the people for change (*Organiser*, 2 February 1986). Contrasting Hindu liberalism with Muslim obscurantism, H. V. Seshadri, a leading ideologue of the Rashtriya Swayamsevak Sangh (RSS) observed:

Those who campaigned for reforms among Hindus have been acclaimed by the entire Hindu society as their emancipators. And no political party has demanded maintenance of status quo and made opposition to reforms an issue in the elections. Those who demand and campaign for reforms in the Muslim community are opposed and even physically attacked by their religious and political leaders and followers. (*Organiser*, 2 February 1986)

The reform of Hindu laws received much self-congratulatory emphasis, which deliberately ignored the opposition to the Hindu Code Bill. The reforms were appropriated as a high achievement of Hindu nationalism and were used to project the progressiveness of Hindus in contrast to the conservatism of Muslims. Yet it is well known that the political ancestors of the contemporary Hindu Right, as indeed of many Congressmen, were the most vocal critics of reform. They condemned the proposals for subverting Hindu ideas, culture, and religion (Som, 1994). The Hindu Code Bill was introduced in 1944 but not passed until 1955. Every clause of the bill was opposed, including the abolition of polygyny, which was objected to on grounds similar to those given by Muslim organizations resisting change in personal laws (Kishwar, 1994). The cry of religion in danger was raised. Clauses giving property rights to daughters were the most vehemently opposed. More recent attempts by the Andhra Pradesh legislature to amend the Hindu Succession Act and make daughters coparceners in joint family property came in for much criticism, and the act's passage was delayed because of opposition by the ruling party at the center (Kishwar, 1994). Such Hindu opposition to reform measures is merely a sign of conservatism, however. Muslim opposition to reform, on the other hand, is also seen as antinational and a threat to national security. Given this equation of reform with nationalism, acceptance of reform by Muslims would signify their loyalty to the nation. Opposition to reform testifies to not only their backwardness but also their obdurate refusal to participate in the national mainstream.

The rhetoric of women's equality and of reform played a strategic part in the vilification of the Muslim community. This is vividly illustrated by the manner in which the concept of legal equality was deployed during the debate to reinforce the stereotypes of Muslims as archaic, obscurantist, and antinational. At one level, recasting secularism as "pseudo-secularism" helped the Hindu Right to gain new adherents in the middle classes, professionals, and the print media, most notably the Hindi media. At another level, the crude rhetoric it spewed forth against Muslim fanaticism helped to mobilize support on the streets. Over time, the double-edged propaganda has helped create a popular "common sense" about Muslims and minority appeasement, through repeated focus on polygyny (thought to be a universal Muslim vice); failure to bring about a uniform civil code even after forty years of independence; the special status of Jammu and Kashmir provided in Article 370 of the Indian Constitution; and Article 30 of the Constitution, which allows minorities to have their own educational institutions (*Organiser*, 2 February 1986). Such examples of government "appeasement" of Muslims were an affront to Hindus, compounded by the government's reluctance to enforce any change in personal law. Yet this comprehensive condemnation of Muslim personal law as a primitive institution is not without its contradictions. Arguably, the Hindu Right's critique reflected not so much a commitment to women's equality as resentment of the special "privileges" enjoyed by Muslim men. As Amrita Basu (1995b: 165) has noted, it often "stemmed from an envy of the Other and his excesses embodied in polygamy, easy divorces, non-vegetarianism," all images that have been powerful factors in the demonization of Muslims.

In many ways, this familiar story is rooted in a century of revivalist thinking and communal politics (Sarkar, 1995, and this volume). The new and striking aspect of the Hindutva discourse is not the denigration of Muslims through such stereotyping—a necessary feature of communal politics—but the way Muslim women were used for the denigration of secularism. From early 1986, the argument shifted from the terrain of women's rights into a full-blown critique of secularism, ridiculed as pseudosecularism. The emphasis on the backwardness of Muslim personal laws and the oppression and exploitation of Muslim women was displaced by a sharper focus on the problem of secularism. From this perspective, the status of Muslim women highlights the pitfalls of pseudosecularism as practiced by the Congress government. The principal target was the preferential treatment of Muslim men and how it constituted a violation of secularism and equality. Hindu middle-class acceptance of this argument delegitimized secularism and opened the space for its renegotiation.

The diminished importance of the Muslim woman's oppression in the Hindutva discourse deserves some consideration. Seeing Muslim women as a plank in building a Muslim hate campaign provides a necessary, but not sufficient, explanation for why the spotlight was on them. Crucially, a discursive shift was required for the accomplishment of the larger and more ambitious project of displacing the Congress Party from the center of Indian politics. By questioning the secular claims on which its legitimacy had rested in the postindependence period, the shift created new opportunities for advancing the political agenda of challenging Congress Party supremacy. The goal is quite transparent, even though it is strenuously presented in terms of reform and women's rights.

By early 1986, there was growing support for claims that the Babari Masjid in Ayodhya rightfully belonged to Hindus because it was the site of Rām's birth (the Rām Janambhūmi). The Hindu Right's reformist impulse faded and the backwardness of Muslim women became its hope for launching the most trenchant critique of the state and its appeasement of minorities. Significantly, they did not demand the withdrawal of the retrogressive Muslim Womens Bill, because their whole campaign would have collapsed had that unlikely event occurred. During this period, the Hindu Right was not primarily concerned about the backwardness and barbarity of Muslim personal law in denying the rights of Muslim women; rather, it advocated a change in personal law as a means of conducting the more crucial struggle against minority appeasement. Muslim women's rights yielded place to personal law as the most effective critique of appeasement and of the pseudosecularism promoted by the Congress. This discursive shift was prompted by the Congress government's attempt to contain the electoral fallout from the All India Muslim Personal Law Board's opposition to the Shah Bano judgment. The introduction of the Muslim Women Bill generated nationwide support for the judgment and a considerable clamor of opposition to the bill from Congress Party members, the middle classes and intelligentsia, women's groups, the media, and the Hindu community at large. L. K. Advani, a BJP leader, declared, "The BJP is in a happy situation in which opposition parties like the CPI, CPI(M), Telugu Desam and overwhelming members of the Janata Dal and Congress are opposed to the legislation" (*Organiser*, 30 April 1986). Noticing that "the majority ruling and opposition party members see the legislation as a surrender to Muslim separatism" (*Organiser*, 13 April 1986), the Hindu Right saw in this its main chance to occupy the political space created by the deeply contentious issue of religious community identity and the concomitant ideological and organizational vacuum in the high ground of Indian politics. "Even those who were silent till now on the Muslim communal problem have come out openly against it. There is a silver lining on the national horizon, nation's conscience is awakened as never before to the menace of Muslim communalism," boasted the *Organiser* (1 April 1986).

The protection of minority rights, an important plank of secularism, was now under critical scrutiny from other political groups and from the intelligentsia, who were showing signs of unease with secularism. The Hindu Right interpreted this as the most serious crisis of the secular state in postindependence India, one that opened up possibilities of negotiation between communities and of the modification of secularism. At that point, the status of women was not being contested; rather, the focus was on the relevance and reformulation of the secular worldview. From then on, the Hindu Right acquired unprecedented strength. At no time before this had it received even 10 percent of the national vote; the average had been 7 percent. By 1991, however, support for Hindu nationalism was rising rapidly in northern and western India. The Shah Bano controversy was the turning point in the Hindu Right's political growth. In this sense, then, the debate on women and reform was an important moment in the group's expansion because it gave a remarkable opportunity for the Hindu Right to press its claims on the disputed mosque site in Ayodhya and simultaneously to launch its attack on secularism by arguing that national integrity is harmed by the pluralism and protection of minority rights entailed in the secular discourse.

The fundamental importance of the rights discourse lay in its capacity to replenish the ideology of political Hinduism by identifying its critique of minority rights with the emerging national consensus on the distortions of secularism. Most notably, it underlined the point that the theory of respect for all religions requires their formally equal treatment. The RSS argued that it had never demanded any special rights for Hindus. At the same time it was against making any concessions to religious minority groups and it opposed religious discrimination (Kapur and Cossman, 1995). A strong antipathy toward the secular state as a political arrangement for the appeasement of minorities was expressed through opposition to the Muslim Women Bill. This damaged the state's legitimacy, for in the process of protecting minority rights it was countenancing the violation of the principle of gender equality. The Hindu Right's strategy attempted to dismiss cultural diversity by setting the equal treatment of all women in opposition to secularism. Indeed, any recognition of cultural difference was considered a violation of the constitutional guarantee of equality. Above all, it perpetuated Muslim minority privileges and the oppression of the Hindu majority. The transformation of these myths, stereotypes, arguments, and propaganda into a national common sense that gained widespread prominence was crucial to the Hindu discourse and to the catapulting of the BJP to the center stage of Indian politics in the mid–1990s.

The transformation makes sense in the context of the sudden expansion of Hindutva politics and the need to break the Congress coalition of Brahmans, Muslims, and Scheduled Castes. In part, this was accomplished by casting aspersions on the vote-bank politics of the Congress Party. Existing political arrangements and structures could be delegitimized by claiming that the Muslim vote bank was solely responsible for the distortions in the politics and culture of the nation. For the Hindu Right, Muslims were particularly objectionable because they (allegedly) acted and voted in unison, as members of one indivisible community with one way of thinking and behaving. By contrast, it argued, there was no Hindu vote bank because Hindus were diverse and divided into numerous castes and communities, and were generally tolerant and naturally inclined toward diversity. The argument ignored the historical experience of the creation of the public sphere in India, in which the politics of numbers and voting blocs has been a part of the democratic experience and is central to the strategies of all political parties and communities. In the Hindu discourse, though, only Muslims think and act in unison. Pandering to the minorities and forging a diabolical alliance with the Muslims were part of a concerted Congress Party design to regain its lost supremacy. During 1985 and 1986, the theme of surrender to Muslim fundamentalism was highlighted in numerous articles in the *Organiser* with headlines such as "Congress wilts under pressure from the fundamentalists," "Congress bending backwards on Muslim personal law," and "Minorities are a pawn in the Congress game of power."

The government was uniformly accused of not caring for Muslim women because Muslim men bring in the votes. Rajiv Gandhi was vociferously condemned for succumbing to Muslim vote power and bigotry: "Rajiv Gandhi by pandering to these bigots is not only strengthening Muslim communalism but endangering the very security of India. . . . Political parties allow this dangerous state of affairs because they crave for the Muslim vote" (*Organiser*, 6 April 1986). The only way out of this quagmire of minority appeasement is a uniform civil code to end the special privileges of Muslims; the continued opposition of Muslims to it "justifies putting them in a subordinate position and even depriving them of the right to vote" (*Organiser*, 11 May 1986).

Gender Justice and Legal Reform

The Congress Party converted women's rights into an issue of minority rights and secularism and consequently avoided the issue of the lived experience of minorities. The Hindu Right built its attack on Muslims by focusing on their treatment of women and completely ignoring the identity concerns of Muslims. These two strategies were mutually supportive, but they were not doing the same thing. The *Organiser* was ostensibly talking about Muslims but was really talking about secularism; the Congress Party was ostensibly talking about secularism but was really talking about communities and minority rights. While espousing different world views, each discourse approached women in terms of their relevance to the ongoing political struggle over control of the state and regime. Those opposed to reform in personal laws emphasized the laws' religious basis and the dangers of intervention. Those in favor of reform stressed the harmful effect of personal laws on national unity. In their own ways, then, both stressed the national unity argument, albeit differently.

In a discussion supposedly about women's rights, the most notable feature of both strategies was the marginalization of Muslim women and the trivialization of their rights. The Lok Sabha debate virtually sidestepped the issue. Some women members did raise the topic, but it aroused no serious interest and women were commonly misrepresented in the debate. Consequently, women's rights—which inescapably made Muslim personal law the key issue in the debate—failed to be highlighted. Yet, the official position was framed entirely around personal law: a crucial issue for the Congress Party was a contextualized notion of citizenship in which community identities are paramount, in contrast to notions of equality before the law, equality of opportunity, or equality of treatment (Mansfield, 1993). This paradox arises because the recognition of religious differences in the application of law can violate the constitutional guarantee of equality, yet the denial of cultural diversity can violate the spirit of secularism, which postulates equal respect for all religions. The legal and political concept of equality occupied a highly contested terrain that intersected and overlapped with the contemporary struggle over notions of secularism and national identity.

Throughout, the Congress Party assumed that Muslim women were passive witnesses to the legislative debate, but they were by no means absent from the various battles being waged in the political domain. They were in the forefront of struggles mobilized by women's organizations to secure and safeguard their rights. Muslim women's opposition was a significant feature of the protest against the Muslim Women Bill in Kerala, West Bengal, Bombay, and Delhi, where the rights of indigent women were reaffirmed in public meetings and *mullās* (Muslim teachers or interpreters of Muslim law) were derided for turning religious law into an instrument of injustice (Hasan, 1993). In Delhi, fifteen hundred Muslim women participated in a rally organized by the All India Democratic Women's Association. The campaign culminated in a spectacular protest with hundreds of women chaining themselves to Parliament on the day the Muslim Women Bill was passed. For the first time Muslim women came out into the streets to fight for their rights in the face of opposition from family, neighborhood, community, and religious leadership. The president of one women's organization, the Janawadi Mahila Samiti, described their activism as "nothing short of a breakthrough in Muslim women's participation."[8]

This urban, educated, and middle-class dominated mobilization of women questioned the interpretations of the *ulamā* about the Sharī'at. Some Muslim women even supported alternatives outside the laws and traditions of the community. Their resistance served to remind both the community and the state that Muslim women would no longer remain silent in the face of obvious injustice and discrimination. But their opposition to the Muslim Women Bill was obscured by the media, which focused on the political actions of Muslim men and seldom paid attention to the activities of Muslim women. Spearheading the crusade against the Shah Bano judgment was the All India Muslim Personal Law Board, which has no representation of women. In the event, newspapers invariably focused on the board's actions and women's voices were completely silenced in the institutional sphere.

Women's important role in these political struggles was also submerged in the generalized dissatisfaction that there had not been enough protest and that the protest had been unable to change government policy or stall the legislation. But the failure to influence government policy should not lead us to disregard and discount women's activism, including the different kinds of activities of Muslim women. Some Muslim women did resist the legislation, but others provided support for it, which was not articulated in demonstrations and protests or in participation in the countrywide anti-Shah Bano movement mounted by Muslim politicians. There is no doubt that many urban Muslim women were worried that the Shah Bano judgment impinged on personal law, but their concern was expressed in private rather than public actions. Large numbers of Muslim women defended religious symbols and identity, and they rallied around the religious leadership's opposition to external interference in community affairs. But the spirited support by some women for the divorced Muslim woman's right to maintenance is a noteworthy contrast to the muted and passive opposition to it by others.

Muslim women's contradictory responses can be attributed to their diverse perceptions of their interests, since broader social and political processes may, at times, produce shifting and cross-cutting loyalties of class, community, and gender (Sangari, 1996). The results of all this activity have been mixed. Nevertheless, they have meant an increased self-confidence for some Muslim women, an expanded political consciousness, and the questioning of community construction of gender roles. The debate over the Shah Bano judgment generated a new trend of women's participation in the struggles and actions of women's organizations such as Janawadi Mahila Samiti (JMS), the National Federation of Indian Women, and other nonparty organizations. A leading JMS activist underscored the importance of women's mobilization against the Muslim Women Bill as a landmark in the expansion of JMS activities: "Even though we failed to block the legislation, we were able to establish contacts and rapport with Muslim women."[9] The campaign encouraged many women to join the JMS, and some of them now form the active cadre of the organization. There are large numbers of women seeking legal help and relief through the Legal Action Cell of the JMS.

Despite all the opposition, however, the government and most political organizations did not pay attention to women's voices. Muslim women became trapped in a contestation over the larger issue of the relationship between community rights and the state. Because so much of the debate was about secularism, legal reform was assessed in terms of its role in the encounter between pluralism and nationalism, not its intrinsic value for women's equality. These displacements and subversions treated Muslim women as emblematic of personal law or minority identity, and the high stakes of real Muslim women in equality were overlooked. Since the Shah Bano and Babari Masjid controversies, legal reform has become even more complex.

Rethinking on the issue has been shaped by the fears and anxieties aroused by the demolition of the Babari Masjid and by the discontents of Muslims in everyday life, which have been aggravated by communal politics since the mid-1980s (Bilgrami, 1993). The implications of this for women are clear. From their standpoint, the difficulty lies in linking the symbolic constructs and political concerns of Muslims to their own lives and actions. Community identity has come to be seen exclusively in terms of the regulation of family matters. In failing to define identity in more positive terms, the Muslim leadership has succeeded in privileging one arena as the essence of Muslim identity: the private sphere. Thus, all efforts at identity preservation are concentrated on Muslim personal law, which has become the refuge of Muslim leaders and politicians. In the present circumstances, this identity is necessarily defensive and leads to the definition and redefinition of Muslim women primarily as Muslims and a minority, which imposes severe constraints on women's rights.

During the 1990s, the sensitivities of Muslims have been increasingly recognized. Discussions about legal reform have taken a new turn, largely due to the interventions of women's groups and the women's movement in general, which have tried to change the terms of debate by emphasizing the primacy of women's rights. As a result, the issue of gender justice is now at the center of debate. Positions in the debate range from favoring legal uniformity and reform from above by the state to advocating legal pluralism, which essentially envisages reform of personal laws from within by communities themselves. All these efforts aim at making laws conform to principles of gender justice. Indeed, several judicial interventions have addressed discrepancies in the law, as for example the recent Supreme Court judgment giving the widow and daughter of a deceased coparcener equal right to property left by him; another judgment granting a divorced Hindu woman the right to sell, use for income, or dispose in any way she likes the land given to her in lieu of maintenance; and another giving a widow full ownership rights on the residence given to her as part of maintenance. These judgments have greatly reduced the discrimination between men and women in matters of inherited property.

The struggle for gender justice and for legal reform has also been strengthened because a uniform civil code (UCC) and personal laws alike have been critiqued on grounds of gender inequity. Furthermore, there is growing recognition that a UCC would be difficult to introduce into a multicultural society. Consequently, most women's groups have relinquished the idea of uniform laws as the central plank of women's equality and have articulated an alternative position based on principles of gender justice and women's rights. In the post-Shah Bano and post-Babari Masjid context, the emphasis is much more on the interplay of secularism, equality, and rights and on reconceptualizing the relationship between social equality and cultural recognition in ways that will support rather than undermine each other. The spotlight on equal rights rather than on a UCC signifies a meaningful shift in favor of equality and away from the uniformity implied by a UCC. The change is evident in the repudiation of a UCC by almost all groups and parties except the BJP.

Enlarging the scope of choice is thus the centerpiece of several alternative proposals. One suggestion is to devise genuinely egalitarian or secular laws for which individuals may opt. A women's rights group in Delhi has attempted to shift the debate from the comparative rights of communities to the rights of women as individual citizens. It has argued in favor of a comprehensive package of legislation providing equal rights for women in terms of access to property, guardianship of children, and rights in the matrimonial home, as well as equal rights in the workplace; antidiscriminatory provisions in recruitment, promotions, and job allocation; and so forth. Under this proposal, all Indian citizens would come under the purview of common laws, but they would have the right to choose to be governed by personal laws at any point in their lives (Working Group on Women's Rights, 1996).

The dichotomies between public and private, nation and religious minority, uniform and personal laws, and group and individual have been major impediments in reconceptualizing the relationship of the state to equal citizenship. The problem is how to arrive at a conception of citizenship based on the principle of democratic choice that guarantees equal rights without jeopardizing minority rights or undermining justice. Arguably, recasting the debate this way could redress gender inequalities without coming into conflict with the claims of communities. In the event of conflict, however, such a project would require the state to jettison the protection of inequalities and its constitutional endorsement of personal laws.

Notes

1. In 1993, a Christian Marriage Act was proposed by the government with the approval of all Christian churches and Christian women's organizations. Despite the Christian community's support for changes in divorce laws, the Bill has not yet been debated in Parliament.

2. Discussion of the Congress Party discourse is based on the Lok Sabha Debates, Fifth Session, Eighth Lok Sabha, Vol. J ON 1986 XVII, Government of India, New Delhi.

3. Separate personal laws for Hindus, Muslims, and smaller religious minorities existed under British rule and were carried forward or replaced by

similar laws after independence. Examples are the 1955 Hindu Marriages Act, the 1956 Hindu Succession Act, the 1937 Muslim Personal Law (Sharī'at) Application Act, and the 1939 Dissolution of Muslim Marriages Act.

4. This attitude was based on several misconceptions. One is the supposed immutability of Muslim personal law. Personal law is a creation of the modern state, more particularly, the colonial state, which began the process of codification of what the Raj called Muhammadan law (Kozlowski, 1993). Independent India's first law minister, B. R. Ambedkar, questioned the notion of an immutable Muhammadan law adhered to from "ancient times." "That law," he declared in the Constituent Assembly, "as such was not applicable twenty years ago" (Constituent Assembly Debates).

5. Chatterjee (1989) makes a similar point with regard to the colonial state's attitude.

6. Far from being pampered, Muslims are among the poorest and least educated in India, besides being discriminated against in public employment, even though they have made some progress. The Gopal Singh Committee, set up by the central government in 1980 to study the condition of minorities, noted that some employment exchanges refused to register Muslims. Indeed, the situation of Muslims has remained the nation's best-guarded secret.

7. This discussion of the Hindu Right's position and interventions is based on the *Organiser* (the official weekly English language journal of the Rashtriya Swayamsevak Sangh) 1985–1986.

8. Interview, Kalindi Deshpande, president, Janawadi Mahila Samiti, 12 February 1995.

9. Ibid.

Chapter Six

Woman, Community, and Nation

A Historical Trajectory for Hindu Identity Politics

TANIKA SARKAR

THE HINDU WOMAN BECAME A POLITICAL RESOURCE for a militant Hindu chauvinism that was composed, from the late nineteenth century onward, largely of ideologues from Bengal, Punjab, and Maharashtra. Notions of sharply delineated and mutually opposed religious communities had already entered the Indian political vocabulary. In a variety of ways, reimaging the woman within the community helped Hindu social leaders to reach out to women of their castes/class as active and consenting constituents of the community. The community came to be vested with a political self-image that cast itself as threatened, weakened and embattled, and, at the same time, inherently superior to non-Hindus. This dualism gave the self-image a doom-laden appeal, the energy associated with a last-ditch battle for survival. It also gave the community a moral right to political power.

The mobilization of the woman within a reoriented notion of community power was important in the context of a wider social crisis that Hindu militant leaders had faced continuously from the late nineteenth century. The new Hindu middle class was inextricably grounded in upper-caste power and land, and in service and commercial privileges. The privileges and the claim to social leadership came under severe strains. In Bengal, the absolute rights that the landed gentry had enjoyed over rent were fractured significantly in the last decades of the century by certain minimalist state programs for peasant protection. From the 1870s, there were tenant agitations against arbitrary taxes and illegal landlord exactions, and self-help movements by low-caste peasants against ritual degradation (Chowdhury, 1967; Bandopadhyaya, 1990). Earlier liberal reforms had already significantly breached upper-caste patriarchal absolutism through some protective legislation for Hindu women. Thus, for the Hindu social authorities, the colonial state and liberal reformers seemed bent on unmaking the securities and controls that the upper-caste landed *bhadralok* (respectable people) had so far been allowed to enjoy.

From the 1870s onward, Punjab became the firm base for Swami Dayanand's agenda for a reformed Veda-based Hindu fundamentalism. The Arya Dharm struck deep roots among a commercial and service elite that also developed small-scale banking and industrial capabilities. In the 1870s this elite was threatened by Brahmo, Christian, and Muslim proselytization from Bengalis and Indian Christians who had a far better grip on the educational facilities with which to negotiate a newly colonized situation, and from Muslims with a more confident hold on a refined Urdu culture. The Arya Samāj promised a modernized existence, in line with the liberal reforms in terms of women's education and caste and gender reforms. These reforms were undertaken by a new community claiming to represent the most authentic sources of Hindu traditions, as well as actively combating other communities' claims to truth and power. Later, its hold on the new administrative posts was shaken by the emergence of Muslim competition, and its plans to invest in the rich new canal colonies were foiled by state regulations. Consequently, the militant Hindu supremacist edge sharpened and prevailed over the impulse toward inner reform (Jones, 1976).

Maharashtrian Brahmans had been secure in their monopoly over admin-·istrative posts from precolonial Peshwa times. Under colonial rule, they augmented their hold on the new education and professions. From the 1860s onward, however, they were confronted by a low-caste upsurge that demanded that the colonial state transfer power from Brahman to non-Brahman hands. Significantly, the anti-Brahman movement developed in the heart of Brahman power—the city of Poona—and found a space in the lower echelons of administration, education, and even some entrepreneurial activities (O'Hanlon, 1985).

In the first decade of the twentieth century, worries of the upper castes about their declining hegemony were heightened by the prospect that Untouchable groups would separate from the Hindu community and seriously reduce the one stable claim to power the Hindus had: their absolute numerical majority. A recent study has traced how these anxieties were systematically fed into Hindu militant reformist schemes to integrate low castes within the community, as well as displaced onto the image of an embattled community fast losing its numerical edge to Muslims (Datta, 1993). Low castes were a tension spot within upper-caste Hindu claims to power, emerging as the absent cause, the silent invisible organizing principle that structured communal stereotypes, anxieties, and discourses. Threatened with the erosion of the community by the possible secession of low castes from the Hindu fold, with a possible shrinking of his authority and with challenges to his power, the upper-caste Hindu began to develop an explanatory system that held the Muslim—rather than his own caste privileges—responsible. Allegedly, Muslims, with their proselytization and forced conversions, their abductions of Hindu women, and their supposed self-proliferation, were throttling Hindu growth.

Worries about disappearing numbers opened up a space for the manipulation of gender issues in Hindu supremacist discourse. Numbers led to a preoccupation with bodies, their growth and their health. The child-wife produced weak progeny, widowhood meant the loss of potential childbearing wombs. Such a preoccupation could turn to internal reform. It also incorporated a rhetoric of Muslim designs on Hindu women, of ceaseless abductions whereby Hindu wombs produced Muslim progeny. Stabilized by the threat from a rival community, the new supremacist agenda was consolidated to achieve a unified community, which would incorporate the low castes and marginalized Hindus within the fold without significantly disturbing the existing power equations within the community.

In this agenda, the upper-caste Hindu woman acquired a threefold importance. She was, par excellence, the object of Muslim design, the personification of the vulnerable community and Hindu nation. Simultaneously, she was the marginal, powerless figure within the community who, like the low castes, needed to generate active consent to the new politics. Also, as a member of the upper-caste/middle-class leadership that was composing the new politics, she needed to be an active inventor of the new imaginary; at least, as mothers of the future leaders of the community, women needed to be taught the lessons and the intentions of the new politics, so that they could convey them to the children at home.

When the supremacist militancy attained its most powerful organizational consolidation with the foundation of the Rashtriya Swayamsevak Sangh (RSS) in the 1920s, a similar sociopolitical crisis was in the making for the Hindu social leaders. By then, however, the stereotypes of communal anxiety were so sedimented in a widely used common sense that the RSS dispensed with the reformism that the early Hindu militancy had generated.

Locating the Hindu Woman

In colonial times, the sphere of domestic practices, ritual, and belief was legally exempted from colonial transformative processes that could operate far more freely in civil society and the political sphere. Change in the domestic domain was to be permitted only when proved to have scriptural and customary sanction. Three very important historical developments followed from this.

First, the domestic sphere became conceptualized as one of relative autonomy. It was envisioned as both the last bastion of a vanished freedom and the site of a possible, emergent nation. Hindu nationalists, increasingly critical of colonial discrimination in the economic, political, and administrative realms, and of their own exclusion or marginalization, insisted on rights to self-determination in domestic norms and practices. Between the 1870s and the 1890s, anticolonial agitation emerged from resistance to proposed changes in the age of consent and to the introduction of divorce and the reform of Hindu marriage laws (T. Sarkar, 1993).

The second development, the conceiving of personal law as a domain of self-activism, led to wide popular involvement with processes of legal change. In fact, a public sphere developed largely out of debates over domestic matters and intimate relations. The new material conditions that structured the discursive field—vernacular prose, print culture, and journalism—enabled a continuous exchange of diverse views by people who simply needed vernacular literacy to express and receive opinions on themes that concerned their own everyday lives. Legal reforms generated an active debate over women's practices. Gender norms were detached from the realm of sacred prescription or unselfconscious common sense and their ideological basis was made completely transparent. Never before in Indian history had such a demystification of domestic values taken place.

The third development, the notion of a coherent, unified religious community, was tied immediately and directly into personal laws, which were assumed to be the concrete expression of religion. Law, religion, domesticity, community, freedom, and nationhood stood in a continuous metonymic relationship with one another to such an extent that they could even be used synonymously. The conjugal relationship held the links in place, since the new laws mostly centered around the figure of the wife. The Hindu wife, then, came to be a figure of unusual political weight and significance (Sarkar, 1992).

In the late nineteenth century, some Hindu nationalists opposed reform and insisted on a proud preservation of the Hindu way of life. To them, the wife's political significance was based on the claim that she was ruled by Hindu scripture and custom alone, and that she had not changed—unlike the Hindu male, who had surrendered his body and his mind to Western pedagogy and discipline. Despite their professed commitment to tradition, though, there was something distinctively modern in their discourse. They insisted that the true Hindu wife accepted scriptural rule out of her own free will and out of love and commitment to the greater glory of the community, for which she embraced the pain of widowhood, child marriage, and a nonconsensual, indissoluble union—a union severely monogamous for herself; her husband had every right to be polygynous. At the same time, this choice must not actually be seen to be exercised in practice; there need not be laws that hold out different possibilities and offer women a practical freedom of choice. The assumption of willed consent had to be sufficient in itself. The woman—the sign and ground of Hindu supremacy—was thus vested with a moral ascendancy over the Hindu man and the non-Hindu woman, an ascendancy simultaneously made nonactivist and nontransformative for the woman herself, even though her passivity indicated a complete transformation for the community (T. Sarkar, 1993). Thus, the woman had *the* political function, but that function was exhausted in her act of embodying unchanged domesticity in an age of flux. Over the age-of-consent controversy of 1890–1891, this language reached such stridency that the justification of the pain of raped and dying or brutally damaged child-wives clashed too sharply with the image of Hinduism as the most nurturant, loving, and joyous form of community life.

In the late 1890s, Vivekananda shifted the patriotic project from the domain of domesticity and conjugality to an exclusively male group of ascetics who would rejuvenate Hindu society through full-time social service (Sarkar, 1992). By the turn of the century, Hindu revivalists had moved away from the figure of the wife altogether and evolved a new project for the salvation of the colonized community. The all-male forms of political practice were, however, a specifically Bengali resolution.

In Punjab and the United Provinces, the revivalism of Swami Dayanand marked out a very different trajectory. The departure lay in his conviction in the centrality of the woman's status within a transformed and purified Hindu community and in the need for drastic changes in current domestic practices (Jordens, 1978). There is, then, a reorientation in the Hindu woman's location. She must transform her practices, not adhere to unreformed norms with great tenacity. Ironically, while Dayanand shared the imperative for reform with the liberal reformers, he overturned every liberal premise, however limited and fraught, on which the reformist agenda had been based. Dayanand propagated widow remarriage, an end to child marriage, and some education for women. Each change, however, denied individual affect and enthroned community commands.

Liberal reformers had advocated widow remarriage for normalizing female sexual desire, which would be gravely distorted if the husband died in the wife's infancy. Dayanand endorsed it only so that a better economy of potential childbearing wombs could be managed. It was also delinked from the exercise of free choice because a widow could marry only a widower, and the relationship ideally had to be terminated after the procreative purpose was adequately fulfilled. The woman was to be educated, not in the interests of companionate marriage—which might humanize patriarchal relations to an extent—but in the interests of better child management and a more disciplined child-rearing process. The mother-child relationship was to have no emotional autonomy of its own, since the mother was instructed to deprive her infant of her breast milk so that she could prepare her body as soon as possible for bearing and feeding the next child (Chakravarti, 1989). There was a heightened accent on the sexual content of marriage, but it was to be monitored and regulated entirely according to the best breeding requirements. Child marriage was discredited on similar grounds (Jones, 1976).

The entire sexual contract was laid bare and made into the object of pedagogy. This stripped it entirely of any notion of pleasure and annexed the sexual aspect of conjugality to racial needs for a strong and numerous population. The instrumentality of personal relationships to authoritarian community needs and demands, the complete subjugation of individual existence to a totalitarian discipline, and an obliteration of emotion, pleasure, and freedom in human relations were finalized through the instrument of reform.

The main differences with the liberal reformers were twofold. Liberal reformers had depended on state legislation as an instrument for social change. Legal identity would give the woman, at least notionally, a sphere of personal rights outside the rule of the family and the community that had so far structured every aspect of her life absolutely. These institutions would remain the primary socializing and disciplining agencies for all women, but potential access to law widened women's options and added a new variable that was relatively autonomous from—and even possibly at variance with—the family and the community. The law could set up counternorms. Within the Arya Samāj, however, the same reform items were not tied to an external agency but were conveyed exclusively through a reformed family and community into which the woman was completely and absolutely integrated. Her new opportunities neither arose from nor created a space beyond the family-community complex. She inherited her new lifestyle as a changed normative horizon prescribed by her old rulers, not as a right on which she, as an individual woman, had an inalienable grasp.

Furthermore, the reformed Hindu community was using the new norms to mark a fiercely asserted claim to superiority over other Indian communities. Here, at last, we have a finalized location for the Hindu woman in communal organizations that was available neither to the sanatanists (who believed in the timelessness of religious truths and endorsed the status quo) nor to the sect of Vivekananda (who delineated a society based on male bonding). The latter would certainly inspire the RSS organizational apparatus, but not its wider social ideology.

The woman's new location does not necessarily or invariably situate her in an increasingly regressive situation. She may have experienced profound transformations in the conditions of her existence, yet the changes would not enlarge the notion of the woman's rights, only that of the community's adaptive capability. At the same time, the woman is given an activism within a political formation already poised for battle against others. Instead of the ideal of embourgeoisement through the principles of liberal individualism, we find aspirations toward an authoritarian and totalitarian community formation on highly regimented lines.

Homogenizing the Hindu Community

The Rashtriya Swayamsevak Sangh (RSS) has been the most effective organizer and bearer of the politics of the Hindu Right, and the founder and teacher of several mass and electoral wings tied to its training program and general guidance. In 1925, when Indian nationalists had already been able to organize one of the largest mass movements in history, the RSS was founded as an alternative to the mass anticolonial struggles. It neither joined nor initiated any anti-British movement, and its activism consisted entirely of anti-Muslim violence (Basu, Datta, Sarkar, Sarkar, and Sen, 1993). Its women's wing, the Rashtra Sevika Samiti, was established in 1936 after Lakshmibai Kelkar, the mother of a Maharashtrian RSS veteran, had persuaded the RSS sarsanghchālak (supremo, or ideological leader) Hegdewar to help her. Elsewhere, I have tried to account for this shift in organizational strategy (Sarkar, 1991, 1995). Here, I very briefly summarize my arguments while developing some new ones.

Between the 1920s and 1930s, Indian nationalist politics went through fundamental transformations (Sarkar, 1989). Gandhi reordered the Congress Party so that peasants, tribals, and women could be incorporated into an erstwhile elitist organization that was beginning to adopt agitational tactics. At the same time, he began to coordinate Congress Party activism with Muslim organizations and movements within a broad and militant anticolonial upthrust: the Non Co-operation and Khilafat movements of the early twenties. Younger, more radical Congress leaders energized the resulting organization and committed it to a democratic ideal of nationhood based on universal adult suffrage and social justice. Suffragist groups emerged, determined to secure adequate representation of women within the democratic scheme (Forbes, 1996). More radical groups, largely outside the Congress Party mainstream, developed visions of class and caste equality that went beyond the more moderate Congress aims of harmony and bourgeois liberal progress. The new communist groups began to work among the industrial proletariat and the lesser peasantry, with visions of class war and social egalitarianism. B. R. Ambedkar threatened that the Untouchables would secede from the

Hindu fold altogether. In the South, the more moderate and relatively affluent leaders of the non-Brahman movement were challenged by the radical, militantly rationalist perspective of lower-caste groups mobilized by Perriyar (Omvedt, 1994). The political imperatives of Hindu militancy seemed threatened with an alarming degree of redundancy in this reoriented context.

A largely unnoticed, yet deeply significant, pattern of constraints faced by the upper echelons of the social hierarchy in the colonial situation needs to be retrieved here. Until the mid-nineteenth century, landowners might claim hegemonic controls in the name of traditional leadership, and the Dharma Sabha might uphold gender orthodoxies with a measure of confidence (Mukherjee, 1975). Yet nationalist rhetoric and its aspirations toward hegemonic authority proved increasingly incompatible with the largely feudal rhetoric and its legitimization of social power, however forcefully the latter might represent its paternalist credentials. The more the nationalists insisted on a generalized deprivation and subordination of all Indians under colonialism, the more they needed to base their claims to power on representing the widest segment of the Indian people, and not in the name of the community, class, castes, and gender from which they themselves originated. Representative capabilities could be claimed only at the cost of masking immediate social interests, by sacrificing overt invocations to inherited authority and social power, and by the rhetorical acceptance of an image of social leveling.

Crucial here were the counterclaims by the colonial state that Indian society was deeply stratified, that the neutral state—not implicated in the indigenous and internal distribution of social power—was the best watchdog for the interests of the underprivileged, and that nationalist demands for greater self-determination derived from a microscopic elite. In addition, there was an authentic (though far too often compromised) nationalist sensitivity to the subordination of women, low castes, and low classes in Indian history, which was driven home by the nationalist leaders' growing impatience with their own subordination under colonialism, despite their occupation of traditional leadership positions. There was a real sense of shared, generalized deprivation as colonial subjects, a sense that dispossession cut across social differences and rendered those differences partly irrelevant (T. Sarkar, 1993). Sectional interests could develop sectional organizations for managing and improving class- and caste-specific interests (Brahman Sabhas, chambers of commerce, the British Indian Association of landowners). In the wider nationalist politics, however, these sectional claims for leadership lost their prescriptive force and needed to operate covertly, enfolded within a rhetoric of consensus and equal representation.

During Gandhi's leadership of the Congress Party, this became a complicated and highly problematic enterprise, since the actual incorporation of the socially dispossessed within the nationalist organization was sharpened by the Gandhian rhetoric, which bestowed an iconic status on the peasant, the Untouchable, and the woman as ideal patriotic subjects. The growth of leftist, lower-caste, and suffragist politics threatened to translate this iconic role into a real and realizable possibility. The relative underdevelopment of a fully artic-ulated Indian capitalist class and ideology (Bagchi, 1972) possibly inhibited the development of any other hegemonic scheme where self-interest could be articulated as general good. These constraints generated a long and powerful tradition of populism in Indian politics that has created profound problems as well as possibilities for Indian democracy. At times, it creates intolerable strains, as proved by the eruption of upper caste anger during antireservation movements against affirmative action for lower castes. On the whole, however, social authorities have been forced to work as much as possible within this rhetorical domain.

These constraints marked the boundaries of the public statements of the new Hindu Right, which had to develop an imaginary based on consensus and unity. And, here, the recurrent Hindu-Muslim violence that leaders of both communities had stoked into life since the late nineteenth century was a particularly potent resource. Promoting intercommunity conflicts had served a similar purpose of strengthening hierarchical power within communities in the name of an alleged consensus against a common enemy. This strategy now emerged as the core of the new organizational activism of the Hindu Right. In the 1920s, not surprisingly, communal violence plumbed new depths, for the specter of violence was essential to invent and realize the image of a shared communal enemy and to secure it most successfully.

Down to the 1990s, counterpoints to established social hierarchies have regularly provoked fresh rounds of communal violence, rendering it a neces-sary and structural feature of right-wing politics. In these bouts of communal violence, the figure of the Hindu woman has emerged as a crucial mobilizing impulse, since much of the violence was composed around allegations of abductions by Muslim criminals. The Hindu community dissolved into the figure of the threatened woman, and violence became a necessary condition of Hindu male honor (Datta, 1995).

There is a further acute example of how sharpening internal divisions among Hindus led Hindutva forces to identify agendas that simultaneously promoted fear of a common enemy and reinforced their own specific power base against internal challenges. Hindu militants of the late nineteenth century had challenged the established cultural ascendancy of Urdu in northern India by conflating a religious and a linguistic community during the Hindi-Urdu controversies. In the process, communities were invented, for Hindi, which they privileged as the Hindu language, was an invention that grew by suppressing a whole range of local linguistic traditions, and Urdu was actually the shared language of the Hindu and Muslim elites (King, 1989).

When the RSS was being set up at Nagpur, Hindi was once again invoked, this time to resolve an internal tension. Hindutva forces were located in a multilingual geography, and the ascendancy of Hindi-speaking groups was being challenged by Marathi speakers. The local power games of the progenitors of organized Hindutva, therefore, neatly coincided with the late-nineteenth-century communalist rhetoric of Hindi-Hindu, which provided a highly empowering tradition with which to counter the aspirations of Hindu Marathi speakers. Hindi supremacism, then, became yet another imperative, taking its place with insidious silence about the class- and caste-based power of these landed, middle-class, Hindi-speaking, upper-caste Hindutva protagonists (Baker, 1971).

If a homogeneous community threatened from outside was a necessary political imaginary, how would gender fit into the scheme? The endangered woman could be an exceptionally potent weapon for violent mobilization, and that tradition continues to this day. Indian history was rewritten by the Hindutva ideologue V. D. Savarkar as a continuous assault on Hindu womanhood by Muslim invaders, whose conquest of the country was motivated by this desire (Agarwal, 1995). The narrative simultaneously merged the woman into the community and made her a cause and a metaphor for the defeat of a Hindu motherland. Women were imaged as perennially threatened—a conviction, according to Rashtra Sevika Samiti accounts, that inspired its creation. Lakshmibai Kelkar, its founder, was haunted by this fear, and wanted Hindu women to have the physical strength to repulse attacks.

The other Hindu communal narrative used a selective and often distorted version of census data to reinvoke the earlier sense that Hindu population growth was drying up and that Hindus would lose their numerical majority within India as a result of Muslim overbreeding. This inspired anxiety about the Hindu female body and its capacity for bearing strong and heroic sons who would grow up as protectors of the community (Datta, 1993). The eugenic imperative legitimized the founding of the Rashtra Sevika Samiti, where a rigorous physical training schedule would build up future mothers. Indeed, anxiety about the leisure-softened, incarcerated bodies of upper-caste women was the reason that Lakshmibai Kelkar's request for a separate organization for the women of RSS families was eventually granted. It also explains why the Samiti devised a theater of warlike gestures, even though there was certainly no plan to send women into direct violent action. Every day, sevikas worshipped the icon of an eight-armed goddess (a figure taken from contemporary nationalist iconography) and spent time meditating on her weapons. The schedule of physical training included a course in martial arts and was a daring departure for upper-caste women of those times. Revolutionary terrorists in Bengal trained their women in martial arts, and the idea probably traveled from there. Unlike women terrorists, however, the sevikas had no agenda for immediate political action, and certainly not one that entailed confronting the colonial state. In fact, the Hindu Right never troubled the colonial rulers with any kind of agitation.

From the outset, Samiti members were projected as mothers (Sarkar, 1991, 1995). Much after the Samiti's founding, M. S. Golwalkar, the second RSS *sarsanghchālak,* described the Sangh's gender ideology as a "call to motherhood." While women's bodies would be shaped up for healthy reproduction, the daily *buddhik,* or ideological training, that the organization provided was to open women's minds to the basic lessons of Hindutva politics, primarily its fierce and aggressive Hindu supremacism. This education, however, was meant to impart an uncritical admiration for Hindu scriptures and customs, without familiarizing women with the texts themselves. Even now, this pedagogic pattern continues: sevikas can narrate eulogies and lists of great qualities and attributes, but their actual exposure to sacred texts of any kind is severely limited.

A conservative form of domestic values also prevails, which encourages some educational and career aspirations, provided they are sanctioned by parents. Parental permission is again vital in marriage arrangements, where self-choice is discouraged. This accent on parental discipline shapes an obedient filial and feminine identity, maintains the caste and class boundaries of the families, and rules out transgressive miscegenation, without overtly referring to caste ideology as such. Thus, social hierarchy is maintained without making the ideological apparatus explicit, for parental counseling is portrayed as an emotional imperative.

The local-level samitis supplement familial and caste controls, yet their mode of discipline is so different that they are seen as a separate and autonomous space. Indeed, they seem to be a kind of playground for sociability, a voluntarily formed peer group whose leisure time is spent in interesting activities (Sarkar, 1991). What future mothers learn there is meant to be transmitted to their children later. The samitis not only fashion mothers and the family but also form preschool pedagogical tools: "Let our mothers make the children wake up early in the morning, make them salute their elders, and offer worship to the family deity." Mothers should teach their children to resist "a blind aping of the West" and their girls to avoid European dress and not to "expose their bodies more and more." They should keep alive the observance of sacred occasions and ceremonies and take children on regular visits to temples. Mothers must also teach literacy, but teaching "noble *samskāras*" (refinements) or a pious disposition was far more useful than formal learning.

Samskāras would include deference to family elders, Hindu historical heroes and deities, and RSS great men. The mother's mediation thus renders the family, the RSS, and the nation into a single all-encompassing yet intimate reality (Golwalkar, 1980).

Apart from mothers, the local samitis train teachers for the RSS-run schools, a large number of which are primary and elementary. The teachers are overwhelmingly women; we were told that most come from RSS backgrounds, and many would be trained by the samitis (Sarkar, 1996). Continuity is thus ensured between what the child learns from the mother and what is later taught at school. Samitis, schools, and homes cluster in the same neighborhoods, which secures an exceptional degree of physical intimacy and overlapping of spaces, times, and persons—mother, teacher, samiti members—who combine their functions in an assembly line to produce ideological reinforcement. The social coherence and homogeneity is formidably well structured, since families that feed into schools and local samitis are necessarily similar in caste and class terms. Other schools, families, and leisure organizations are similarly exclusive and tightly knit, but they seldom feed into one another at the level of personnel and ideas to quite the same extent, and they usually do not have a strong and monolithic ideological underpinning. By contrast, the samitis provide mothers and teachers, and the entire enterprise is held together by a single cluster of practices, ritual, and politics.

The sheer economy of political investment is remarkable, but the economy does not stop there. Samitis have exercises for training their members to become informal counselors and leaders among the women of their kinship groups and neighborhoods. Samiti members make a point of family visits among the households of sevikas, where they insert themselves by helping during distress, illness, or family crises (Sarkar, 1991). Through kinship networks, they penetrate non-RSS households as well, say, when a sevika marries into such a family, or when a girl of such a family marries into a samiti member's own family. For the latter, the local samitis run special sessions. For the former, the samitis train sevikas carefully not to foreground samiti contacts or resume samiti attendance after marriage but to forward the Rashtra Sevika Samiti's task by becoming docile wives and gaining the confidence of the women of their new family. For instance, the samitis teach the battered wife to accept her lot and to blame herself for her own failure to achieve harmony. To the wronged wife, they say that men are necessarily faithless and one has to live with this biological fact. They discourage talk of divorce or legal help, and they silence protest through persuasion and through invocations of Hindu patriarchal examples—the legendary wives who accept conjugal tyranny with a smile. They teach impatient or rebellious daughters that they lack the age and experience to evaluate their own decisions and that their parents love them most (Sarkar, 1991; Anitha et al., 1995). One can see how easily they capture the confidence and respect of their new families and neighborhoods, and how well they advertise their organization, whose political commands are thus insinuated into a new and fresh environment without any additional mobilizational inputs. Through their everyday dispositions and normal activities, the sevikas win new territory.

Flavia Agnes has acutely remarked upon the difficulties for radical women's organizations in merging with their surroundings. They ask women to protest against injustice, to question what is given as common sense, to think and act for themselves. This often leads to social isolation, emotional deprivation, loss of anchorage and mooring. Radical organizations cannot replace the lost world. New convictions cannot combat the weight of inherited norms (Agnes, 1995; see also Shaheed, this volume). By contrast, the retrogression and gender insensitivity of the sevikas guarantee their safety, acceptance, and merging within the broader caste-class milieu—even if they do nothing to help the battered wife or the rebellious child. The Rashtra Sevika Samiti gender ideology, then, is a form of surrender to patriarchy, in which the Samiti forwards the cause of the RSS. At the same time, the local samitis do offer some valuable resources for women integrated with the family and the community: physical training, a political identity, acceptance and even encouragement of education and jobs if their parents agree. The samitis help women to achieve the transition from a domesticated to a more public domain with the support and consent of the family and with the comforts of the old, inherited, safe, and uncontested values intact.

In their new kinship and neighborhood groups, then, women merge and later emerge as accepted leaders and advisers, transmitting the domestic, gender, and political ideas of the RSS. The women's activities are restricted within a confined circle of a homogeneous class-caste cluster, but their mobilization within this boundary is exceptionally powerful. A fundamental peculiarity of RSS politics is that mobilization within the same milieu, even the same family, is initially more important than mobilization among other social groups and spaces. A very wide range of RSS activity is restricted to the upper-caste, middle-class, urban, service and trading or small manufacturing community. The sevikas are essentially an auxiliary force in this realm.

The ideal of Samiti motherhood acquires a heroic dimension. It strips itself of earlier softer and more emotional attributes as the sevikas are pulled into a violent politics of pogroms against Indian Muslims. Traditional Hindu and nationalist icons are redrawn to serve as the source for a new kind of inspiration. In the years immediately preceding the demolition of the Babari Masjid in 1992, the Vishwa Hindu Parishad (VHP) woman ascetic leader Sādvī Rithambhara reiterated the same message in her famous audiocassette. The nationalist martyr Bhagat Singh's mother, she narrates in her apocryphal story, wept after the son's execution, not because her son was dead but because she had no other son who could die a similar death. The accent was on her lack of motherly grief and her eagerness to reexperience the loss—a transgressive departure from the model of natural or ideal motherhood, one stripped of all libertarian or larger human possibilities.

Rithambhara's use of motherhood was not a particularly original one within a militaristic politics. A ruthless warrior ideal usually develops a heroic-woman ideal on similar lines. But the Samiti does make some new departures in norms and conventions by expanding the horizons of domesticity and adding serious, politicized dimensions to femininity. At the same time, the thrust of the transformation obliterates the notion of selfhood and erases concern for social rights and gender justice.

Hindutva Women, Consumerism, and Gender Rights

The quiet, routinized, and largely informal work of the local samitis continues. They follow the expansion of RSS *shākhās* (daily-training branches) and schools in urban, middle-class, and upper-caste milieus in north Indian cities and towns, and they have some reach in Maharashtra and Karnataka. They were very instrumental in training women in the other RSS affiliates for militant and violent action in the Babari Masjid campaigns (Sarkar, 1995).

Although the samitis provide the backdrop and the underpinning for the recent and very sizable entry of Hindutva women in violent campaigns, the leading roles of right-wing women in public politics is a new phenomenon that requires some explanation. Women ascetics have been pivotal in whipping up riots, and RSS affiliates and subaffiliates have spawned a number of women's wings (Sarkar, 1995). Women have endorsed specifically male forms of Hindu violence. Krishna Sharma, the leader of the Delhi Vishwa Hindu Parishad (VHP) Mahila Mandal, has justified the tearing open of wombs of pregnant Muslim women by Hindu rioters and the gang rapes of Muslim women that are said to have been videotaped (Anitha et al., 1995). Uma Bharati, Sādvī Rithambhara, and Vijayraje Scindhia of the Bharatiya Janata Party (BJP) and the VHP—both affiliated with the RSS—have been as important icons of the movement as male leaders like L. K. Advani. Simultaneously, the movement among the women of the Hindutva brigade has outstripped the orbit and boundaries of the Rashtra Sevika Samiti and other organizations. The range of active consent among the middle and upper-middle castes and classes increased enormously during the Babari Masjid campaigns from the mid–1980s onward. Clearly, the work of the women's organizations cannot entirely explain the resonance of RSS messages and values among this enlarged constituency.

The enlargement of active consent and support coincides with certain structural changes in the social base of the constituency itself. The slow but steady growth in the state bureaucratic apparatus since independence has created the basis for a tremendous expansion of an affluent middle class with high aspirations. To some extent, the Green Revolution and the consequent growth of agro-industries have bridged the gap between rural areas and small towns. We interviewed a large number of RSS supporters from north India who have links with both. From the mid-1970s onward, the state has encouraged, with credit and other facilities, the growth of small manufacturing units. Simultaneously, the salaried middle classes in several sectors have experienced a rise in wages (Basu et al., 1993). The whole phenomenon was grounded on an immense stimulation of purchasing and the promotion of commodity distribution through aggressive advertising campaigns and media techniques. Much of the production and distribution of commodities relates to women's fashion items and to household gadgets that are meant for women's use. The trend toward a specifically feminine consumerism increased dramatically after India was launched on the new career of liberalizing its economy under World Bank and IMF guidelines, particularly since 1991. Cable TV networks daily recreate innumerable spectacles of Western life styles. The market is simultaneously inundated with growing numbers of foreign consumer products that are distributed and consumed within precisely those reoriented upper and middle classes that are the RSS's terrain.

The female support base is changing fast. Women are wooed as privileged consumers, urged to spend money on themselves for an endless flow of nondurable goods that undercut the traditional domestic values of the self-effacing woman who lives not for herself but for her family. A rather aggressive new consumerist individualism is generated, and a new identity fashioned. Significantly, the new Hindu upper-caste, middle-class woman now has the ability to respond independently to the seductive calls of the advertising culture, since she is often educated and employed.

What are the problems and the possibilities for the RSS when it faces the changing figure of the new Hindutva woman? A public identity generated by jobs, education, and a new self-image might tend to push her toward a discourse of gender equality and rights and toward a wish to negotiate the new opportunities further. She might resent the new forms of discrimination that her public roles force upon her, and she might start questioning domestic inequalities and the prescriptions handed out by the samitis to deal with them. Her very immersion in consumerist preoccupations might create new strains. Her new identity might impose impossible new demands. And the advertising culture, with its relentless campaigns against aging and loss of desirability, with its continuous insistence on constant purchasing, might not make for a satisfyingly stable and tranquil sense of individuality.

Here, the RSS and the Rashtra Sevika Samiti face formidable rivals in the much larger, dynamic Left and radical, and militantly secular women's organizations. Unlike the Samiti, these propagate and work for the discourses of gender rights and link them with broader agendas of social egalitarianism. They systematically publicize gross and violent gender injustice among oppressed social groups, and they link patriarchy with larger patterns of social injustice. A woman might learn to interrogate too many things: the home, the workplace, and the overall system of oppression, discrimination, and marginalization, which she still experiences as a woman, despite her new opportunities and privileges.

There are, however, certain countervailing possibilities for the RSS. The Indian government's new economic policies of structural adjustment—to which the RSS also subscribes despite its occasional rhetorical flourishes of svadeshī and self-respect—significantly widen the economic and social gaps between women. A small segment of the middle-class experiences enhanced opportunities and expanded privileges, but the mass of lower-class women find employment shrinking in the formal sector, job securities vanishing, and social benefits and trade union possibilities becoming chimerical (Patel, 1994). Class interests would then undercut a shared gender identity.

Again, a woman's entry into the public domain of jobs and status binds her more firmly to her male class and caste counterparts. During the anti-Mandal agitations of 1990, when the government promised job reservations in public services for Other Backward Caste categories, upper-caste women students and employees were as strident in protest as upper-caste men. A new commitment to social privileges develops that is not available to the purely domesticated woman. The woman thus emerges as an integrated class-caste subject with an active, informed solidarity with her menfolk.

The Hindutva movement negotiates the new situation with a threefold strategy. It does not deny the privileges of consumerist individualism to its women. It incorporates women as leaders of the anti-Muslim violence and allows them a new role in activism that was earlier withheld. And it simultaneously constructs a revitalized moral vision of domestic and sexual norms that promises to restore the comforts of old sociabilities and familial solidarities without tampering either with women's public role or with consumerist individualism. Murli Manohar Joshi, the Bharatiya Janata Party leader, writes about the dangers of the erosion of old values: divorces, widow remarriage, lesbianism, feminist ideas, women's movements (Joshi, 1995). Samiti leaders reiterate the virtues of Hindu patriarchal traditions (Anitha et al., 1995). Older forms of gender ideology are merged with new offers of self-fashioning and a relative political equality in the field of anti-Muslim and antisecular violence. Patriarchal discipline is reinforced by anticipating and accommodating consumerist aspirations.

Part II
The Everyday and the Local

Chapter Seven

Women and Men in a Contemporary Pietist Movement

The Case of the Tablīghī Jamaʻat

BARBARA D. METCALF

THOSE WHO HAVE FOLLOWED POLITICS IN SOUTH ASIA in recent years have seen an acceleration in the use of religious symbols in public life: in Pakistan, where the issue of Islamization has been debated since the seventies; in Bangladesh, where the secular thrust of the immediate postindependence period of the early seventies has been abandoned; and in India, where the rise of Hindu nationalist parties has seriously challenged the tradition of secularism associated with leaders like Nehru. A striking feature of this change has been the activity of women in religious parties and movements. Not all religious activity is focused, however, on public life. The subject of this paper, the Tablīghī Jamaʻat, is a widespread Islamic movement active in all three countries, in which women and men participants alike remain aloof from public political life and debate.

Why do contemporary women participate in religious movements? Liberals and feminists have usually assumed that religious or right-wing movements are detrimental to women's interests, and that women participate only at the behest of their menfolk, who exercise overall leadership. Nonetheless, it has become clear that women themselves often take independent initiative in participation and may see these movements as serving their own interests, much as women have in fundamentalist Christian movements in the United States.

To imagine this kind of independence for Muslim women is even harder than to imagine it for Hindu or Christian women because of the distorted lenses through which outsiders typically view Muslims and Islam. The work of Edward Said, of course, has played a crucial role in sensitizing scholars to these distortions. His seminal book, *Orientalism* (1978), argued that ideas of the "Orient," forged in the West from a position of political and technological power, depicted Muslim cultures in particular as uniform, unchanging, and inferior in ways that legitimized and explained Western power. Islam as a religion, it has been argued, has long been deemed uniquely unfavorable to women, virtually the limiting case for oppression and social inequality on the basis of gender. The symbol of women's head coverings, or veils, is heavily charged and is typically taken by observers as a sign of oppression by Islam or men imposed on women.

If Islam has occupied a powerful place in the European imagination, it has played an even more dramatic role in the political imagination in India.[1] As Ritu Menon argues in this volume, many Indians imagined Pakistan in the immediate postpartition period as the opposite of what they wanted their own new state to be. Thus Pakistan was feudal and backward, its men oppressive toward their own women, lascivious toward others. The Muslims of India were assimilated into this construction. These attitudes have taken on new salience in the past decade, fueled by the debate over the Shah Bano judgment (Hasan, this volume) and symbolized above all by the destruction on 6 December 1992 of the Babari Masjid in Ayodhya by Hindu nationalists defying government restrictions. It is tempting to see the Tablīghī Jamaʿat, which holds aloof from all issues of state and the organization of society, as a reaction to these Indian events. Yet the movement is equally widespread in both Pakistan and Bangladesh, both of which in recent years have espoused explicitly Islamic state ideology.

In this chapter, I discuss male and female gender roles in the Tablīghī Jamaʿat as a way of seeing some aspects of the movement's appeal for women and men alike. These issues of gender represent only one theme in a complex, long-lived, and widespread movement. And while the teachings about gender persist, they obviously take on varying emphases and meanings in the different time periods and contexts in which Tablīgh has flourished.

The Historical Background of the Movement

In the post–World War I period, when the promises held out by the colonial power during the war and the solidarity of the activist political movements withered, many people in India turned to the formation of voluntary associations focused not on political action per se but, in varying degrees, on individual and emergent community regeneration. Tablīghī Jamaʿat was first conceived by Maulana Muhammad Ilyas, a pious, learned religious leader based in Delhi, who died in 1944. The origin of the movement is typically dated to 1927. Today its annual meetings in Pakistan and Bangladesh draw well over a million people, and although meetings in India are smaller, participants may be as many (Qurashi, 1989). Tablīgh networks extend throughout the world, not only to places of Indo-Muslim settlement like North America and Britain but to continental Europe, Africa, Malaysia, and elsewhere.

Clearly in this long period, participation in the movement has had widely different implications. The movement was started by the very class of religious clergy that at the same time was forming the Jamiyyati 'Ulama-yi Hind as a supporter of the Congress Party: Tablīgh leaders held aloof from that organization, as they did from all political expression. The context of the movement changed dramatically with partition, and one scholar has identified the immediate post-1947 period as the first occasion of real growth (Aggarwal, 1971). A third significant stage came with the creation of a Muslim diaspora population from the sixties onward, with Tablīgh becoming truly transnational while serving as a counterculture to the dramatic economic changes of recent decades. The third stage is particularly relevant here.

Throughout this long period, the central tenet of Tablīgh has been that all Muslims could teach others the key values and practices of Islam and that the very act of teaching others would in fact best teach the teachers. In effect, any sincere Muslim could, by going out to offer guidance to other Muslims, undertake what had heretofore been the province of men distinguished by education, saintly achievement, and, often, notable birth.[2] Participants start with inviting others to join them in the congregational prayer and regard nothing as more important than this. They also teach other fundamental obligations, including Qur'anic reading, the fast (*rozā*, the requisite alms giving (*zakāt*), and the ritual visit to Mecca (*hajj*). They do not engage in any disputation or abstract discussion but simply focus on these positive injunctions. Persons associated with the movement do not, moreover, offer any social or political program; it is not a political movement now nor does it have a utopian vision of a polity and society to come. All that is left to an unexplored future; the urgency of the moment is faithfulness to individual Islamic teachings.

The tour—the central feature of the movement—consists of a jama'at, or party, of perhaps ten or so individuals who go out for an evening, a few days, or a prolonged journey. During the tour the participants support one another in ritual fidelity, stay in a mosque, and read out loud and pray with those who come for house-to-house visits. The tour is the occasion for a radical break with all the usual enmeshments, including those, typical for most people, of intense face-to-face hierarchies of family and work. That break allows the far-reaching change that was Maulana Ilyas's goal, for he was explicit that it was the journeyer, not the audience, who would be most significantly changed (Muhammad Zakariyya, n.d.: 23). Everything in the tour is meant to inculcate humility, not least the fidelity to prayer that renders a Muslim humble before Allah. Travel, moreover, encourages a state of permanent vulnerability and uncertainty in which, outside one's normal moorings, one learns to be dependent on God. The humility that is the movement's goal is further encouraged by the priority given to proselytization so that each participant places himself continually in a situation that risks rebuff.

Beyond all this, however, a range of practices foster a leveling among the participants, a leveling modified in principle only by degrees of fidelity and faith. In a society, for instance, where dress is a clear mark of status and particularist identities, all tablīghīs dress alike in the simplest garments. In a society where to open one's mouth is to betray great hierarchic gaps, above all, that between English and the vernaculars, and, among the vernaculars between elegant Urdu and simple language, all *tablīghīs* cultivate simple language. In a society that looks down on manual labor, on tour everyone carries his own bag and does the most menial tasks.

The very openness of the group further diminishes hierarchy. There are no criteria for membership or entry. Any Muslim who seeks to join is welcome in a way that is virtually unknown in highly institutionalized, highly stratified societies. No priority is given to intellectualism. Each member is seen to have the very same capacity for full participation by the simple step of embracing readily accessible teachings and committing himself to spreading them. Each person, by virtue of being Muslim, is assumed to be a potential participant worthy of respect.

Among those on a tour, the elimination of hierarchic distinctions is relentless. Decisions are made through a process of consultation known as *mashvarā*. The *amīr*, or leader, himself is chosen by the group. He ideally should be distinguished by the quality of his faith, not by worldly rank; a peon or servant can be an *amīr*. There are echoes of *sūfī* notions that the least likely person may be one of the spiritual elect. Thus authority is, in principle, no longer based on outward attainments or birth, and charisma is vested in the group as a whole.

Different roles are assigned to members of a mission. Key to these roles, and to Tablīghī thinking generally, is the concept of service, or _khidmat_ (Altaf Husain Qasimi, 1968: 14). Ideally, roles are shifted and a single person may act as teacher or preacher on one occasion but humble cook or cleaner on another. The movement's focus on divine reward motivates this service, as it does all else. Maulana Ilyas argued that to do service was in fact to attain two rewards, that of serving one's companions and that of freeing them to engage in tablīgh (Muhammad Zakariyya n.d.: 36).

Maulana Ilyas preserved in his papers the letter of a university graduate describing the _khidmat_ of one jama'at's *amīr.*

He looked after everyone's comfort throughout the journey, carried the luggage of others on his shoulders, in addition to his own, in spite of old age, filled the glasses with water at mealtimes and refrained from sitting down to eat until everybody had been seated comfortably, helped others to perform [the ablution] on the train and drew their attention to its rules and proprieties, kept watch while the others slept and exhorted the members to remember God much and often, and did all this most willingly. For a person who was superior to all of us in age, social status and wealth to behave as the servant of everyone was the most unforgettable experience of the tour. (Nadwi, 1983: 150)

Tablīghīs ideally pay their own way; no one is patron and no one is dependent (Metcalf, 1994a). All of this marks a dramatic departure in societies characterized by structures of subordination and hierarchy.[3]

Although there is some degree of organization and some mosques and schools associated with Tablīgh, there are no paid staff members. Tablīgh offers no career path in itself. The local jama'at group, described above, is the fundamental building block of the movement, and could, in principle, operate and reproduce itself even if there were no center at all. For women and men alike, the only source of status in the movement is meant to be piety and faith, with leadership resting not on birth but on personal work and qualities.

Women's Participation

Women are scarcely visible in this movement. It is men who go from door to door in college hostels; men who approach other Muslim men to invite them to pray in airports; men who can be seen, traveling in small groups on bus or train, in Indian cities as part of their monthly or yearly sacrifice of time for proselytization, or *da'wa*. It is men one sees in subcontinental cities, dressed in simple white loose pants, long shirt, and cap, modest bedding on their backs, disappearing into a mosque where they will spend the night. However, women also participate, not only seeking education and practicing piety as individuals but also by going out to teach, provided only that they do not mix with unrelated men. They are expected to engage in *da'wa* in their own sphere of women and members of their family.[4] Women's *jama'ats*, when they do go out, are accompanied by their menfolk; in number, they are far fewer than those of men. There are, however, invariably *jama'ats* of women at the large annual meetings, settled amidst various homes where, as in one home I visited, furniture had been cleared out to allow for bedding to cover the entire floor. Pakistani women described visits not only from expatriates and other South Asians but even of women visiting from such distant countries as France.

Maulana Muhammad Ilyas, the movement's founder, is remembered as encouraging work among women from the very beginning. He turned first to the wife of one of the teachers at his school at Nizamu'd-Din in New Delhi, Maulana 'Abdu's-Suhban, who was from the area of Mewat, southwest of Delhi, where Tabli͞gh influence first spread. This woman was herself described as "a very pious, pure, religious woman, adorned with purity, a person of understanding (*sahib-i fahm*) and judgment." She began work among women in Delhi, and, at Maulana Ilyas's instruction, formed a *jama'at* to go to Mewat, each member accompanied by a close male relative. Ilyas had sought the approval of other religious elders, who were, apparently, very worried that such activity was inappropriate and conducive to women's using Tablīgh as a pretext for license. He persisted, gradually winning the support of people like the respected Mufti Kifayatu'llah (Muhammad 'Isa Firozpuri, n.d.: 105–6; his *fatvā* is in 'Abdu'sh-shakur, 1981: 8).

Women were to be lodged in a private dwelling where they would be secure. The rule was set from the very beginning that the house had to have an indoor toilet, a custom unknown in Mewat but now common, as one history writes, "through the blessing of Tablīgh" (Muhammed Isa Firozpuri, n.d.: 102). As this example suggests, Tablīgh, in a variety of ways, generalized the customs of the respectable and the urban, here replacing with interior toilets the custom of nighttime trips to the fields.

Most important, and more common than distant travels, have been the neighborhood meetings for women that are occasions for the committed to assemble and for others to be drawn in. In some places these meetings are daily; in others, less frequent. One striking aspect of women's participation is in fact the opportunity Tablīgh offers for women to congregate. Among South Asian Muslims, women are discouraged from even going to the mosque and, in some traditions, to the saintly shrines, which have nevertheless been well attended by women. Even in homes, they have typically gathered in large numbers only on occasions of marriage or death. Now in the Tablīgh, they have regular occasions for congregational gatherings and common worship. In Karachi, for example, women meet on Fridays at the Makki Masjid in the heart of the city for the hours between noon and late afternoon prayer; when I attended a meeting there in July 1991, perhaps a thousand women were present. First a woman spoke, then a man (over a loudspeaker). The warmth, gentleness, and simplicity of the discourse was palpable as women were reminded of their responsibility for their own piety, for guidance to their family, and for support to those going out. In the final prayer, the speaker implored God for guidance, forgiveness, and mercy. Women listened, prayed, meditated, and chatted as they gathered their wraps to depart. Women's neighborhood groups gather in Delhi in Muslim areas like Nizamu'd-Din and the walled city.

Printed materials primarily discuss and are directed toward men. Still, the movement's basic text, Muhammad Zakariyya's *Faza'il-i A'mal* (*Teachings of Islam*, n.d.), includes a section on women in its important collection of exemplary incidents from the lives of the Prophet's companions. Other books used by tablīghīs may summarize women's activities or include specific directions for women's Tablīgh. One list, in an "unauthorized" pamphlet of rules for Tablīgh tours written at his own initiative by a sympathizer (Muhammad 'Isa Firozpuri, n.d.: 107–111), offers five "conditions" and fourteen "principles" for women; for example, the practical suggestion that proselytizing should begin in houses where people are known to be sympathetic. Only married women, accompanied by a male relative, should travel to a different town, "since this is an age of disorder." Women are to observe seclusion from unrelated men and make use of the men accompanying them to spread the word of their presence and schedule meetings.

Women, Muhammad 'Isa Firozpuri, must learn, read, and in turn teach the *Fazā'il* texts, which deal with the fast, *hajj*, prayer, Qur'anic reading, meditational practices, and the normative stories (*hikāyat*) mentioned above. The teaching is to be done without long discussion. "However experienced someone claims to be and to have the last word from *Hazratjī* (the Delhi-based leader descended from the founder), she should be silent." (This limitation, of course, also applies to men because the whole modus operandi of the movement is to emphasize faith and example, not disputation, debate, or elaborate argument.) Women, he continues, must arrange that during the tour they offer the canonical prayer, supererogatory prayer, and Qur'anic recitation and litanies; they are to arise early in order to pray for guidance for the *ummat* (of Muslims) and for all humankind. Women's meetings should include ordinary people (*'awām*) in order to instruct them, to awaken their religion, and to organize *tashkīl*, the identification of men from their families who will go out for Tablīgh. This entails writing down the names of male relatives, the time they should spend on tour, and the expenses they can meet. The local women should be encouraged to undertake instruction in their own homes and to hold weekly meetings. Women, he explains, choose their own leader (*zimmedār*, the same term used for men); but they should also consult the amīr of the male jama'at when they are on tour. To do this, a woman zimmedār is to send queries through her own male relative, "just as in Madina the women chose Hazrat Asma to be present with the Prophet." Women should not give speeches heard by men. The final principle is that women should go out wearing plain clothes and no jewelry except simple earrings, whether going to a neighboring house for an instruction session or on a journey: "This protects you from danger." (Although the concern for danger may be specific to women, the emphasis on simple clothing, of course, equally applies to men.)

Within this framework for women's activity, it is clear that women may be responsible for men's participation. Indeed, members of a jama'at of women whom I met were indignant when, hearing their stories, I suggested that it appeared that either husbands or fathers had introduced Tablīgh into the family. They insisted I was wrong and told stories of women companions who, like women they knew, had first practiced true Islam and made sacrifices that ultimately influenced their menfolk. "Not that we are like them," they added, "Our sacrifices of time, money, and leaving our children, sad as we may be, are nothing in comparison to them, and nothing in comparison to the opportunity we now have for uninterrupted obedience to Allah." They told me of a woman who read aloud each night from the *Faza'il* collection of *hadīth* in the movement's basic text (Muhammad Zakariyya, n.d.; Metcalf, 1993), despite her husband's disdain. One night she did not pick up the book to read. Disconcerted, her husband asked why; she replied that she saw no reason to, since he ignored it. He then commenced to read the book aloud himself. Thus a woman had led her husband to proper Islam.

Another story, told to me by the person involved, also exemplifies women's initiative. This man serves as the president of his local union as well as of his national federation. For several years, his mother, to whom he was devoted, had faithfully attended a weekly women's *bayān* (discourse) in the movement's central mosque, and had frequently volunteered his name (as women are asked to do for their relatives) to go out with a *jama'at*. Because of the heavy demands and unpredictable hours of his work, he never went. In 1984 she died, a loss he took very hard. His brother, a man in his early twenties, was equally stricken, to the extent that his health declined and within the year he too died. At that point, this person, who had never been involved in the Tablīgh before (and was known, other people told me, as secular and "leftist"), committed himself on the spot to go out for four months—and he has never looked back, sustaining a full schedule of Tablīgh activities including leadership in the city council (*shura*) of the Tablīgh, responsibilities for a large family, and obligations as a labor leader. Again, we see the influence of a woman in setting the course for a male relative. Presumably, however, men also tell stories of recalcitrant women whom they attempt to influence, like the village women described by Patricia Jeffery and Roger Jeffery in this volume, who chafe at attempts by their menfolk, influenced by Tablīgh, to check their customary songs.

Gender Roles in Tablīgh

Even this brief sketch suggests central themes in the ideals upheld for gendered behavior. Tablīghīs are meant to be humble, pious, consultative, simple in their living habits, and unconcerned with hierarchy. Men are not meant to cultivate cleverness, ambition, verbal dexterity, physical prowess, knowledge of cultural trends—qualities that would be valued in other contexts. Although they do not withdraw from society but hold down jobs, they eschew many ordinary activities. They should not watch television, listen to the radio, go to films; ideally, they live modestly. They do not discuss or participate in politics. Particularly in the course of the tours, male participants take on the humble domestic tasks that are typically done by women or, in the case of the more prosperous, by servants: Tablīghīs on tour cook and serve food, nurse the ill, and wash and repair clothes. The basic personal style valued by the movement is not taught intellectually but is inculcated through prolonged practice and mutual correction. Nor is the ideal personal style limited to the tours. One of the most striking vignettes of teaching on gender is represented by a talk at an annual meeting using as its text the *hadīth* of the Prophet permitting women to refuse to nurse their suckling infants for whatever reason. On that analogy, the speaker argued, men certainly could not decline to provide child care for a task as important as Tablīgh.[5]

These ideals of male qualities and roles influence female roles in at least two ways. First, the emphasis on humble relationships among men encourages more egalitarian relationships between women and men. This does not mean that women and men are expected to play the same social roles. Women are emphatically meant, ideally, to remain in the home. Overall leadership of the movement is male, but as relations among men change, those between women and men change as well. It seems an almost psychological imperative that as practices of hierarchy in one set of relations are modified—those among men—the hierarchical structure as a whole—which includes relations among women and men—will also be modified. Thus, some participants I have spoken to have described how the atmosphere in their household has improved. One young father of two small children criticized his society generally for widespread harshness, including physical punishment of children, and even suggested that in this respect behavior in the West was more humane. In his own case, he felt that the personal traits he was learning in the Tablīgh had made his family life far more cooperative and harmonious. Another man said he was less likely to get cross with his wife, for example, over cooking, since he now knew how easy it was to do things like add too much salt. The standard set for women's segregation from unrelated men is, to be sure, rigorous.[6] But the fact of segregation is clearly not sufficient to describe the quality of relationships within the family.

Second, the Tablīgh ideal means that there is less distinction between what men and women do. At the core men and women share what they consider their most important life's activity, namely, faithful adherence to religiously sanctioned practice and its dissemination to other Muslims. Men, of necessity, may hold outside jobs but tend to avoid much else in public life: politics, films, the *akhārā* (club), and so on. Thus, differentially favorable opportunities for men matter less in the Tablīgh movement than in more politically oriented movements because neither the men nor the women seek out public roles in the society at large. If differences in men's and women's behavior in public are reduced, so too may differences be flattened within the family. Just as men in the course of travel on missions experience some redrawing of gender roles as they cook and wash, the women left at home, like women in the homes of migrant workers, may take on a range of previously male responsibilities in order to sustain the household. Tablīgh, moreover, eliminates whole arenas of customary ritual and ceremonial life that have been the purview of women: all the customs, social exchanges, and song, now regarded as religiously deviant, that had characterized their separate sphere (see Gardner, and Jeffery and Jeffery, this volume). No occasion is more important for such customary observances than marriage. Yet participants in an annual meeting have described to me that marriages are celebrated there by proxy, dozens at a time. Marriage has typically entailed the enactment of elaborate interactions that bolster social relationships and interdependencies. Tablīghīs are, presumably, people who opt out of those social enmeshments. Women's honor, then, would not be measured by the number and sorts of people who participate in cere-monies they organize nor by the lavishness of the hospitality they offer but, as should be true for men as well, by piety and commitment to the movement.

Underlying these common roles for women and men is, implicitly, the theory of the person cultivated by the larger reformist movement from which the Tablīgh movement derives. This movement revitalizes an old theme in Islamic thought that postulates a shared essential nature between women and men: both have the same constitution, the same responsibilities, the same potentialities. This does not mean they have the same roles or even the same status within the family; it is not a socially egalitarian theory. What it is becomes clearer by emphasizing what it is not. It is not a theory that elaborates female specificity, that accords women unique qualities of sensitivity or spiri-tuality or delicacy on a Victorian model; it is not concerned with a distinctive female physical makeup. It thus has no notion of complementary or opposite sexes. Women are to cultivate the same qualities, take on the same role models, read the same books as men (Metcalf ed. and trans., 1990). The women enjoined as models in such cherished texts as the "Tales of The Companions," *Hikāyatu's-sāhabā*, the first section of Muhammad Zakariyya, n.d.), are cele-brated for being just what it is that men should also be: humble, generous, pious, scrupulous in religious obligations, brave in the face of persecution, and so forth. The ultimate ideal of human behavior, understood as that exempli-fied by the Prophet, in fact resonates with qualities we typically associate with being feminine: everyone, male or female, should struggle to be gentle, self-effacing, and dedicated to serving others.[7]

Modern political Islamist movements like the Jama'at-i-Islami founded by Maulana Maududi in the 1920s (Nasr, 1994) cultivate the perspective of a unique female personality and capacity characteristic of broad trends in Victorian thought. Some Tablīgh writers seem to do so as well, utilizing a language of opposite or complementary sexes, with the woman as queen of the home and possessing a warmer, more easily influenced, temperament (Muhammad 'Isa Firozpuri, n.d.: 102–7). But the dominant attitude in the Tablīghī Jama'at seems to emphasize an essentially shared nature and shared responsibilities. Much more work needs to be done to differentiate attitudes about women on the part of tablīghīs over time, as well as in regard to what may be different attitudes and interpretations of women's role by women and by men. Two recent studies of contemporary religious movements suggest how important such differences may be: Chandra's (1994) work on the BJP (Bharatiya Janata Party), which shows how significantly the party's ideology differed before and after 1985; and Bacchetta's (1996), which suggests the differing ideologies of the men's and women's wings of the RSS. One crucial element in preserving the Tablīgh single-sex model is its apolitical character. By contrast, nationalist ideologies typically embrace a gendered vision of the nation as a brotherhood of males, sometimes as sons of a mother, with women sharply distinguished in personality and capacity from men and destined to make their contribution precisely by producing more sons for the nation.

Critics of Tablīgh

It is significant that Tablīgh has not produced a distinctive literature for women in contrast to politicized, Islamist movements like the Jama'at-i-Islami. There is nothing like the spate of publications on women associated with Maulana Abul A'la Maududi (1939) or more recent writers like Sayyid As'ad Gilani (1982) (Metcalf, 1987). It is, on the contrary, critics of Tablīgh who talk about women a great deal. I concentrate here on these issues in Pakistan, where, among Westernized circles, angry opposition is invariably articulated by criticism of what is taken to be Tablīgh treatment of women. Here is a string of examples where the underlying theme is that men are not behaving like men:

- A retired government official, trained as a psychologist: "tablīghīs treat women very harshly. A nephew of mine became a tablīghī and basically starved and beat his mother. They treat their wives and daughters badly."
- A professor, also a retired government official: "My neighbor, an active tablīghī, went on a mission at the very time of his daughter's wedding. He was in Bangladesh and she was getting married. Who would leave at such a time?"

- A fortyish, Western-trained, university professor: "There was a case of a little girl abducted while her father was away on a tour. He would not even come back."
- A young woman in development work strikes the theme of male domination: "In Karachi I went to condole with the widow of a close family friend. This was an open, pleasant family. . . . One of the sons, a bit older but always *bhāī* (brother) to me had become a tablīghī. As I walked in, he just walked out and didn't even speak to me. He keeps his wife hidden away. His mother said to me that now that this son was head of the family, she didn't know what would happen to her."

Opponents have other themes. In Pakistan, some lump tablīghīs with other religious groups, and denounce all who would purport to tell people what is and what is not Islam. They may also criticize tablighis as lazy, fanatic, dirty, and corrupt. More specific critics denounce Tablīghī withdrawal from politics in favor of religious obligations at the cost of worldly affairs. But the theme that runs through many of these objections, and is particularly marked in the comments about women, is the assumption that tablīghīs neglect what should be their basic responsibilities, whether toward their family or toward development. Thus, an MBA from Michigan State University (seated next to me on a Pakistan International Airline flight) grew angry on the subject of tablīgh absenteeism; committed to economic growth and development, he would not give his subordinates leave to go on tour; when they came to his door, he said, "I lock the door" ("*Mai tālā lagātā hun*").

A final comment from an opponent strikes a somewhat different note. A journalist in Karachi, associated with the Jama'at-i-Islami, the Islamist party that is often seen as the Islamic alternative to Tablīgh, blamed tablīghīs for corruption and for failing in their requisite duties. What bothered him most, however, seemed to be what he presented as gender confusion: tablīghīs act female. He was very distressed about the state of a friend's son, of the more concern, he explained, because his own son "had almost fallen into Tablīgh clutches." The friend's son, he continued, "now behaves abnormally. He acts like a Pakistani girl!" At this he bowed his head, pressed his knees together, and folded his hands. "They become abnormal," he repeated. A colleague in the office shortly picked up the thread, speaking with more respect but implicitly continuing the theme: "I have never seen a Tablīghī Jama'at person lose his temper. This is astonishing given the way, for example, we used to react to them in the hostel when they would come around, especially in Ramzān, to invite us to come to the mosque. Normally people in any religious sect will react very strongly if you oppose them." He was at once respectful and bemused. It is women who are supposed to be bashful, reticent, and nonconfrontational.

That talk about women in relation to Tablīgh should be such a central theme is not surprising. Issues related to women have occupied a central space in public discussion of law and politics in Pakistan, particularly from the late seventies onward. For many people, women have, quite simply, become a powerful public symbol of what Islamists call an "Islamic order." This is an extraordinary change in Muslim discourse, for, while the control of women has always been important, the notion that women bear a special burden of embodying Islamic teachings and norms is new. The assumption that women should therefore be secluded and their activities highly constrained has, more-over, been challenged by an active, articulate professional class represented by such movements as the Women's Action Forum. Some of the opposition to Tablīgh is a spillover from opposition to Islamization.

What, then, is going on in the Tablīgh movement? Participants present a very different interpretation of what critics see as mistreatment and neglect of families and irresponsibility toward jobs. First, from their perspective, every-one should be engaged in Tablīgh. If women and children are an impediment for men in fulfilling this responsibility, men and children are equally an impediment for women. The biography of the son and successor of Maulana Muhammad Ilyas, Maulana Muhammad Yusuf (1917–1965), describes his frequent absence from his ill wife (Muhammad Sani Hasani, n.d.). But how is that absence interpreted? One recalls the spiritual forbear of many tablīghīs, Maulana 'Abdu'r-Rahim Raipuri, unwilling to let his dying son distract him from his disciples who had undertaken the *hajj* in his company (Metcalf, 1982: 168). If Raipuri's life is a positive model, Yusuf's behavior deserves praise, not condemnation, in this perspective. Similarly, the woman who refuses to nurse, or the women mentioned above who leave their children behind to go on a tour, should be praised.

Tablīghīs would deny that women's interests are damaged when men go out. At the least, women gain spiritual merit for sustaining the household. When asked about their families, moreover, participants are likely to tell stories, like those collected in interviews by the Delhi-based sociologist Muhammad Talib (1990), that tell of how at the very time that a participant absented himself for a tour, a family crisis—irresponsible children, an ill parent, a pend-ing lawsuit—was transformed for the good. Clearly, critics and participants have differing ideas of what is in individual and family interests and what is the nature of family responsibility. Tablīghīs do respond to some criticism. Thus a work on issues of *sharī'a*, or normative codes related to Tablīgh, begins with a letter from a revered disciple of Maulana Thanawi, Maulana Shah Muhammad Masihu'llah Khan, setting for Tablīgh the same conditions as those for the required *hajj* pilgrimage to Mecca, in which tours should be undertaken only if the participants can do so without incurring debt or hardship to the family or other dependents ('Abdu'sh-shakur, 1981: 5–7).

Whatever the reality, it is clear that the simply dressed, noninstrumental, humble tablīghī challenges much that the rest of the society holds dear—worldly progress, family wealth, national or community politics. Men inclined to Tablīgh are thus thought to be failures as men, as signified by their "effeminate" behavior and presumed neglect of women. It is not surprising that Tablīgh behavior elicits such an emotional response. Yet Tablīgh participants, women and men, find in the movement ample space for meaningful action, comradeship, leadership, new skills, and even travel.

Recently the historian Leila Ahmed has suggested that if we define "feminism" as movements to enhance opportunities for women's independence, choice, and solidarity, we need to specify two streams of feminism: one, that associated with Westernizing, liberal trends; and a second, that associated with a wide range of Islamic religious or Islamist movements (Ahmed, 1992).[8] I would consider it inappropriate to describe a feminist theme in the Tablīghī Jama'at, for the very significant reason that women's roles are not a focus of discussion, but I do think it is possible to recognize that the implications of the movement for female education, independent activity, and solidarity with other women do represent a range of behaviors we are likely to miss if we assume only a static, monolithic tradition on the one hand and liberal Westernized roles on the other. From this we see that what is often assumed to be the only model of change—again a lurking part of our common sense—namely, that movement to the kind of public roles held as an ideal for women in contemporary Western society is not the only source of change, but that other kinds of change can and do transpire in societies that turn out to be less uniform and static than one may assume.

Notes

I am grateful to many people, above all participants in the Tablīghī Jama'at, for discussions that have contributed to this paper. I had many conversations about Tablīgh in the course of trips to India in 1990 and to Pakistan and, on two occasions, to Britain in 1991. Thanks to Khalid Mas'ud for helpful conversations and encouragement throughout. An essay by me, partially overlapping with this chapter, is forthcoming in a volume on the Tablīghī Jama'at edited by Dr. Mas'ud. I am grateful to Amrita Basu, Patricia Jeffery, and Katy Gardner, in particular, as to all the participants, for their comments both at the Bellagio conference and after.

   1. Perhaps surprisingly, this role of Islam is evident to a modest extent in China as well. Recently, Dru Gladney (1994) has argued that the Muslim populations of China also play a charged role in the popular imagination. Looking at not only language but fine art and posters, he suggests that the Muslims of western China in particular have come to be seen as representing the primitive, the erotic, the romantically seductive—the last the more

ironic when he juxtaposes such representations to photographs of modestly dressed "real" Muslim women. Those creating such representations intend to depict themselves as the opposite: as progressive, modern, disciplined, forward looking. As Gladney argues, the representation of the minorities has more to do with constructing a majority discourse than it does with the minorities themselves.

2. For the Indian origins of the movement, see Wahiduddin Khan (1986) and Haq (1972), which is based on Nadwi (1983; 1964 ed. (Urdu original written ca. 1948)). See also Troll (1985), which includes references to important Urdu sources. Also useful are articles in Lokhandwala (ed.) (1971), especially Faruqi (1971), Akbarabadi (1971), and Waheeduzzafar (1971). For the late-nineteenth-century origin of the Deoband movement, see Metcalf (1982).

3. See the text translated in Metcalf (ed. and trans.) (1990). First published at the turn of the century as a guide for girls and women to the reformist Islam that also produced the Tablīgh, the book *Bihishtī Zewar* is an excellent source for understanding hierarchy. See, for example, the sample letters in Book One, where a girl learns the appropriate diction for writing to superiors, inferiors, and equals; the content of the letters reviews such issues as appropriate names for elders and behavior before them. At the same time the book points to the kinds of changes in transcending conventional hierarchy that the Tablīgh further develops. The book was also recommended for men, a striking contrast to books written for women in Europe or the United States at that time. For an evocative picture of the social norms of the Urdu-speaking wellborn, see Lelyveld (1978: chap. 2).

4. See my introduction to Maulana Thanawi's *Bihishtī Zewar* (Metcalf (ed. and trans.), 1990), where I contrast this inclusive conception of women with the discussion of women by the Jama'at-i-Islami that elaborates a more differentiated view of women as "complementary to men" or even the "opposite sex."

5. I am grateful to Syed Zainuddin, Aligarh University, for describing this and other experiences encountered when he attended a Tablīgh *ijitima'* (assembly) in Dewsbury, June 1991.

6. In the very limited circle of people I met, however, this did not preclude, for example, university-level education or marriage of daughters to husbands settled in the West.

7. See the essay on the Prophet's character, given as a preface to a hundred tales of model women—in itself significant that the Prophet is a model for women as for men—in Metcalf (ed. and trans.) (1990: 255–58).

8. For South Asia, an outstanding contribution to this position, based on excellent fieldwork, is the thesis of Huq (1994), which analyzes the female university movement, the Bangladesh Islami Chatri Sanghstha, which sees itself as using female modesty and segregation to secure women's rights.

Chapter Eight

Gender, Community, and the Local State in Bijnor, India

PATRICIA JEFFERY AND ROGER JEFFERY

RESIDENTS OF BIJNOR DISTRICT in western Uttar Pradesh pride themselves that it is an area notable for its communal harmony. On 30 October 1990, however, the first assault on the Babari Masjid took place and Bijnor was the site of serious communal violence. Communal disturbances are often regarded as essentially urban phenomena, dramatic disruptions of a basically non-communalized (though not necessarily nonviolent) order sparked off by outside agents provocateurs.[1] Outsiders certainly were involved in Bijnor, but responsibility cannot be entirely deflected away from the local processes that provided a fertile soil on which outside actors could work (Jeffery and Jeffery, 1994; Basu, 1995c). If we focus on the violent and tragic aspects of communal disturbances, we may bypass the grinding and routinized aspects of communalism that pervade people's daily lives (Billig, 1995).

Social life in rural Bijnor is not structured solely by communal difference. Indeed, gender relationships are premised on some striking commonalities that fail to provide equality of opportunity for males and females, whether Hindu or Muslim, rich or poor.[2] In terms of control over resources, the labor process, and fertility and of how males and females are valued, normal domestic life constitutes an important site of routinized sexism. Moreover, women are key to the *izzat* (honor) of their families, and casting slurs on another man's womenfolk or subjecting them to sexual harassment are means through which males compete for dominance. All women, then, regularly experience controls over their mobility and demeanor that structure their experiences of the world beyond their homes, including their access to state services (such as health care and schooling) and employment. Women's vulnerability may be especially overt in communally charged contexts, but gender issues are important in other aspects of communalism too (Das, 1990; Sarkar, 1991; Chakravarti et al., 1992; Basu (ed.), 1993; Sarkar, 1993; Mann, 1994, Moghadam (ed.), 1994a).

Communal identities are, of course, fluid, and boundaries between competing groupings are time-bound, not primordial. Political dominance is historically specific, and communal identities are socially constructed rather than natural or essential (Barth (ed.), 1969). Claims about fundamental loyalties must be continually reasserted if they are to withstand challenges from cross-cutting and competing sources of identity (gender, class, caste) or countervailing tendencies that stress people's common humanity. "Hindu" and "Muslim" are socially constructed and contested categories, sometimes internally fragmented, sometimes not. The term "Hindu," for instance, may include or exclude the Scheduled Castes.[3] In Bijnor, the Hindu Right's attempt to develop an all-encompassing Hindu category as part of its larger political strategy against Muslims is often treated with skepticism by the Scheduled Castes.

In this chapter, though, we mainly concentrate on the intersections of gender and communal identities and have put class and caste identities on one side. We focus on the "local state" in Bijnor—the facets of the state operating at District level—and how it helps to sustain (rather than challenge) local-level gendered communalism (Cockburn, 1977). Communalism does not necessarily result in violent death or serious bodily injury, nor does it merely erupt episodically. Rather, it structures people's life chances on a daily basis in deeply gendered ways (Jeffery and Jeffery, 1997). In rural Bijnor, long-standing processes that are both gendered and communalized have been especially detrimental to Muslim women.

Gendered Communalism and the Local State

Liberal feminists tend to regard the state as a potential ally and see pressing for legislative and policy reform as a key feminist strategy to protect and enhance women's citizenship rights. Sometimes, indeed, the state does respond to popular pressure, if only to attract votes. But many feminists (and others, of course) note that the state more often endorses than undermines inequalities. It is usually controlled by dominant sectors of the population and cannot be a neutral arbiter of all its citizens' rights. It may abuse some or all of its citizens' rights, and it may control the populace even in the course of providing social services. Sometimes, too, official national policy may promise far more than the local state functionaries will ever deliver. Many feminists, then, are skeptical about what women can reasonably expect from state action ostensibly on their behalf.

In India, much national and state-level government policy—such as agriculture and health—is framed in *apparently* secular and class- and gender-neutral terms (although we cannot assume, of course, that policy makers intended the disinterested application of policy). The different systems of family law, of course, are conspicuous and important exceptions on both communal and gender counts (Parashar, 1992; Engineer, 1992). In South Asia more generally, many analyses of the nation-state's involvement in communalism and gender issues concentrate on the state at the center and particularly on its legislative and policy-making activities (Chhachhi, 1989, 1991, 1994; Hasan (ed.), 1994 and this volume; Mukhopadhyay, 1994; Mumtaz and Shaheed, 1987; Jalal, 1991; Mumtaz, 1994; Kabeer, 1991). Commentaries on the Shah Bano and Roop Kanwar affairs in India, for instance, tend to portray gender issues as entangled in the central state's attempts to buy off fundamentalist or communalist pressures (Engineer (ed.), 1987; Hasan, 1989; Pathak and Rajan, 1989; Qadeer and Hasan, 1987; Kumar, 1994: Sangari and Vaid, 1996).

We should not, however, essentialize the state by implying that it acts in unison from a central point in pursuit of a single set of goals. The state at the local level is not simply a microcosm of the national state. State institutions react to diverse pressures, and different levels of the state and different sectors (law and order, social and economic development) cannot be assumed to act in harmony with one another. Indeed, any local discretion in policy formulation and implementation makes this highly unlikely. National policies are experienced in people's everyday lives only after being mediated through local state institutions. National policies—whether seemingly neutral in relation to gender and communalism or not—are superimposed on local settings that may be marked by gender and community (as well as class and caste) inequalities. The outcomes can be systematically (if maybe unintentionally) biased, and belie national level proclamations of equal opportunities.

The daily workings of the local state, however, have not been analyzed with the same sophistication as the Indian national state (as in Bardhan, 1984; Vanaik, 1990).[4] Accounts of lower-level state functionaries (extension workers, policemen, health workers, teachers) are generally managerial in emphasis, or else examine their roles in factional and party politics and the class biases in their work patterns rather than exposing gender and communal biases (Banerji, 1972). Yet gender and communal discrimination operates in several ways; perhaps most overt are the intentionally discriminatory acts of prejudiced individuals. But, in addition, normal and apparently gender- and community-blind institutional procedures can dramatically signal inequalities of opportunity and result in structured inequalities. Such institutional sexism or communalism is deeply embedded in the daily workings of many social institutions, including the state apparatus.[5]

Discussions of communalism that have examined the local state have mainly focused on the police, the Provincial Armed Constabulary, District Magistrates, and the army. It is certainly vitally important to understand how state control and repression may be deployed locally in gendered and communally biased ways. Yet focusing on the law-and-order facets of state activity, especially during crises and their (apparent) resolution, underplays what happens between one crisis and the next and seemingly implies that there are no other sites of gendered communalism within the state. In any case, gender issues have only rarely been seriously addressed, even in accounts of local riots that explore the underpinnings of discrimination against minority groups (Engineer (ed.), 1984, 1991; Das, 1990; Chakravarti et al., 1992; Pandey, 1991; Banerjee, 1990; Akbar, 1988; Saberwal and Hasan, 1984).

Crucially, the local state encompasses all aspects of the interface between state and civil society, not just the judiciary and the police. Thus we should examine how the local state not only enforces public order but also protects and provides. Accordingly, we consider here the health and education sectors, both (ostensibly) features of the state's caring and paternalistic face rather than its controlling and punitive one, both (supposedly) concerned with the disinterested provision of services irrespective of gender, class, caste, or community. Both sectors, too, have considerable scope for local discretion, which, in the absence of adequate monitoring, allows space for gender and communal discrimination to be part of normal procedures. Decisions about the siting of educational and health facilities are formally allocated to government staff posted at District level, but strings may be pulled by locally dominant groups, at District headquarters or in the State capital. Rules and work plans for the lowest-level workers—village school teachers, primary health staff—also allow considerable leeway in their working practices, which anyway cannot be effectively scrutinized by supervisors. Briefly, the education and health sectors are important sites of gendered communalism, both intentional and covert. The local state's role in sustaining—if not actively promoting— structured inequalities while apparently serving the whole populace is a particularly striking litmus test of local state processes.

Like several other Districts in western Uttar Pradesh, the towns of Bijnor District have a Muslim majority, with 60 percent of the urban population. Bijnor District is distinctive, however, for having the largest proportion of *rural* Muslims—about 35 percent—in Uttar Pradesh. About 25 percent of the rural population are Scheduled Castes, with 40 percent other Hindu. Some villages are dominated by particular Hindu castes and others have no substantial settlements of Muslims; many have evenly balanced Hindu and Muslim populations; and yet others are exclusively or largely Muslim. There are distinctive and separate Muslim institutions and class and caste structures, to a greater degree than in areas where Muslims form a small minority. Bijnor Muslims are diverse and located in a range of class positions, from (mainly small) landowners and businessmen to landless laborers, from cattle traders to barbers and midwives. Muslims, however, are much weaker politically than their numbers in Bijnor would suggest. Brahmans dominate trade and commerce; Jats dominate agriculture and small-scale rural industries (like sugar production). The Scheduled Castes have access to several government schemes and also benefit locally because Bijnor is a "reserved constituency" (restricted to Scheduled Caste candidates) in the Lok Sabha elections. Mayavati, a leader of the Bahujan Samaj Party (which defends Scheduled Caste interests), represented the seat in the 1980s. In the 1991 elections, however, the constituency was won by the BJP, which retained it in 1996.

In 1982–1983 and 1985, our research focused on Dharmnagri and Jhakri. In 1990–1991, we worked in Dharmnagri and Jhakri again, as well as in Nangal and Qaziwala. Summary population distributions are provided in Table 1. As part of our research, we collected general economic and demographic data about the four villages from village men and women, and interviewed staff in the schools and health facilities. We also conducted intensive interviews with almost one hundred women, most of whom were born and reared in other villages in the District. Thus, although the material presented here primarily pertains to the education and health facilities in the four villages, our argument is backed up with information about numerous other villages in the locality.

Schooling in Rural Bijnor

A major concern of the 1950s and 1960s Community Development Programmes was to extend schooling. By 1971 Bijnor had one primary school per 2,000 rural population (or one for more than 300 children aged 5–9). Despite

Table 8.1. Population by Caste and Religion, Fieldwork Villages, Bijnor District 1990–1991

Caste/Religion	Dharmnagri		Nangal		Jhakri		Qaziwala	
Hindu: Jat	35	(4%)	1,150	(28%)	nil		nil	
Other Hindu	460	(58%)	550	(13%)	nil		21	(1%)
SCs: Jatab	274	(35%)	1,787	(43%)	nil		205	(7%)
Other SCs	19	(2%)	105	(3%)	nil		56	(2%)
Muslim: Sheikh	nil		18	(1%)	352	(74%)	1,488	(51%)
Other Muslim	nil		550	(13%)	125	(26%)	1,148	(39%)
Total	788	(100%)	4,160	(100%)	477	(100%)	2,918	(100%)

Source: Censuses conducted by authors.
Noye: SC = Scheduled Castes; percentages are of the total population in each village and do not all add to 100% because of rounding.

a widespread school expansion program in the 1970s and 1980s, the 1991 figure was one school for 250 children, and about 65 percent of the 5–9 age cohort—90 percent of boys and only about 40 percent of girls—were enrolled in government-recognized and—aided primary schools (District Statistical Diary, 1991–1992).

Scholarships and fee waivers are readily available for Scheduled Caste children, who are now represented in primary schools roughly in proportion to their population. There are no special programs for girls or Muslims. In the four fieldwork villages, only about 30 percent of primary-school-age children were attending state primary schools and roughly 40 percent were attending no school at all. Facilities in state primary schools are meager, teachers are often irregular in their attendance, and teaching is sporadic—but despite these well-known inadequacies, schools have long been a key facility promised by rising politicians. *Panchāyats* (village councils) with wealthy, well-connected landholding groups have been most able to bid for government support, for instance, by donating land on which a school can be built. Within villages, such groups vie for schools to be located within their own controlled space.

In Dharmnagri, the two-room government primary school in the middle of the village has two teachers. Notionally, it serves a population of 2,200 in Dharmnagri, Jhakri, several mixed Muslim/Hindu villages, and two colonies of Hindus resettled from East Bengal. In 1991, only one Muslim boy (and no Muslim girl) was attending the school. Near Qaziwala, the government primary school (again, two rooms and two teachers) is equidistant from three mixed Muslim/Scheduled Caste villages; the total population in 1991 was about 3,800, with Muslims the overwhelming majority. But in 1991, only seven Muslim boys attended and all fourteen girls in the school were Scheduled Caste. In Nangal, a mixed-sex and a girls' primary school were originally in the Jat and Brahman section of the village but are now on the edge of the village farthest from the Muslim and Scheduled Caste sections. With eight teachers in all, they serve a population of around 5,000 in Nangal and neighboring villages. Again, only 5 of the 174 boys were Muslim and none of the 98 girls. The Dharmnagri government junior secondary school (classes 6–8) serves Dharmnagri and Qaziwala primary school graduates, among others. It now has eight classrooms and teachers. The pupils reflect the primary schools that feed it: very few Muslim boys (none from Jhakri or Qaziwala) and no Muslim girls. Nangal has no government junior secondary school, and children must travel at least five kilometers in one of three directions. Higher secondary schools (classes 9–12) are all sited in towns.

Generally, few Muslim villages, or Muslim or Scheduled Caste *muhallās* (wards) in large, multicaste villages, have government primary schools. Where they do exist, they are smaller, have fewer teachers, and serve a larger population.

This communal bias affects accessibility and thereby school attendance. Children straying into territory dominated by other castes or communities feel vulnerable to physical attack. To avoid such civilian policing of access, they may be willing to attend school only in neutral or friendly territory, or if they can create security in numbers. Territory may be perceived in class and caste terms, but the presence of Scheduled Caste children in all the government primary schools in our research villages suggests that such considerations do not prevent their attendance. The low levels of Muslim attendance suggest much stronger inhibitions for Muslim children.

The siting of schools also has gender implications because of gender differences in mobility. For girls, all public space is, in a sense, foreign territory. Unless protected by a brother or cousin, a girl may be fair game for sexual harassment by boys from her own caste and community, let alone others. Parents prefer to send daughters to girls' primary schools, or ones with female teachers. Even girls from locally dominant castes are vulnerable, especially as they approach puberty. Few continue beyond fifth class, since this often involves travel beyond the village. Only the wealthiest landowners school their daughters beyond the age of fourteen (eighth class).

Even if a school is accessible to its potential pupils, however, it may be difficult to ensure adequate staffing. Fear of sexual harassment makes rural postings problematic for women teachers from outwith the immediate vicinity who cannot be protected by male relatives—and local girls are unlikely to obtain sufficient schooling to train as teachers, especially if they are Muslim. For instance, the primary-school teachers in Dharmnagri and Qaziwala (all women) and the junior-secondary-school teachers (all men) commuted daily to work, and they were all Hindus. At all the government schools serving our fieldwork villages, considerations of siting and staffing lead to the exclusion, withdrawal, or irregular attendance of Scheduled Caste and Muslim children—especially Muslim girls—beyond primary level.

The commonest response (even among dominant castes) to the systematic limitations in the accessibility and quality of government schools is to establish facilities under caste or community control, or to use private schooling. Most private provisions are in towns, and only wealthier families from surrounding villages can send their children. School fees (usually Rs 15 per month per child, a day's wage for a male laborer), uniform (about Rs 80 a year), and schoolbooks (around Rs 50 a year) are beyond the pockets of the poor and landless. Nangal has two Jat-and-Brahman-controlled Montessori primary schools (one of which is run by the RSS), a government-recognized private junior secondary school, and an Ambedkar secondary school in the Scheduled Caste muhallā. Only one Muslim boy and no Muslim girls attend these schools, and no Muslim children in Nangal attend schools elsewhere.

Muslim girls are also almost totally absent from the Muslim-run private school near Qaziwala: just 33 of the 219 pupils are girls, only 9 of them Muslim. Rather, sensing their effective exclusion from government schools, Muslims in Qaziwala, Jhakri, and neighboring villages generally opt to send their children to the *madrasā* in Begawala, one kilometer from Qaziwala and two from Jhakri.

In 1991, the Begawala *madrasā* had eight hundred registered students. Fees are nominal because most funding comes from postharvest donations provided by Muslim landholders in surrounding villages. The *madrasā* teaches Urdu and Islamic studies to the level required for admission to the Deoband seminary for qualification as a *maulvī* (prayer leader) (Metcalf, 1982), but advanced classes are restricted to boys. Most Muslim parents see the *madrasā* as a means of ensuring that their children know at least the basics of Islamic doctrine and morality. The *madrasā* only recently began to teach Hindi, vital for access to government or other employment and for other dealings beyond the village. After the BJP came to power in Uttar Pradesh in 1991, the *madrasā* committee withdrew its application for government recognition and assistance with equipment for the higher classes because it expected to be prevented from providing the schooling that its members, as Muslims, wanted for their children. There are more girls than boys in the elementary classes for learning to read the Qur'an Sharif and in the Hindi classes. This is hardly because of policy, for girls are taught in cramped classrooms, whereas boys are taught in several large airy halls. The staff say that the boys are involved in farmwork from the age of eight or nine, but girls' involvement in housework is less incompatible with school attendance. Few girls, however, attend the *madrasā* long enough for literacy in Urdu (let alone Arabic) to be firmly established, and all are excluded from the *madrasā* at puberty. In both Jhakri and Qaziwala, *maulvī* also teach young children to read the Qur'an Sharif in the village mosques, and some literate women teach children in their own homes. The *maulvī* in Nangal supposedly took classes, but during the communal tension of 1990–1991, no Islamic schooling was taking place there.

Gender, Community, and the Culture of Schooling

The culture of the state schools is also problematic. The formal curriculum's stress on a literary language and urban skills has little relevance to most rural children. Schools provide basic literacy and numeracy (locally acknowledged as the everyday advantages of schooling) but rarely the technical skills useful in village life (Jeffery and Jeffery 1994a, 1996b; Jeffery and Jeffery, 1997). The hidden curriculum aims to produce docile minds and bodies. Children learn the rudiments of reading, writing, and arithmetic by rote, and are physically punished or humiliated if they make mistakes or speak out of turn. Hindu children learn bodily displays of modesty and respect. And the *madrasā* teaches rules of washing and bodily deportment with respect to handling the Qur'an Sharif and prayer, and bodily modesty for girls through their use of *dupattās* (shawls) when reading the Qur'an Sharif.

Apart from these general issues of curriculum and style, most Muslims perceive government schools as communal in their daily functioning. Local teachers are all Hindus, who often display their distaste for things Islamic, for instance, refusing to make allowances for Muslim students fasting during the month of *Ramzān*. Muslim students believed that Hindus were more likely to be accepted as private pupils for tuition by the teacher, and given preference in marks or other privileges in class. Such beliefs—which we cannot evaluate—are further reasons why Muslims rarely take state schooling seriously. Many Muslims also believed the state was trying to undermine their religious allegiances by making it hard for them to learn Urdu and therefore Arabic (cf. Brass, 1974; Farouqui, 1994).[6] Other issues (such as the evaluation of Muslim rule in India) highlight the curriculum's role in creating and sustaining communal identities. Muslim children outwith the state system are not exposed to official versions of history, but *madrasā* texts reinforce particular interpretations of Islamic doctrine and Islamic and Indian history. Similarly, the private schools in Nangal portray very different (and often more avowedly anti-Muslim) views from those formally espoused by the state schools (cf. Sarkar, 1996).

Furthermore, schooling and school texts largely reflect rather than challenge conventional gender relationships (Kishwar, 1991; Karlekar, 1991; Minault, 1986, 1993; Mann, 1994; see also Ray, 1988, on girls' resistance). Hindu and Muslim girls alike are educated for marriage, not employment. They need homemaking skills to perform their domestic obligations capably (Papanek, 1979; Sharma, 1986; Mukhopadhyay and Seymour (eds.), 1994). Muslim parents explicitly send their daughters to the *madrasā* to become *rozā namāz lāyaq* (capable of fasting and prayer) so that their future in-laws will be unable to say they are incapable of raising children correctly. The Urdu texts used in *madrasās* include many selections (for instance, from Bihishtī Zewar) that emphasize women's duty to be pious (Metcalf (ed. and trans.), 1990).

By contrast, boys' schooling reflects their (perceived) job chances. In Bijnor, Brahmans and "big caste" Hindus such as Jats and Rajputs have used their head start to help their sons monopolize "good" jobs (meaning secure, government, or white collar) (Jeffery and Jeffery, 1994a; Jeffery and Jeffery, 1997). Muslims believe their sons will not obtain "good" jobs, so secular schooling— locally viewed as a preparation for employment—is considered almost valueless for them. In Bijnor, at any rate, the marked class differentials in school attendance among Hindus are not reflected in comparable differences among Muslims. Muslim (and Scheduled Caste) boys drop out of schooling earlier than "big caste" Hindu boys in comparable economic positions. And while *madrasā* education offers Muslim boys little chance of successfully competing for secure white-collar employment, it might lead to employment as a *maulvī*—one of the few routes to nonmanual and possibly urban employment for able rural Muslim boys.

For several reasons, accordingly, Muslim girls are very unlikely to attend secular schools. They tend to live in villages without state schools or to find their access to nearby state schools curtailed because of harassment. Further, many Muslim boys now want educated brides—but not more educated than themselves. Thus secular schooling would not enhance (and might even damage) Muslim girls' marriage chances. Generally, then, Muslim girls in rural Bijnor are educated either at a *madrasā* or at home, and this is unlikely to change unless the employment prospects for Muslim boys improve.

Health and Family Welfare in Rural Bijnor

Among Muslims and Hindus alike, gender differences in health status and access to health services are closely associated with the sexism of domestic life. Recent discussions of the routine workings of government health and family welfare facilities, indeed, have emphasized gender issues, along with class issues, but communal issues have rarely been addressed. Nevertheless, access to health and family welfare services in rural Bijnor is systematically skewed along communal and gender dimensions.

The siting of health facilities and the allocation of doctors to at least the larger clinics (Primary Health Centres, or PHCs) can be a focus for intense political activity. Villages with political connections may offer plots of land and obtain clinics, despite poor locations or nearby existing facilities. Elsewhere in Uttar Pradesh, a Block was even divided so that two powerful Congress Party politicians could each have a PHC in his home village (Akhtar and Izhar, 1986). In Bijnor District, Mandawar, with a population in 1971 of 10,000 (70 percent Muslim), has excellent road communications and is in the center of the Block containing Jhakri, Dharmnagri, and Qaziwala. It would have been the obvious place to locate the PHC for the Block. But the PHC was sited at the far north border of the Block, and sees very few patients. Similarly, the Dharmnagri hospital (established in the 1950s) was expanded steadily and now has impressive buildings—despite the very small demand for its services. Dharmnagri is on no bus routes and people from many surrounding villages can more easily use the hospitals in Bijnor town, five kilometers away. Begawala, on a main road, and with a well-attended weekly market and several small private pharmacies, would be a much better site. Jhakri, as a small village, has no government health facility. Qaziwala (with three times the population of Dharmnagri) has only a small subcenter, in a tumbledown rented building. Nangal has only a subcenter, and more health facilities are available in the larger villages or small towns a few kilometers away in three directions. But the Nangal clinic has excellent premises located under the residence of the wealthy Jat landowner who was *pradhān* (village headman) when it was established.

As with schools, the location and staffing of health facilities also have gender implications. Dispensaries and outpatient clinics are open to all at a nominal cost, but most people who use government clinics come from within five kilometers, and females (especially girls) are underrepresented among clinic users (Kielmann et al., 1983; Visaria, 1985). Women's own work is time-consuming, and they can easily use only clinics a short walk from home. It is hard for a chaperon to take time to accompany them any great distance—and we heard about instances of harassment by village men that prevented Muslim women from using their local clinic. In addition, women patients generally prefer to consult female staff, who themselves are anxious about being sexually harassed in the villages. In rural health facilities, the residential quarters supposedly provided for female staff do not always exist or are seriously inadequate in terms of security and comfort. As in many villages, the doctors and female staff appointed to the Dharmnagri hospital generally commute from Bijnor rather than live in their quarters, so round-the-clock service (for events like childbirth) is impossible. Many staff report for duty irregularly, and clinic hours are not routinely observed. During our frequent visits to Qaziwala, for instance, we never saw the subcenter open. The Auxiliary Nurse-Midwife (ANM) was married to the District Medical Officer's driver, and treated her posting as a sinecure that enabled her to live in Bijnor with him.

In practice, local populations often depend heavily on the (illegal) private practices built up by clinic pharmacists, who (it is rumored) use drugs stolen from PHC stock and bribe District medical staff to turn a blind eye. In addition, untrained village-based practitioners (all male) have thriving practices administering allopathic medicines, as do the small number of Ayurvedic, Unani, or folk healers (again, almost all male). Even poor women prefer to consult female private practitioners (all Hindu) or the government women's hospital in Bijnor town, if time, money, and permission from their affinal kin allow.

Gender, Community, and the Culture of Health Services

In contrast to education policy, government health policy requires many health activities to be specifically targeted at women and children because most preventable untimely deaths are of children. Health staff should supplement clinic-based maternal and child health care by seeking out clients—especially pregnant women, infants, and young children—for immunizations and other preventive health services.

As with education, however, the health staff tend to reflect the greater access of some sectors of the population—men and Hindus—to training for medical and paramedical employment. Women patients, especially minority women, may be poorly served by government staff unsympathetic to their situations. Since we began our research in 1982, all the Dharmnagri health staff have been Hindu or (for the lower positions) Scheduled Caste. Only one Muslim, a woman trained as a birth attendant, was in government employment in the four fieldwork villages. Generally, doctors and ANMs have urban upper-caste backgrounds. Their conspicuous disdain for village practices tends to result in authoritarian dealings with villagers, most pronounced in relation to Muslims and Scheduled Castes. Moreover, in their outreach activities, health workers cannot visit all the homes in their area and hence generally develop good social relationships with only relatively affluent, upper-caste Hindu households (Jeffery, 1988; Narayana and Kantner, 1992). Partly, this reflects their origins, but ingratiating themselves with influential village leaders can also enable them to influence where they are posted and help female staff to avoid harassment (Banerji, 1972). Consequently, preventive care is also biased.

The male worker responsible for Dharmnagri, Jhakri, and Qaziwala, for instance, was a Bengali Hindu and worked mainly with Bengali migrants. During an immunization drive in 1991, the Dharmnagri PHC doctor checked the male worker's records and found that all the children listed as immunized had Hindu or Scheduled Caste names. In Nangal, Hindu and Scheduled Caste women attended the regular child health clinics in a Jat area of the village to obtain immunizations and other care for their children. Muslim women rarely did so, nor were they visited at home; their children had very low immunization rates. Overall, our maternity history data from the four villages indicate that rates of child immunization and tetanus toxoid protection of childbearing women are substantially lower among Muslims and Scheduled Castes than among Hindus.[7]

In addition, since the mid–1970s, much routine health work has been subordinated to government health workers' needs to "motivate" women to become family planning accepters (or "cases"). Meeting family planning targets is the main criterion on which health staff receive approval or punishment from superiors; this has had both gender and communal implications.[8] The government's most favored methods are female sterilization, intrauterine contraceptive devices (IUCDs), and most recently, hormonal injections. Hormonal pills and condoms are considered vulnerable to client error, and (like other spacing methods) are often not offered to clients. Many village women perceive the family planning services as coercive, and particularly aimed at poor women and those of minority communities. During the political Emergency (1975–1977), indeed, rumors of the coercive tactics used to obtain sterilization cases (mainly male sterilizations at that time) were rife. Very few men in the four villages were sterilized then. Of these, pressured or not, almost all were Hindus. Yet fear of coercion is central to the resistance and hostility to health staff among Muslims in Jhakri and Qaziwala (Jeffery, Jeffery, and Lyon 1989; Jeffery and Jeffery, 1997).

Islamic theologians take different stances on contraceptive use, but Muslims in Bijnor generally believe that sterilization—though not necessarily spacing contraceptive methods—signifies lack of faith in Allah's ability to provide for however many children are born. They believe that a sterilized person cannot pray and will not be admitted to Paradise. Crucially, moreover, because educated rural Muslim men rarely obtain appropriate employment, few Muslims are investing heavily in their children's education and Muslim couples tend not to perceive children as economic "costs." Health workers consider Muslims, lower Hindu castes, and the poor much harder to convince of the benefits of small families than members of the locally dominant castes (Jeffery and Jeffery, 1997; Jeffery and Jeffery, 1996b). Understandably, ANMs want postings where their sterilization targets can be met relatively easily. Within mixed populations, they concentrate on the people most likely to be easily motivated. In 1983, for instance, the Dharmnagri ANM was not visiting Muslim households in her area because, she said, they had provided no family planning "cases."

Overall, Muslims in rural Bijnor have poorer access to government health services than comparable Hindus. They have been less able to influence the siting of facilities, and there is greater social distance between Muslim villagers and the predominantly Hindu medical staff. Women's mobility and access to health services are more restricted than men's, but the family planning program makes the government services especially problematic for Muslim women.

Gendered Communalism and Rural Women's Activism

Clearly, government education and health services discipline those they ostensibly serve. Parents and children often complain that teachers physically punish pupils and compel them to learn their lessons by rote. Some women, indeed, had not been sent to school in order to protect them from such treatment. Others had refused to go, preferring to replace the combined punishments from parents and teachers with chastisement from their family alone. Similarly, health workers may persuade patients to accept interventions—especially contraception—without adequate monitoring for side effects or consideration of the patient's best interests. Sometimes ANMs help women through pregnancy and delivery only if the women promise to be sterilized afterward. Sufficient drugs are not available at government health facilities, and women often comment on the scant curative health services and how demeaning their style of functioning is to patients.

Many of the health service's inadequacies impinge on all women, and the widespread local view—held by Hindus as well as Muslims—is that curative services are merely sweeteners to encourage people to accept contraception. But the prioritization of family planning places Muslim women in an especially difficult position. Most Muslims believe that they are specially targeted by the family planning program, which they regard (in effect) as "ethnic genocide" practiced by the "Hindu Raj." Muslim women complain about the local state's intrusive and coercive approach to family planning and its failure to meet women's perceived health care needs. Many Muslim women fear how government health workers will respond to them, and they often prefer to consult private doctors who have no family planning targets to meet. Muslim women do not see the state as a reliable protector of their reproductive health and other rights.

Arguably, given such negative facets of state education and health services, Muslim women's lack of access to them—at least as they are currently provided—might not be regarded as such a deprivation. Yet, although people in rural Bijnor critique the local state's activities, schooling and health care are valued—and scarce—resources. Schooling can widen employment opportunities, if only for some. Muslims' belief that their educated boys cannot obtain good employment (except possibly as *maulvī*) was often expressed in tandem with resentment over the lack of educational and employment reservations for Muslims on a par with those available to Scheduled Castes and the Other Backward Classes.[9] Without literacy in Hindi, negotiating the world beyond their villages is a serious challenge, for men as well as women. Like other nonliterate women, individual Muslim women often describe themselves as "a thumbprint person," as "a blind person," or "like a beast." They lament their inability to read, not because this had restricted their employment opportunities but because nowadays girls' education affects their marriage chances.

Similarly, Muslim women in rural Bijnor often complain about frequent childbearing, which they see as debilitating (or even life-threatening) for themselves and their children, as well as likely to create financial difficulties in future. But most Muslim women cannot easily obtain modern contraceptives because of the pronatalism of domestic and religious authorities. Many, though, requested medical and contraceptive advice from us (rather than from government health staff) (Jeffery, Jeffery, and Lyon, 1989; Jeffery and Jeffery, 1997).

Muslim and Hindu women make many complaints about the local state in rural Bijnor. Moreover, their commentaries often assume that women on both sides of the communal divide face similar difficulties and dilemmas in their daily domestic lives: problems protecting married daughters; conflicts between mothers-in-law and daughters-in-law; anxieties about medical symptoms, dowry problems, or wife beating. Could their grievances provide a focus for gender-based resistance and activism that might undermine communal alignments?

In practice, women's critiques are equivocal and leave substantial elements of the status quo unchallenged.[10] Marriage migration is not resented, but distant marriage is because a woman cannot easily maintain contact with her natal kin. Women rarely consider their lack of land rights and their dependence on their in-laws problematic, yet they are outraged by harassment of brides over their dowries. Women often bemoan having too many children and their difficulties in obtaining contraceptives, yet they do not critique local preferences for sons. Complaints about women's situation jostle with critical and unsupportive behavior toward other women. Women expostulate about how men devalue their work—and about women's inability to cooperate in the sharing of household tasks. Critical commentaries on marital violence are often tempered by assertions that men should not tolerate willful and defiant wives. Pride in women's capacity to work hard and to endure the pains of childbirth coexists with self-deprecation in relation to reproductive physiology, such as menstrual and childbirth pollution. Women's voices provide a window on their dissatisfactions and their wish to ameliorate their present situations rather then reframe them entirely, but their endorsement of negative and shameful images severely hampers the forging of allegiances to one another as women.

Moreover, within a single household, women have divergent interests and conflicting loyalties. Older women are often in authority over others. Younger women compete for scarce household resources. The continual repositioning of individual women (as daughter, sister, mother, or wife) undermines women's capacity to mobilize. And women's workloads and divisive class and caste loyalties further compromise their identification qua women. Thus women do not speak in unison and their perspectives are unstable, inconsistent, and contradictory. Alliance building is an uncertain enterprise, achieved (if at all) in the face of considerable organizational difficulties (Sharma, 1978). Not surprisingly, when women resist their situations, they generally deploy individualistic methods typical of the "weapons of the weak" (Scott, 1985).

In any case, although women often foreground gender issues, they do not consistently exclude communal ones. Some elements of women's self-perceptions belittle women's qualities, but communal identifications generally entail self-aggrandizement and negative stereotypes of the Other, which contaminate women's contacts across the communal divide and make collaboration to press for their interests as women difficult (Jeffery and Jeffery, 1994b; Jeffery, forthcoming; Shaheed, this volume). By the late 1980s, the anti-Muslim rhetorics of the Hindu Right had penetrated rural Bijnor. At the same time, the Tablīghī Jama'at were more actively trying to purge Muslim religious practice of supposedly Hindu accretions, such as women's singing and dancing at weddings or after a boy's birth (Gardner and Metcalf, both in this volume). Often, women's songs humorously critique domestic authorities, husbands or mothers-in-law (Jeffery, Jeffery, and Lyon, 1989; Jeffery and Jeffery, 1996a; Raheja and Gold, 1994). Since songs might be catalysts for empathy between Muslim and Hindu women, efforts to eradicate "women's culture" should not be lightly dismissed (Minault, 1994; Banerjee, 1989; Gardner, this volume). Such obstacles to women's mobilization around gender issues help to explain why rural women have been unable to exert much influence on the local state.

Equally, the lack of woman-friendly state services in the rural areas has implications for women's mobilization. Girls' schooling does not necessarily remedy women's domestic situations, provide economic independence and autonomy, or enable women to mobilize (although distance communication is undoubtedly more difficult for the nonliterate) (Jeffery and Basu (eds.), 1996). Nevertheless, the very low levels of school attendance by girls in rural Bijnor—particularly Muslim girls—leave them little room to maneuver. Most Muslim girls are shielded from the communalist aspects of state schooling but are encapsulated within their own community. Their *madrasā* schooling (if any) reinforces the sexism of family life and their economic dependency. Quietism rather than activism may be their most realistic political response (Kandiyoti, 1988). Equally, low fertility or improved health in themselves do not liberate women, but without access to good health care, women whose lives are devoted to childbearing, child rearing, and domestic and farming work have insufficient energy and time for political activism.

Muslim Women and the Hindu Right

The Hindu Right often portrays Indian Muslims as "pampered" and "appeased" by Congress governments intent on securing their "Muslim vote bank." Yet, the Muslim woman as victim of her own menfolk also figures centrally in the Hindu Right's rhetorics (Bacchetta, 1994; Basu (ed.), 1993, and this volume; Basu et al., 1993; Kapur and Cossman, 1995; Sarkar, 1993; Hasan, this volume).

During 1990–1991, Hindus in rural Bijnor often reiterated the Hindu Right's allegations that Muslims are "backward" because few Muslim girls attend state schooling and separate *madrasā* schooling prevents their integration into the mainstream. Muslim women's purported backwardness is much more complex than this, though. Any systematic differences between Muslim women and others do not arise from intracommunity processes alone, for everyday domestic life continually endorses and replicates gender inequalities in all communities. In that respect, Hindu women are no better placed than Muslim women to ensure that their priorities are met. Muslim women, however, are additionally disadvantaged by a pernicious combination of sexism in their domestic life and the gendered communalism integral to local state processes in which upper-caste Hindus are deeply implicated. Locally dominant groupings have a greater say in decisions that affect the accessibility of state schools, and the lack of pressure from Muslims for secular girls' schooling is linked to their belief that certain groups—especially upper-caste Hindus—have a hold over desirable job opportunities for young men in the District. And by responding to Muslim pressure to protect Islamic culture by officially recognizing *madrasā* schooling, the local state also (in effect) endorses the *madrasā* curriculum's failure to provide Muslim children with the credentials (especially literacy in Hindi) necessary to become full-fledged citizens.[11]

Again, the Hindu Right—as well as upper-caste Hindus in rural Bijnor—portrays Muslims as willfully unpatriotic in their resistance to family planning and their purported determination to outnumber Hindus. That polygyny is permissible for Muslims but outlawed for Hindus is yet more "evidence" of government pampering of Muslims (or, rather, Muslim men) (Hasan, this volume). Government family planning slogans proclaim "we two, our two" (a couple and two children). According to the Hindu Right, Muslims respond with "we five, our twenty-five" (a man, his four wives and twenty-five children). Polygyny, however, is extremely rare among Muslims in Bijnor. Indeed, it is more common among Hindus. The maternity histories we collected do indicate somewhat higher levels of fertility among Muslim women of all classes than among wealthier Hindus, and Muslim men tend to oppose family planning. But high levels of fertility within monogamous marriages are general in Bijnor (and Uttar Pradesh as a whole), and Muslim fertility patterns are comparable to those among lower-caste and poor Hindus. Further, levels of child mortality are significantly higher among Muslims—partly because of differential access to health care—and their completed family sizes are only slightly bigger than those of their Hindu counterparts. Indeed, the prospect of having no support in old age is one reason that many Muslims (and others too) are hesitant about adopting contraception (especially sterilization) (Jeffery, Jeffery, and Lyon, 1989). Our data provide absolutely no support for the Hindu Right's contention that Muslims are purposefully outbreeding Hindus, nor that upper-caste Hindus opt for a small family out of a concern for the national good. Rather, lower fertility among dominant groups reflects their dominance and their wish to maintain it. Making good marriages for daughters and investing in education and careers for sons require wealth and few children. For those—including Muslims in rural Bijnor—who believe that good jobs are inaccessible, education seems an expensive and fruitless investment, and there is little financial impetus for family limitation.

Clearly, Muslim patronage of *madrasās* and their fear of the family planning program help to perpetuate this state of affairs, but these are just part of a much more complex choreography. For many years before the Ayodhya affair, the ability of locally dominant groupings to influence the siting of government facilities, their greater access to training and employment, and the day-to-day discretion that local-level state employees exercise in their work had been sustaining and generating systematic biases in local state services. Minority populations and women were weak constituencies that could not compete effectively for scarce public resources. The appalling drama of communal riots has rightly attracted much attention, but mundane processes in times of apparent communal peace have systematically worked to the disadvantage of Muslim women. And, moreover, in driving a wedge between communities, politicized religion thwarts women's potential to mobilize across the communal divide and to challenge both the sexism in their daily domestic lives and the sexism and communalism engrained in the provision of public services.

Notes

Our research was funded by the Economic and Social Research Council (1982–1983 and 1985) and the Overseas Development Administration (1990–1993). Neither agency bears any responsibility for the views expressed here. Our thanks go to everyone in Bijnor who has helped us throughout this time. A longer version of this chapter was presented as a paper at the Bellagio workshop; many of the points omitted here are in P. Jeffery (forthcoming). We are very grateful for numerous helpful comments from the participants at Bellagio, as well as from colleagues in Edinburgh, Delhi, and London.

1. For criticisms of this view, see Bastian (1990); Pandey (1991); Spencer (1990, 1992). Many "riots" are better described as attacks (often involving the police) against Muslims; see Das (1990); Engineer (ed.) (1984); and Saberwal and Hasan (1984).
2. In rural Bijnor, few women control substantial economic resources or are economically independent. Most are not employed but are family workers in domestic units where they are subordinated to men and older women. Employed women may have seasonal agricultural work or be domestic servants in wealthy households. Fear of sexual harassment, lack of education and job opportunities, and the shame of women earning are all potent disincentives, even for very poor women, to looking for employment. For more on Bijnor, see our publications listed in the bibliography; see also Mandelbaum (1988); Wadley (1994); Agarwal (1994a); Dyson and Moore (1983); Raheja and Gold (1994); and Sharma (1980).
3. Few Scheduled Caste people in Bijnor described themselves as Dalits

("Oppressed"). A few were neo-Buddhists. Scheduled Castes used to be called Untouchables or Harijans.

4. Of more general political discussions, Kohli (1987) is unusual in taking seriously the developmental activities of the Indian states, but he is primarily concerned with regional, caste, and class dimensions, rather than community and gender.

5. As Rex (1986: 108–18) indicates, "institutional racism" has a wide currency but several interpretations; all, however, connote indirect discriminatory practices, hard to identify and to legislate against because it is so taken for granted, insidious, and all-pervasive. The concept was first used in the civil rights movement in the United States and later extended to the women's movement. Generally, the institutions encompassed by the term "institutional discrimination" are public ones, including business as well as state organizations. Normally the family is not included, although (arguably) it is an important locus of institutional sexism.

6. In 1992, however, the Uttar Pradesh Janata government under Mulayam Singh Yadav gave more support to Urdu in schools.

7. Health status is, of course, much more than a matter of what government health services provide. Son preferences and dowry lead to the neglect of girls and to their much higher child mortality rates overall. Class and community profiles are complicated by many variables—notably nutritional status and environmental threats—that affect a child's chances of survival to age five. These, too, are themselves skewed by community, class, and so on. In mortality, gender seems to outweigh community and class.

8. Sterilization targets have also been set for workers in other sectors of the state, such as schoolteachers and land records officers. Health-sector staff often assert that they put all the effort into "motivation" work only to find that another state functionary poaches the "case" (especially if that functionary can offer land to the person sterilized).

9. Our discussions in Bijnor in 1990 were generated by the Mandal Commission proposals, which were to give Other Backward Classes educational and employment preferences similar to those already in place for Scheduled Castes and Tribes. The implementation of these reservations was the focus of (largely) upper-caste Hindu anger over the difficulties their own sons would face in obtaining college places and employment after graduation. Such special programs are very controversial for other reasons, but we cannot explore them here.

10. See P. Jeffery, R. Jeffery, and A. Lyon (1989); R. Jeffery and P. Jeffery (1993a, 1993b); and P. Jeffery and R. Jeffery (1994a, 1996a, 1996b) for further discussion of the following points.

11. In Britain, multicultural education is criticized by the Right on grounds that it dilutes British identity, but also by some on the Left because respect for minority cultures in practice disadvantages minority children through its focus on the "3 Ss" (saris, samosas, and steel bands) at the expense of the "3 Rs" (reading, writing, and arithmetic).

Chapter Nine

The Other Side of the Discourse

Women's Experiences of Identity, Religion, and Activism in Pakistan

FARIDA SHAHEED

THIS CHAPTER LOOKS AT THREE INTERLOCKING BUT DISTINCT ISSUES: the increasingly religious idiom of political expression in Pakistan since the mid-1970s; women's accounts of their everyday experiences of gender and religion during the intensive state-led Islamization campaign of 1977–1988; and the ability of activist women's groups emerging during this period to cut across class and other identities. Even separately, documentation and analysis on these subjects are limited. Without women's recorded narratives of their lives and of their relationships with religion, analysis has often conflated people's experiences with the political use of religion in the public arena. But these two phenomena are not synonymous. Indeed, the women's accounts presented here indicate that they operate at different levels and that their disconnections need to be examined.

The ability of the women's movement to bridge women's distinct identities of class, ethnicity, and urban-rural locations has so far been analyzed in terms of the class background of activists and whether the feminist discourse was secular or not. Class—though significant—is not enough, however, to explain the current women's movement's inability to cut across other identities. The reasons may have less to do with the language of feminist discourse than with the public political nature of the women's movement: the marked tendency to focus on national-level legal rights almost excludes women's personal lives, where definitions of gender and attendant control mechanisms are experienced on a daily basis. Further, developments taking place simultaneously at different levels do not necessarily take the same direction and their contradictory impact needs to be borne in mind.

I draw here upon my own continuing involvement in the debates and activities of women's advocacy groups, on women's experiences of everyday life collected during a yearlong study, "Women, Religion, and Social Change," and the "Women and Law Country Project" being run by Shirkat Gah (the urban-based women's resource center where I work).[1] The latter included a nationwide survey documenting women's knowledge of statutory laws and the actual practices that govern their lives. Since 1993, the project has worked with women in numerous grassroots groups on issues relating to law and rights.

The Politicization of Religion

Until General Zia ul Haq's martial law regime in 1977, the central elite's attitude toward religion vacillated between regarding religion as a personal matter irrelevant to the national project of modernization, attempting to appease (or silence) the small but extremely vocal politico-religious groups, and opportunistically using religion to further its own political power (Mumtaz and Shaheed, 1987; Rashid, 1985).

The populations of the colonized territories were politically heterogeneous and fragmented by class, culture, and geographical location. Numerous social and cultural entities coexisted, whether in harmony or in competition for legitimacy and supremacy. Delegitimized in the era of nation-states and modernization, however, such diversities were ignored or suppressed in the nationalist struggles (Lateef, 1990). Thus, the class acceding to state power in 1947 had internalized the premise of the colonial discourse that any religious/cultural tradition deviating from the approved Eurocentric Christian tradition was incompatible with the desired goal of modernity and progress (Nandy, 1983).

Nevertheless, after independence, substate bonds of community have proved resistant to attempts by central elites to promote markers of identity that would justify their own leadership (Brass, 1979) and distinguish this "nation" from others. Indeed, such bonds have strengthened as people's responses to unequal economic and social development and blatant injustices take the shape of a "re-tribalization of society" (Rashid and Shaheed, 1993b). In Pakistan, this continued fragmentation is perhaps best exemplified by the parallel systems of law and governance that continue to flourish, while, on the ground, the operational law is rarely that of the state, particularly in family and gender matters (Shaheed, 1994).

Concepts of gender are intrinsic to any definitions of a collective self. They reflect the dominant ideology and accompany contests for political supremacy and their attendant cultural battles, from the international to the subnational level. Leila Ahmed (1992) and Lata Mani (1989) have shown that women and gender issues occupied a special place in the discourse between the imperialists and the colonized. Consequently, contemporary attempts by politico-religious elements to appropriate definitions of gender are a continuity, not a radical break, with the past. How religion defines the possible for individual actors, particularly women, cannot be reduced to the use of religion as a mobilizing force in the political arena, however. Indeed, the capacity for political mobilization probably hinges on the personal and social roles that religion performs. For many people, religion is not only a faith but an essential marker of self-identity, a code of ethics and behavior, and part of the prism through which they view the world. Attitudes toward and practices flowing from any given religion are, however, determined only partially by doctrine. Collective memories, existing social structures, and power relations are also crucial, as evidenced in disparities across class, ethnicity, and sects. In each community, religious beliefs are so tightly interwoven with cultural practices that customs unconnected to (and sometimes blatantly contradicting) doctrine are practiced as religious (Shirkat Gah/WLUML, 1994, 1995a, 1995b; Balchin (ed.), 1996). Yet, within these cultural entities, the boundaries of the acceptable are not fixed but part of a dynamic process.

People's responses to the shifting parameters of their lives involve more than a mechanical accommodation to external forces. Interaction actively engages people's perceptions and worldviews (continually modified in the process), and religion plays a greater or lesser role depending on historical experience, social grouping, political preferences, and so on. Adaptation is a dynamic two-way process, and the ongoing ability of religions to reinterpret traditions in the light of altered circumstances allows religious continuity.[2] The real question, perhaps, is why religion is such an appealing idiom for political expression today (Rashid, 1985, 1994; Kandiyoti, 1989). This chapter cannot discuss this issue fully but focuses on some developments that have helped promote a conservative religious discourse in the public arena in Pakistan.

The modernists (liberals and dictators alike) who ruled Pakistan until 1970 failed to achieve any major improvement for the majority. Zulfiqar Ali Bhutto's Pakistan People's Party (in government 1972–1977) co-opted leftist groups or harassed them to the point of redundancy. But Bhutto's own populist ideology of "Islamic Socialism" (liberally mixed with nationalism) itself foundered on the basic issues of economic progress, social reforms, and human rights. By the mid-1970s, however, in the wake of the petrodollar boom, the idea of an international Muslim identity as an alternative axis of transnational alliances had found a positive response that opened a space and provided justification for the creation or re-creation of a collective identity in the likeness of those with oil power.[3] While Zulfiqar Ali Bhutto was in power, Pakistan maintained close links with Libya, Iran (ruled by the Shah), and Saudi Arabia—linkages that also marked a deliberate reorientation from South to West Asia.[4]

The use of religious discourse was not new to Pakistan's political arena, but a *conservative* politico-religious discourse acquired a legitimacy in the mid-seventies, especially through the activities of the Jama'at-i-Islami, one of the motley collection of political parties opposed to the PPP.[5] In their antagonism to Bhutto, mainstream secular parties (such as the Awami National Party and the Tehrik-e-Istaqlal) went along with this discourse for reasons of political expediency. In combination with a general disillusionment with the political process, these developments prepared the ground on which General Zia ul Haq was to erect his Islamization program.

Sometimes described as the high point of fundamentalism in Pakistan, Zia's decade (1977–1988) witnessed the convergence of interests of the military rulers and politico-religious groups—the former seeking political support to enhance their credibility, the latter seeking access to the power consistently denied them through the electoral process. The alliance gave the emerging class of traders and entrepreneurs an opportunity to make their mark on political structures, and the religious idiom found its greatest support among them. The religious discourse emerged against the backdrop of a much wider crisis of national identity. Like other regimes, Zia's politically illegitimate martial law regime turned to religion (Islam), possibly to contain intrastate conflict, but definitely to cloak its ever more repressive and undemocratic measures. While regional tensions within Pakistan remained unaffected, the state's policy visibly immobilized opposition to the regime (Rashid, 1985). The regime gave currency to religiosity as a route to political power. With politicians bent on proving their "Islamic credentials," the ensuing battle royal for the mantle of religious leadership saw heightened sectarianism, violence, and deepening intolerance (Rashid and Shaheed, 1993a).

Women as actors were peripheral to the contest for political power. Yet gender definitions were central to this new politico-religious discourse, and women became easy targets of Zia's version of Islamization. For the first time, the state led an offensive against women's rights through legislation and administrative directives, and attempted to restrict women's mobility, visibility, and access to economic resources (Rouse, this volume). Women, of course, are heterogeneous and they experienced the contradictions between self and other individuals and institutions (including the state) through class, ethnic, and religious identities, as well as through gender. Discourse and debate on women remained almost exclusively urban, however. Moreover, the Zia decade, marked by the retrogression and the rhetoric of the religious right, saw the largest number of women entering the formal labor market and the informal sector (Pakistan Institute of Labour Education and Research/Shirkat Gah, 1993; Mumtaz, 1988; cf. Feldman, this volume). Female applicants for higher education increased. So did the number of technical training institutes for women. In urban areas, even as dress codes became more uniform, an unprecedented number and new class of women started appearing in public places such as parks and restaurants.

Women's Relationship with Religion

Toward the end of the Zia era (1988), the study "Women, Religion, and Social Change" documented women's everyday experiences to identify women's participation in religion and patriarchal structures. The research included a 139-household survey, in which all resident women aged fifteen and above (totaling more than 400) were interviewed. The research was primarily qualitative in nature rather than concerned with statistical validity, and it explored how women think about and express themselves on different aspects of their lives. Interventions that might challenge the women's answers or stop the flow of their narratives were consciously avoided. Women were asked to describe their houses, their neighborhood, their city/village; their typical day and religious and secular holidays; personal events; what they enjoyed, whom they admired, places they visited and avoided. They were asked about their families, their views of authority patterns within them, and about being a woman. Women were not asked their opinion about religion directly, in order that its significance could emerge unaided.

To capture generational changes, households with at least two generations of women were selected. Interviews were mainly conducted in Karachi (Sindh) and Lahore (Punjab), with one village from each province included as a counterpoint. The study covered Christians, Parsees, and Muslims, the last subdivided into ethnic groups, religious sects, and villages that, for the purpose of the study, were taken to be "communities."[6] In Lahore, Sunnis and Shias were looked at separately. In Karachi, we looked at Muslims from the dominant Urdu-speaking community (originally from what is now India) devoid of any attachment to a rural hinterland; migrant Pakhtuns with strong links with the distinct (and conservative) tribal/cultural identity and mores of the North West Frontier Province; and indigenous Sindhis. A rough classification of families into three classes (upper, middle, and lower income) was based on a combination of place of residence, the views of community informants, and observation.[7] Respondents' interview transcripts and those of other family members provide a fairly detailed picture of women's daily lives, including the level of harmony or discord within a household. For this chapter, the most interesting and significant features are the family's paramount role in women's experiences of gender definitions, the living reality of religion in women's lives (through prayers, rituals, and practice), and the cognitive disconnection between those two.

The family is the fulcrum for many activities, the location of honor (*izzat*), and the anchor of women's identity (see also Weiss, 1992). Most women's face-to-face interactions and relationships are located there and joys and sorrows are shared within it. The extended family and the immediate neighborhood define the outer limits of mobility and social interaction for the vast majority of women. On a daily basis, individual women experience female identity in tasks assigned (or assumed), through interactions with others within the family (and to a lesser degree outside), and in the restrictions placed on women's potentiality. Women's comments were to the effect that they have no identity except that of their families, or that "a woman is identified (by people outside her family) in relation to the men of the family." Many women spoke in general terms but specifically mentioned individuals were predominantly male: "Which family? In-laws or my *māykā* (consanguineal family)? If anyone asks about my in-laws, then I will speak about my father-in-law, my husband and *dewar* (husband's younger brother), what they do, what their names are, or I will speak of my mother-in-law. And if the question is about my *māykā*, then obviously I will speak of my father and brothers, because a woman is recognized by the men of the family"; "I introduce my family with my father's or father-in-law's name"; "I will tell them about my husband and brothers"; "Our family is good, my father is . . ."; "Our family is very good because my father-in-law was . . ."; "It is a very good family. Two of my *jeths* (husband's elder brothers). . ."

The family's centrality is also obvious in women's view that the character of family members and a woman's good or bad fortune in marriage are essential determinants of the quality of her life. A young unmarried woman, for example, said: "My brothers love me. Everything is provided for." A married woman commented: "What greater benefit can there be than a good husband?" Another wished that her "husband [had been] broadminded, then the atmosphere [of her home] would be good." Two sisters married into the same family and living together in one household illustrate how a woman's married life depends on her husband's character. Subjected to violence, the younger one said: "[Being a woman] was never a problem at my parents' home, but having come to my in-laws, I have learnt how women themselves use other women, and how men mistreat their wives whenever they want. It is not without good reason that people cry at the birth of a girl." In contrast, her elder sister (with a more reasonable and certainly less violent husband) said: "No particular problem. Whatever God has made, he's made well. Only men are of no use at all. Whatever my heart desires, I fulfill it." Women also spoke of how mothers, mothers-in-law, and sisters-in-law intervened in their lives and also of their own authority over their children and younger siblings of both sexes.

The control exercised by parents, siblings (particularly but not exclusively brothers), and in-laws determines a woman's freedom of movement, access to resources, and definition of self. The dynamics of a class-based society mean that poor women—already disadvantaged in many other aspects—also have the narrowest base for negotiating space for themselves as women. Upper-class women tend to experience less-rigid controls, and their greater access to education and resources often permits them to expand their reference points and take greater initiative in shaping their own lives. Parsee women were most likely to say that no one had authority over them (50 percent); they were also the best educated, were concentrated toward the upper brackets of Pakistan's income levels, and had the highest percentage of employed women. In sharp contrast, few Pakhtun and Sindhi women felt able to make this statement (3.6 and 7.5 percent, respectively).

Descriptions of what women do when they disagree with decisions made by others confirmed the dissimilar spaces available to different women. Younger Pakhtun women most frequently remained silent. Unmarried daughters made comments such as "Our views are not accepted," "Talking back to parents is not liked in our family," and "In the end, elders have to decide everything, especially my father and brothers." Married women said, "My husband decides everything in consultation with his elder brother" or "My husband never asks my opinion on anything; what difference can be made?" In other communities, mutual consultations and women airing their views were more common. Older women had a greater say in everyday matters, although "important" decisions were still made by the male authority.

Generally, women accept the status quo and the way authority is exercised because "he is my husband," "they are my parents," "I am their mother," or "they are younger." Sometimes women justified their parents' authority (occasionally including that of in-laws) on grounds of their greater experience. Men's authority over their wives was accepted "because he is my husband," "because one has to," "because he knows more about the outside world/official matters," or "because he earns and provides for me."

Many women said they would not and could not speak badly of their family to outsiders "even if my relatives were bad." Yet women are not blind to the gender- and age-based structures of control and authority that operate in the family, or to the resulting problems faced by women. Many do criticize and condemn the restrictions imposed on them by family members. Younger unmarried women were more likely to question the system's gender biases. More than half of those critical of the authority structure were unmarried women; 44 percent were aged fifteen to twenty-four years (36 percent of the sample). Only 14 percent of those questioning authority were forty-five or older, but this age group—largely coinciding with the category head or female head of household[8]—were also most likely to say that no one has authority over them (65 percent compared to 26 percent of the sample). All the young unmarried women who accepted no one's authority had at least a bachelor's degree, as did the rare daughters-in-law who expressed similar sentiments.

Women's narratives, however, point to the difficulty of challenging the gender definitions dictated by their families in the minutiae of everyday life. The family is a woman's main support base, and most women do not have access to any nonfamily support systems. Terms would have to be renegotiated with the primary support base. Thus, changing a woman's everyday life (which depends largely on redefining gender rules within the family) is a risky enterprise. Indeed, a woman can be completely cut off and even killed.[9] As one woman said, "And if I didn't accept [my husband's authority], where would I go?" Isolated by zealously enforced patterns of mobility in small family- or kinship-centered social circles, women rarely interact with wider circles that could provide models of different lives and selves. In addition, an intensely male-centered society curtails women's ability to hope and dream of altered lives because it provides so few positive female role models. Women's limited horizons are reflected in the sizable number of rural women unable to name any woman whom they admired, as well as in the male-dominated landscape the women's voices conjured up.[10] Even the personal acquaintances women admire tend to be men, although upper-class women—whose circles provide women with the greatest opportunities for fulfilling potentials—mentioned more admired female acquaintances than the poor (18 percent and 8 percent, respectively). Women politicians, particularly Benazir Bhutto (who contested elections and became prime minister during the study), inspired the poor more than the rich; without politically significant leaders, the pool of women who inspire others would shrink drastically. The wider the point of comparison, the greater is the potential for women to change their life patterns and seek to redefine the contours of their lives. For instance, women whose families had migrated from small towns or villages to large urban centers had not questioned the only definitions of gender visible to them prior to migration, but their families suddenly appeared conservative in the new environment and their own lives more controlled than those of their peers. In the words of one woman, "Since coming here I have seen that there is much strictness in my family."

In Karachi, a middle-class woman stated: "After God, woman is that being which is called 'mother', which is called *dhartī* (mother-earth), which is called earth. . . . The disadvantages of [being a woman] are created by a class society. The woman is disadvantaged only by the system. In a broadminded, free, and social democratic society, there is no sex discrimination. This only happens in our imperialistic, materialistic, ignorant, and backward society." Others also commented that "in the present society, and seeing the position of women, being a woman is a problem in everyday life"; "men don't regard women as human beings"; "a woman is considered inferior to men and she has to do everything with their permission," or "the values and norms of our society are such that women are given less respect than men and . . . have no independence to make decisions." "If I had been a boy/man . . ." was the litany that often preceded women's reflections on the disadvantages of being a woman: "I would have been able to work outside," "I could have done all those things I could not do being a girl," "maybe immediately after being divorced I would have remarried," "I would have been able to go about where I liked," "I could have the freedom to study or do a good job and go on tours," "I would have done great things," "I would have been happy," or "I could have lived like I wanted to."

A persistent complaint was that strictly controlled mobility affected women's leisure, socializing, studies (where relevant), work possibilities, and coping with crises. "Nowadays I am alone, I cannot go out for anything. If my children are sick I cannot take them to the doctor, etc." Time and again, younger women spoke of discriminatory attitudes toward girls and boys in their families and outside. Brothers were allowed out and not questioned (or questioned less). Men did not need permission to go anywhere; women could be refused permission even to attend a mother's funeral. Women were prevented from pursuing their studies and holding jobs. They were expected to do chores for their brothers, and to live according to the desires of others in their families.

Younger women complained more than their elders. But at least some women from all age cohorts, classes, and communities echoed complaints that, as one poor urban mother put it, being a woman "is a problem because we have to accept a man's word." About her husband, one woman explained, "Because he is earning, I have to agree with him halfheartedly on many matters." Others clearly located the problem in their families or community, for example, "*In our family* we have to obey the men, who are very strict"; "*In our family* educating girls is considered a bad thing. Also girls do not get freedom to move about as they will"; "It's a great problem *in our family*. Women do not enjoy liberty nor can they go out of the house, nor can we do anything according to our wishes" (emphases mine).

In specifying the family or community, women imply that change is possible for some women, if not for themselves. Families imposing many restrictions were characterized as conservative and narrow-minded or as following the pattern of a particular community or of Pakistani society. Women did not consider that the structures and relationships operating within the family, the problems they faced, or the disadvantages of being a women were ordained by God's word or derived from religious tenets. They simply did not connect religiosity per se with strict control over women. Just one woman, a fifty-five-year-old doctor, mentioned her family's religious conservatism in describing her personal struggle for independence—but religion was only one factor in a list headed by cultural norms. She described her family as "a custom-bound conservative Pathan family which has a fundamentalist religious, feudal and superstitious mind." In contrast, a forty-one-year-old woman saw her family as "educated, religious and liberal." The crucial factor is whether the family is custom-bound or liberal—and religion can be a part of either scenario.

The only slight exception was husband-wife relationships. Five urban women each attributed her husband's authority over her to his position of "god-on-earth" (*majāzī khudā*). Four, aged forty-three to fifty-five, were from economically better-off families; the fifth was a thirty-five-year-old from a poor family. Two elderly village women spoke of their husbands as their "lords" (*sir da saīn, mālik*). But these are only seven women out of a total of 407, less than 4 percent of those ever married. In any case, this belief—now increasingly rare—derives from local custom rather than religious doctrine; indeed, it is antithetical to the tenets of Islam.[11] The extent to which the view that women are duty-bound (or obliged) to obey their husbands reflects their acceptance of everyday reality or derives from religious underpinnings obviously needs further exploration.

At the close of a decade-long intensive Islamization campaign, then, women's narratives certainly conveyed feelings of impotency and frustrated desires. But their analyses pinpoint traditional culture (including but not equivalent to religion), societal norms, and male control rather than religion as the root cause. Not even women's movement activists identified religion as the source of everyday oppression. Most women failed to refer to religion at all. Examples of those who did: "In the period of Hazrat Mohammed and Hazrat Zainab, the role of Hazrat Fatima-tu-Zehra and Hazrat Zainab are both very clear. . . . Following her footsteps, we can come onto the street and fight for our rights"; "Their self-confidence is so fragile that men just cannot accept that their women, too, have the right to go out. It's actually their own problem and they are the ones who have started all this issue of *hijāb* (the veil) etc. Pakistani men are mentally sick." Across communities, nonactivist women distinguished between religion and the dictates of a male-dominated society. One elderly villager said, "Women are the mothers of prophets. . . . God has given her much honor. Other things depend on our [level] of understanding." A sixty-year-old city dweller felt that "although God has made all men and women the best of living things, the woman is very oppressed. You can say she is a second-class citizen. Women cannot do many things, though they wish to do so for their children and for society. Our way of life is such that every sacrifice is said to be a must for women and not for men. At times like this I feel hurt." In sum, these women's voices do not fit easily into the strain of feminist analysis within and outside Pakistan that views religion as a primary factor in women's oppression.[12]

Further, in contrast to women's apparent need to project their family positively, women did not seem to feel any compulsion to project their own religiosity. Most women's accounts of their daily routines indicated an inwardly focused relationship with religion and did not mention religious practices at all. Yet women's answers to a direct request to describe any religious activity engaged in on a daily, weekly, or monthly basis dramatically illustrate the extent to which religious rituals and practices—as much as responsibilities for housework, childcare, livestock, agriculture, studies, or a job—shape and structure most women's days, irrespective of religion, rural or urban setting, and income level. For women, religion bridges the spiritual and the social. Women tend to welcome daily and episodic religious events because religious occasions of prayer, *dars* (lectures), _khatms_ (collective readings of the Qur'an Sharif or celebrations marking an individual's first complete recitation), and so forth provide social interaction that is unsanctioned and unattainable in any other form for most women. For men, by contrast, tea shops and streets, cattle markets and lunch in the fields, and work and leisure activities in the cities all provide settings for social interaction and support groups. Periodic religious events, then, provide a vehicle for women's reaffirmation of community membership. Yet the participatory nature of religion is neither limited to nor dependent on social bonding. The individual woman, in and by herself, is the pivot of daily prayers, and many women expressed a sense of communion and peace in praying that—aside from the spiritual and psychological aspects—provides a break from daily routines and chores and gives women space that is theirs absolutely. Religion is unique in its capacity to provide self-affirmation, at the level both of personal psychology and the social collectivity. Through its rituals, practices, and structure, religion provides a most immediate sense of participation and belonging that is unavailable to vast numbers of women in other aspects of their lives (Ahmed, 1991).

This participatory aspect of religion is crucial for the individual woman but is rarely taken into account by feminist analysis. The activism of women's groups in Pakistan fails to provide women at large with comparable participation in a meaningful alternative framework, without which women are unlikely to abandon willingly the self-affirmation and social participation that religion currently provides (compare Sarkar, this volume). Women's own narratives of their everyday experiences do not speak of oppression as either emanating from or ordained by religion. Women's accounts certainly suggest that religion is interwoven with cultural traditions, and colors and shapes the contours of their lives. But they attribute the avenues that are open and the barriers imposed, the restricted repertoires of permissible female experiences, and the resulting sense of frustration or impotency to socially constructed gender identities that are imposed by men and differ according to class and ethnicity.

Of course, as part of people's worldview, religious beliefs and tenets are bound to play an important role in justifying existing patriarchal structures and informing attitudes toward gender and, specifically, women. My point here is that women did not express such a linkage when they could have. One could have expected women to say that "our religion teaches us that men are the *hakīm* (guardians, keepers) of women." Instead, the interviews indicate women's resistance or resignation to social reality, not discourse. Hardly any referred to the political discourse so evident in the mass media and the focus of activist women's groups, much less to laws, directives, and policies. Just a few exceptional activists referred to the negative impact on women of recent state measures and the religious discourse, and that too, indirectly. This absence of a narrative connection between women's everyday realities and the ideological discourse suggests that gender identity is experienced and defined at two distinct levels: the public arena of political discourse and the more tangible personal everyday existence of women.

The Religious Discourse and Women's Responses

Women were not all affected equally by the politico-religious discourse ascendant during Zia's period. Rural women (the majority) were affected least directly, though they felt the impact of some measures and legislative changes.[13] Indirectly, they suffered from the reduced expenditures on and general neglect of women's development programs, especially in education and health. But the discourse of prescribed dress codes, demands for gender segregation, and campaigns to push women back into their homes had little impact in the rural areas. Rural women in more wealthy families were already secluded, and poor women had to continue their agricultural and livestock activities side by side with their menfolk. Indeed, neither the state nor the politically ambitious religious elements focused on rural women, who, if anything, were regarded as the embodiment of truly authentic and indigenous womanhood. The leaders of the political discourse were notably not (and still are not) interested in the conditions of women working in the fields, or the exploitation of women in brick kilns or construction sites. Their primary concern, of course, was how to obtain and retain power. And women and gender issues were relevant only insofar as the issue was how to cope with (and control) the implications of changing social and economic circumstances. As Fatima Mernissi (1975a: 8–9) insightfully notes, calls on women not to work outside the home but to veil and behave in a particular manner themselves bear testimony to the reality that (some) women have succeeded in redefining traditional notions of gender in their favor to a degree that provokes a response.

Like most political debates, the discourse was loudest in medium to large cities. For many men and women, though, the official discourse of Islamization, couched in the language of the justice of Islam, respect and protection for women, and so on, must have sounded quite familiar. Indeed, in its echoing of popular culture, it would not have been perceived as a cause for alarm. Few women were aware of how the discourse was being translated into practical measures with repercussions for women.[14] Undoubtedly, employed women faced harassment in public spaces and in the workplace, but it is difficult to gauge whether incidents significantly increased or whether they received more attention, thanks to the emergence of vocal women's advocacy groups. Similarly, the general misogynist atmosphere probably further reduced women's self-assertiveness and resulted in even more precarious terms and conditions of work. But in Pakistan, factory shifts and work floors have always been gender segregated; married women, discriminated against; and female workers, assigned the least skilled and most poorly paid tasks. How much better conditions would have been without Zia's Islamization is a matter for conjecture. Conversely, despite a decade of official emphasis on gender segregation, some factories started integrating floor shifts in the early nineties, for reasons of economic efficiency rather than concern for modifying gender rules.[15]

Professionally employed middle-class and upper-middle-class women were the most outraged by the antiwomen collusion of state measures and religious discourse. Convinced that they were the main targets of the religious rhetoric, these women formed the main vociferous opposition to state policies (Shaheed and Mumtaz, 1992). Daily, they encountered the new conservative discourse, in their homes through the state-owned television that blamed working women for the disintegration of values in the family and the (real and visibly rampant) corruption in society; and in their workplace and in the streets going to or returning from their employment, where every man seemed to have been granted a state license to pass judgment on women's dress and therefore—by a quantum leap—their morality. In cities, nonemployed elite women, too, were shocked out of complacency by the government's adoption of the discourse of the politico-religious parties that, until then, had been disparaged as antimodern and insignificant.

During the nationalist movements and in the early decades after independence, both these categories of women had made important gains. The Family Laws Ordinance (1961) enhanced space—if not actual rights—within the family. A limited number of women gained the right to choose or have a say in whom they would marry. Higher education and remunerative work became acceptable for many, and, by 1975, all branches of the civil service had been opened to women. Unfortunately, however, these redefinitions of the parameters of women's personal lives were largely insulated by boundaries of class privilege in metropolitan locations. Class identity shielded the women who embodied these changes from public visibility and overt criticism. For other women, changes were far less dramatic, the most important being the increased access to and acceptability of education, with its bonus of increased mobility.

Led for a decade by the Khawateen Mahaz-e-Amal (Women's Action Forum or WAF), the limited women's movement could not catalyze a mass movement that bridged class boundaries and the urban-rural divide. Women activists confronted a stifling atmosphere: a martial law regime that—among other things—had abrogated the Constitution, suspended fundamental rights, and banned political parties, demonstrations, and pamphleteering; an incessant use of state-owned electronic media to project a distorted definition of female identity; a veritable onslaught of administrative measures, government directives, and legislation all seeking to reverse—or at least control—advances made by women in redefining their identity and space. Under such circumstances, it is commendable that WAF succeeded in its self-defined role of a "lobby-cum-pressure group": putting women on the national agenda; actively and publicly mobilizing to resist discriminatory laws and directives; helping to amend proposed legislation and delaying the enactment of certain laws; and catalyzing new women's advocacy groups, which are now making their mark (Mumtaz and Shaheed, 1987; S. Zia, 1994).

In the prevailing conditions, though, many women felt unable to join openly in activism and public protest. Lower-middle-class women at WAF meetings I attended drew attention to the differential impact of activism on themselves and on upper-class and professional middle-class women. For less-privileged women, losing jobs was a greater danger than for upper-middle-class activists who were better equipped to handle the consequences. If jailed, poorer women were more likely to be raped than better-connected activists. And upper-class and upper-middle-class women beaten up during their activism could expect accolades from their own family members, whereas lower-middle-class women could experience further abuse at the hands of theirs. Upper-middle-class women activists recognized the validity of such points and accepted that their own activism needed to be much more visible because they were better positioned to take the risk—but this did not translate into strategies for addressing differences among women.

Activist groups, then, failed to mobilize women across class and other identities when WAF opposed particular laws (justified through religion) from within the framework of Islam (1981–1991). Perhaps, given the pressures under which women activists were mobilizing at the time, this is understandable. Why this failure was not, on the whole, remedied after WAF declared itself secular in 1991 is another matter. Women's groups spent considerable time and energy hotly debating whether the framework they adopted should include or exclude religion, without considering that the principal obstacle to building women's solidarity might be something other than the religious/secular nature of their discourse.

Some of today's stumbling-blocks are rooted in the conditions prevailing in the late seventies and eighties. Activism was led by upper-middle-class professionally employed women, precisely those who had most successfully redefined the parameters of gender for themselves. They stood to lose the most from a narrowing of those parameters. They also felt gender-based discrimination most acutely. Class privileges, urban living, and class integration had all cushioned them from other identity-based discriminations, such as ethnicity. By contrast, women who suffer oppression by virtue of class, religion, or ethnic identity, in addition to gender, necessarily have concerns not premised solely on gender. Sharply defined classes and marked rural-urban disparities accentuate the very real differences in women's lives. And the greater these differences, the more difficult it is for women of one class (especially those who have most successfully altered their lives) to transcend their own experiences, encompass the realities of other women's experiences, and provide effective leadership and mobilization across classes. Unless the dominant feminist groups address women's diverse concerns in their discourse and activism alike and consciously include leadership from different backgrounds, the base of the movement will probably remain small or fragmented.[16]

This period of activism materialized in direct response to a state-sponsored onslaught on women's rights. Activists had to counter the agendas of the state operating in tandem with the discourse of right-wing religious groups. The pace was energy-sapping. There was little time for theorizing, and even less for setting their own agenda. Instead of being shaped by an independent feminist analysis, women's activism came to resemble a negative mirror image of the discourse it opposed. In addition, the urgent need to counter the laws and other state initiatives kept the focus of activism on legislative changes. The proposed laws had, of course, to be resisted; they drastically reduced women's formal rights and had far-reaching, disastrous implications (Mumtaz and Shaheed, 1987; Jehangir and Jilani, 1990; Zia, 1994). Yet, as a recent survey confirms, family and many other matters continue to be ruled by customs (Shirkat Gah, 1994). The formal law is unknown to the vast majority of Pakistan's women and has little meaning except for those personally confronted by its—usually unpleasant—implications (such as the Enforcement of Zinā Ordinance). Consequently, many women may not have identified with the legal issues that dominated women's groups' discourse and activism. Moreover, whether related to law or not, campaigns—then as now—have focused on exceptional situations. Campaigns about violence against women (including domestic violence) have been launched on worst-case scenarios, and many women may be reluctant to see the connections between such horrifying cases and their own lives. Nor have most high-publicity campaigns included concrete measures to support women survivors and victims.

It is far easier to mobilize animated support against blatantly unjust laws or the consequences of violence than for more mundane issues such as education, but a focus on law or exceptional situations neglects the sources of women's everyday oppression. The "Women, Religion, and Social Change" study, however, identifies daily control mechanisms: low mobility that curtails and controls interaction with others and impedes access to medical facilities, educational institutions, and employment opportunities, and exclusion from household decision making, including choosing a husband. I have witnessed many interactions between Shirkat Gah and several grassroots organizations in squatter settlements, small towns, and villages. The middle-class professional women's groups that currently dominate feminist discourse should listen carefully to other women's articulation of their own needs and support them in their own agendas rather than imposing preconceived ideas and priorities that stem from our own experiences and locations.

In "Feeling Foreign in Feminism," Maivan Clech Lâm presents a wonderfully articulate criticism of how the dominant "white 'professional' or bourgeois feminism" in the United States has appropriated the right to conceptualize the lives of women of color and speak on their behalf from a position of power and privilege. The same criticism can be made in Pakistan—and probably South Asia more generally—about those who dominate the activist discourse. She says:

> Certain white feminist agendas in the United States appear not only off target but decidedly filmic. That is, they come across as too cleanly and detachedly representational, with little connection to the lives of women I know best, or to the difficult consequences that these women face when they try and change. . . . I certainly do not assert here that white bourgeois feminist accounts of their own lives are filmic; I state only that theirs of mine, on the occasions when they presumptively universalize their accounts of the lives of women, often are. (Lâm, 1994: 867)

I could not agree more with Lâm's view that feminists exercising the privilege that springs "from their relatively unproblematic access to authority and resources, which in turn have a way of generating one another" must learn to unlock the grip of arrogance when evaluating and analyzing what Isabelle R. Gunning calls "culturally challenging" practices. To do so, Gunning suggests a self-examination of "the limitations imposed on her consciousness by her own homegrown subjectivities and needs"; a coming "to terms with her given status as heir of an . . . order" and learning what that status signifies to other women "subjugated by that order"; and training "herself to hear, rather than talk, the lives of these women, in the fullness of their complexities—lives that these women hope to modify, even radically, but not jettison, at least not in the majority of cases" (Gunning quoted in Lâm, 1994: 871–72).

Without learning these lessons, urban-based activist women cannot be a meaningful reference point for others, though their discourse can still be heard. Middle-class activists are better read in feminist literature, better linked to international groups and concerns, and the most likely to debate the theoretical basis for action. Certainly, there must be theory—but it needs to be rooted in the realities of women's lives. Better-connected, less-oppressed, and more-visible and vocal women must ensure that the diversities of women's experiences and locations are not leveled (or perpetually put in parentheses). They should not impose their own analysis and reality as the only ones for all women—something that, unfortunately, seems to be happening in regard to women's relationship with religion.

Perhaps the most significant contribution of urban middle-class women's groups has been catalyzing ideas and groups elsewhere. Connections must be built between different groups of women and between initiatives addressing women's basic needs (that tend to ignore the question of rights) and those promoting women's rights (that tend to bypass basic needs). The growing links between urban women's groups and grassroots organizations have great potential, providing that communication is two-way. Unless grassroots women's groups can start shaping feminist discourse in Pakistan, it will probably be impossible to forge a broad-based women's movement that can effectively overcome the barriers and distances imposed by identities other than gender.

Understanding the interlinkages between women's everyday lives in the private or domestic sphere (the "personal") and the institutions of the public sphere (the wider economy and other institutions, including the "political" as conventionally understood) is intrinsic to feminist analysis. Yet, in Pakistan, advocacy groups have thus far concentrated, almost exclusively, on strategies and structures for public political intervention.[17] This seeming mismatch between feminist theory and feminist activism is a fundamental issue. Many of today's most vocal women's rights advocates first experienced activism when the need to place women on the national agenda and to resist retrogressive trends encouraged them to focus on issues that caught both the public imagination and the attention of policy makers. But women experience patriarchal controls through mechanisms simultaneously operating in the public and the private spheres. Hence, to be effective, women's activism must evolve a broad variety of complementary strategies.

Conclusion

The gaps in consciousness and analysis between women's everyday experiences of patriarchy and religion on the one hand and their "political" dimensions on the other have far-reaching implications for the women's movement in Pakistan. Feminists need to examine why women's narratives of the everyday make little or no reference to the forces operating in the public arena. Feminists must also be conscious of—and their activism must also be informed by—the disparity between women's own accounts of their relationship with religion and the dominant thread of women's activism, which sees religion primarily as a source of oppression.

Two further challenges face the women's movement. The first involves rethinking its almost exclusive reliance on structures and styles of activism borrowed from political movements that feminists so often criticize precisely for ignoring the personal aspects of women's oppression. Without renouncing the public-political dimension of the struggle, women must devise creative strategies for meaningful change in the private-personal realm, so that individual women can redefine gender relationships within the family and loosen patriarchal controls in their daily lives. Second, women are united across class and ethnicity by the limitations and oppression of being female, as poignantly exemplified by their choruses of "Had I been a boy, I could have, I would have, I may have." There are no positive definitions of the female gender, aside from those premised on women's reproductive powers. By contrast, community identities (whether ethnic or religious) allow women and other oppressed classes to participate in myths of greatness and strength, not just oppression. This may partially explain why community has a stronger appeal than either gender or class, a phenomenon that probably has political repercussions for both gender- and class-based political struggles (see Jeffery and Jeffery, this volume). Moreover, implicit in the concept of community is the tacit or overt assurance that community members (however defined) will be protected. Existing women's groups, whose visions of a better future usually depend on successful negotiations with state structures, cannot make an equivalent claim. In systematically integrating development issues into their activism and discourse, women's advocacy groups will need to devise mechanisms for direct interventions that do not rely exclusively on the—often discredited—state apparatus.

Like patriarchy, religion operates at both the personal and public levels and poses a similar challenge. Women's narratives suggest that the interface between religion and politics in the public sphere is not the primary—and certainly not the only—context in which women relate to religion. Yet the political manipulation of religion undoubtedly affects women profoundly. The ascendancy of religion in the political sphere has less to do with gender issues than with political bankruptcy in the pursuit of state power and with the failure of the state to fulfill, and of politicians to pursue, the social contract.

In their bid to monopolize the public discourse, politico-religious groups have been alarmingly successful in shifting the terms of debate, and gender issues have been central to this enterprise. Meanings have become progressively more dichotomous and do not reflect the plurality on the ground. The strident voice of the politico-religious parties is steadily eating away the space for the autonomous definitions and experiences of religion previously open to women. Increasingly, vast numbers of women whose faith is a living reality must choose between giving up their faith altogether or conforming to the dictates of groups whose political agendas are cloaked in religious discourse.[18] Such attempts to straitjacket definitions of gender must be vigorously and vociferously opposed, by all means and at all levels. But women activists should avoid counterposing feminism and secularism on the one hand and religion and women's oppression on the other. Such rigid either/or thinking imitates the male-dominated political elements who use it to further their own ends. It also fails to answer the needs at hand. To reconfigure their lives successfully, women simultaneously have to redefine markers of identity and self other than gender, markers that are not identical for all women. For some women, the marker may be class; for others, religion or culture; for yet others, profession.

I see no reason that these should have equal salience for all women. As feminists, we reject external impositions of "womanhood" and insist on exercising our right to self-definition. It is illogical to dictate to other women and reject their right to define—or redefine—gender in ways that have meaning in their own lives, even if not in ours. Feminist groups need to promote autonomous choices for women, and to respect the differences that arise. Undoubtedly, women who insist on retaining (or not opposing) certain practices or beliefs (including religion) may be "culturally challenging" for others. But women—and men, too—must have the right to challenge both the doctrinaire, legalistic version of religion and the ethnic and religious chauvinism currently ascendant in the political arena without being *obliged* to renounce either their religion or their ethnic identity. Instead of headlong confrontation, a focus on concrete issues and desired changes can bridge the distances and differences between women. By becoming reference points for identity and self other than those promoted by the dominant male ideology (whether politico-religious or secular), the networking and actions of women activists and autonomous women's groups can catalyze changes in which women formulate their own justifications and priorities.

I have highlighted the personal aspects of gender because these are neglected in Pakistan, both in scholarship and in activism. Political and legal issues are important, of course, and I certainly do not mean to undervalue the role of urban-based middle-class activists. Indeed, had such women not aggressively opposed both the religious discourse and the policies adopted under Zia (the former continuing after his death; the latter still in the statutes), the prospects for women's equality in Pakistan would have been even bleaker than they appear today. My concern here, however, is that self-professed feminists in the broader women's movement should not allow their own existential realities to be the sole reference for feminist struggle. The movement must not become exclusivist to the point that many women feel "foreign in feminism." Women do daily battle within very disparate realities that are the contextual springboards for their engagement in the broader political struggle for women's rights. If feminist discourse fails to recognize and accommodate the differences between women, there is a danger that it—like the religious discourse—will not resonate with women who see in it little connection with their own lives.

Notes

My thanks to Patricia Jeffery, Cassandra Balchin, Amrita Basu, and Neelum Hussain for inspired help and feedback; to Durre S. Ahmed for discussions on women's relationship with religion; to the women linked through Women Living Under Muslim Laws, whose many divergent analyses inform and enrich my work; and to Shirkat Gah Lahore for sharing experiences and analyses, and allowing me the luxury of writing.

1. The Pakistan Women and Law Country Project is part of the multicountry action-research Women and Law in the Muslim World Programme of the network Women Living Under Muslim Laws. The regional study was conducted in Sri Lanka, India, and Pakistan under the aegis of the International Centre for Ethnic Studies (Colombo). Research has been completed in Pakistan, Bangladesh, Sri Lanka, Nigeria, Fiji, and Turkey, and is under way in many other countries.

2. Nandy (1983) regards the greatest tradition as the tradition of reinterpreting traditions.

3. In Pakistan, the 1974 Islamic Summit in Lahore was a means of launching the Muslim alliance axis internationally and of recognizing Bangladesh and closing the civil war chapter.

4. After the Shah of Iran was replaced by Khomeni in 1979, Pakistan strengthened its ties with Saudi Arabia.

5. The most popular slogan was "Nizām-e-Mustafā," literally the rule of the prophet Muhammad.

6. Even such loosely defined "communities" provided insights. Parsees and Pakhtuns had the most cohesive identities. Lahori Christians did not seem

very different from other Lahore groups. Shia respondents had a strong sense of community based on religious affiliation, not geographical location. But Sunni was too broad a religious category, and Punjabi ethnically too vague.

7. The upper-class Lahore sample is biased toward families with at least one woman activist because of the snowball technique used to draw up the sample.

8. Others were widowed or single women living with other relatives.

9. Newspaper reports about women mutilated or killed by brothers, fathers, or other male relatives for presumed illicit sexual relations testify to the extreme control of women within the family. Exercising free will in marriage can provoke equally violent reactions. Oppression in the family is vividly portrayed in women's accounts of their lives, and also in fiction (see Badran and Cooke, 1990).

10. One-third of the Punjabi village women could think of no women they admired.

11. Women also referred to religion in the context of sexual relations within marriage. Several said sex was a religious duty, but this was almost inevitably accompanied by statements that it was a pleasure, natural, part of marriage, etc. One woman, believing that sex was a religious duty because of the man's financial support, obtained employment and denied her husband sex because he no longer maintained her.

12. Some feminists in Pakistan say that people are not religious because their religion includes aspects that are unorthodox or contradict doctrine (e.g., belief in the supernatural power of shrines or trees etc.). But people who practice such rituals *perceive* them as integral to their religion and so such actions cannot be regarded as "nonreligious" in their lives.

13. Women were most affected by the Enforcement of Zinā section of the Hudood Ordinances (1979). In 1993, 75–80 percent of women prisoners in four main jails were charged with Hudood offenses (Human Rights Commission of Pakistan, n.d.: 58). See Jehangir and Jilani, 1990.

14. In 1988–1990, the Pakistan Institute of Labour Education and Research and Shirkat Gah–Women's Resource Centre jointly carried out a study, Female Participation in the Formal Labour Force, interviewing approximately one thousand women. The vast majority knew nothing about the text or implications of the new legislation, directives, and ordinances. When told about the discriminatory Hudood Ordinances (covering extramarital sex, including rape), women responded that if it was Sharī'at (Muslim jurisprudence), it must be all right.

15. Personal observation during a survey of the leather industry in 1992. Several sports apparel and accessories factories in Sialkot (Punjab) and a footwear producer in Karachi had integrated their floor shifts, and managers of some footwear factories in Lahore were considering similar action.

16. Razack (1991, 1994) presents a lucid discussion of the implications of multiple sources of oppression (culture, race, and gender).

17. Women's groups in Pakistan have yet to organize collective support mechanisms for dealing with personal oppression, even for women of their own class. Only very recently has an initiative been established by a new women's group, Bedari, in Islamabad.

18. I am not questioning the religious sincerity of members of politico-religious groups (indeed, I have no reason to presume a lack of conviction) but theirs is a *political* agenda, whose significance outside the political framework would be minimal.

Part III
Agency and Activism

Chapter Ten

Hindu Women's Activism in India and the Questions It Raises

AMRITA BASU

Some of the most powerful images and sounds that live on, since the storm over the Babari Masjid in Ayodhya has abated, are those of Sādhvī Rithambara and Uma Bharati. Their shrill voices filtered through cassette tape recordings goaded Hindu men into violence against Muslims in the course of many riots between 1990 and 1993. On 6 December 1992 these women openly celebrated the destruction of the Babari Masjid. Women's activism has not only found expression among the movement's orators and spokespersons but has also taken hold at the grassroots level. In the early 1990s, thousands of women became skilled in organizing demonstrations, campaigning for elections, and using arms and ammunition.

Perhaps the most startling form of women's activism is their complicity and often direct participation in Hindu violence against Muslim families. In October 1990 in the town of Bijnor in western Uttar Pradesh, Hindu women led a procession through a Muslim neighborhood with *trishūls* (tridents) in hand, shouting bigoted, inflammatory slogans. In the aftermath of the violence in which several hundred people were killed, these women radiated pride at their actions (Basu, 1995c: 35–78; Jeffery and Jeffery, 1994; Jeffery and Jeffery, this volume). In the riots in Bombay in January 1993, Hindu women often justified violence against Muslims. Following police killings of Muslims in the Pratiksha Nagar Housing Colony in Bombay in January 1993, some Hindu women stood on their balconies looking down at the dead bodies of two Muslim women and insisted that these women had died of natural causes, and in any event, "Muslims deserved to die." Hindu women employees of a state-owned corporation threatened to boycott their jobs until the government destroyed a nearby Muslim slum.[1] In a riot in the outskirts of Bhopal during this same period, a woman who was a member of both a municipal corporation and the Bharatiya Janata Party (BJP) had rushed to the scene of the violence and goaded Hindu men into violence against Muslims.

In the first part of this chapter, I ask whether Hindu women's activism derives its distinctive features from the peculiarities of "communalism," and in particular, traits that distinguish "communalism" from "fundamentalism."[2] Women's activism may be partially explained by the fact that the BJP, which typifies the attributes of "communalism," has supported certain women's rights on the basis of political expediency. However, in the second part of the chapter, I suggest that by overemphasizing the distinctive attributes of "communalism," we risk neglecting its affinities with "fundamentalism." The BJP's "modern" political project resuscitates antimodernist forces, and fundamentalists' claims of authentically representing religious traditions are often shaped by the prevailing political context.

The leadership for Hindu women's activism comes from three women's organizations: the Rashtriya Swayamsevak Sangh (RSS)-affiliated Rashtra Sevika Samiti; the Vishwa Hindu Parishad (VHP)-affiliated Durga Vahini; and the Bharatiya Janata Party (BJP)-affiliated women's organization. While the activities of these organizations are so closely interconnected as to be virtually indistinguishable at the local level, their national personas are quite distinct. The Rashtra Sevika Samiti consists of a small, highly dedicated cadre of women whose lives are guided by RSS principles. It refrains from direct involvement in party politics and concentrates on educating girls and women in the principles of Hindu nationalism and on training them to fight for a Hindu state (Sarkar, this volume). The Durga Vahini's mission is to create Hindu solidarity by helping families during periods of hardship and by providing essential social services. Formed in 1980, the BJP's women's organization remained dormant for many years. Since 1989 it has galvanized women around the Babari Masjid or Rām Janambhūmi issue and the BJP's electoral campaigns.

I observed the events of the tumultuous period 1990–1992 while in India studying the growth of Hindu nationalism. I interviewed numerous women who were associated with the Hindu nationalist campaign from the leadership level to rank-and-file members of the three affiliated women's organizations. I visited several towns that had experienced severe riots and interviewed victims and participants in the violence. I joined processions of women as they marched from door to door, campaigning for the BJP in the 1991 parliamentary elections. This chapter draws upon those observations and experiences.

Women's Activism and "Communal Politics"

Certain distinctive features of Hindu "communalism" appear at first glance to promote women's activism. The movement that has emerged since 1989 is led by the BJP, a political party. It is neither controlled nor even deeply influenced by Hindu priests, scriptures, or doctrines. The BJP's major objectives since it was formed in 1980, but with increasing urgency, have been no more complicated than attaining power in New Delhi and in India's regional capitals. The BJP's independence from religious orthodoxy seems to be a key ingredient of women's activism. It frees the party to assume positions that might conflict with Hindu conservatism and to support women's independence when the BJP finds this politically expedient. Other questions, like female seclusion, that are often a staple of "fundamentalist" movements do not figure on the BJP's agenda.

Several scholars have noted that although "fundamentalist" movements are far from monolithic, they tend to converge in their opposition to women's autonomy (Hélie-Lucas, 1994). Most "fundamentalist" movements share a preoccupation with regulating women's sexuality and reproduction (Papanek, 1994). By contrast, Hindu "communalism" is not currently obsessed with controlling Hindu women's sexuality and fertility (though see Sarkar, this volume), although as I suggest below, it is obsessed with Muslim women's fertility. It does not oppose abortion and birth control or seek to regulate the number and spacing of children. It has not differentiated itself from other political parties with respect to its positions on premarital sexuality, adultery, and widow remarriage.

An excellent example of how the BJP's expediency may serve women's interests is evident from its attempt to steal the thunder of the Congress Party on a scheme it was considering in 1995 to improve the position of women. The Congress government in the State of Haryana announced that it would invest Rs 2,500 (approximately $78) in the name of a newborn girl in a savings scheme that would yield Rs 25,000 when she turned eighteen, the legal age of marriage. (The scheme is restricted to unmarried girls in families with annual incomes below Rs 11,000 and with no more than two children (*Economist*, 11 March 1995: 40)).

Once Congress Party chief Narasimha Rao recognized the electoral potential of this issue and promised to extend the scheme to the whole country, the BJP claimed that it had thought up the idea and implemented it first. The BJP government in Rajasthan had in fact launched a similar scheme in 1993 as a population control measure, not to improve girls' conditions. The Rajasthan government had provided a stipend for girls whose mothers or fathers had undergone sterilization, a condition that the Haryana government does not impose. However, the BJP is sufficiently concerned with electoral success that it was happy to broaden the scheme so that it would be more beneficial to women if this entailed electoral advantage.

Expediency has also meant that the positions the BJP women's organization assumes are often inconsistent. Although its members voice the party line on the Rām Janambhūmi movement, it is difficult to identify a single one of the vital issues before the women's movement—dowry, *satī*, female feticide—on which it holds a unified position. Thus contrary to what one might expect, neither its positions nor its actions on women's issues are all conservative. Kusum Mehdre, an active member of the Madhya Pradesh women's organization and Minister for Social Welfare, felt that women should attain economic self-sufficiency by assuming nontraditional roles. Accordingly, she had provided them employment in the production of generators, electronics, and leather goods.[3] Purnima Sethi, the convener of the BJP women's organization in Delhi, reported that she had created an agency that provided women with free legal counsel on marriage, divorce, and dowry, so that they could extricate themselves from abusive domestic situations.

This lack of consistency is also evident in the BJP itself. Although the BJP brought India to the brink of disaster over the question of where and when Rām was born in Ayodhya, it has not articulated a position on questions that "fundamentalists" consider vital in developing a coherent worldview: how to govern the economy, reform the legal system, and create a religious state. Dipankar Gupta (1991: 579) argues:

> Fundamentalism dictates how criminals should be punished; how business should be conducted; what sartorial ensembles are acceptable; in short all the relevant aspects of secular life are now imbued with religious sanction. . . . Unlike fundamentalism, which represents ethnic identities in a near full blown fashion, communalism picks on one or two important characteristics and emotionally surcharges them.

"Communalism" also offers a striking contrast with "fundamentalism" in its relationship to secularism. Whereas most "fundamentalist" movements reject the separation of religion and state, Hindu "communalism" accepts this separation in principle and rejects a religious alternative to the secular state. Partha Chatterjee (1994: 1768) argues:

> The persuasive power, and even the emotional charge the Hindutva campaign appears to have gained in recent years do not depend on its demanding legislative enforcement of ritual or scriptural injunctions, a role for religious institutions in legislative or judicial processes, compulsory religious instruction, state support for religious bodies, censorship of science,

literature and art in order to safeguard religious dogma or any other similar demand undermining the secular character of the existing Indian state.

This point has crucial implications for women because the major alternative to secular law is community-based religious law. In general, safeguards against sexual inequalities are greater in secular than in religious law. By virtue of its supposed commitment to secular principles, the BJP can uphold constitutional protections of sexual equality. The best example of this is the uniform civil code. The BJP has not only emerged as the champion among Indian political parties of a uniform civil code; it has taken over what was historically a major feminist demand. Many feminists now balk at joining hands with the BJP on this issue.

The BJP uses the language of legal and constitutional rights to pit women's rights against minority rights. As Kapur and Cossman (1995: 101) point out, it interprets secularism to mean that Muslims and Hindus should be treated alike, thereby disregarding the vulnerabilities to which Muslims as a minority community are subject. One consequence of juxtaposing the interests of women and minorities is to undermine solidarity among Hindu and Muslim women. "I feel for my Muslim sisters," Uma Bharati commented, "but they do not seem to feel for themselves. Why do they agree to wear the *burqā* (veil)? How can they abide by Muslim law?"[4]

The issue of the uniform civil code provides a lens on some of the most distinctive attributes of Hindu "communalism." Islamic "fundamentalism" in South Asia and the Middle East is inseparable from nationalist opposition to Western domination in its various guises. Women may exemplify what is authentically indigenous and traditional or its antithesis, Westernization and modernity. Deniz Kandiyoti notes that although colonial authorities intervened extensively in the economic and political domains, they provided the colonized greater autonomy in the private sphere. This was the arena that "fundamentalists" claimed as their own (Kandiyoti, 1991b: 8; Devji, 1991). "Fundamentalists'" desire to veil or reveil women in Bangladesh and Pakistan has been a reaction to the supposed Western "unveiling" of women (see Feldman and Rouse, this volume). Similarly, Valentine Moghadam (1994: 13) notes that "fundamentalists" in Iran consider the veil an antidote to the virus of *gharbzadegi*, which is variously translated as "Westoxication," "Westitis," "Euromania," and "Occidentosis."

Hindu nationalists in India, unlike their counterparts in many predominantly Muslim countries, identify their principal enemies as internal rather than external. Even as India has engaged in the process of economic liberalization, and Western economic and cultural influences have grown, Hindu nationalists have not openly expressed anti-Western sentiment.

The issue of the uniform civil code provides the BJP with a means of challenging the legitimacy of the Indian state. Debates about the uniform civil code dating back to the 1950s provide the BJP with an instance of the state's willingness, under Nehru's secular left-leaning leadership, to "appease" religious conservatives. As Zoya Hasan (1993: 7) points out, Nehru passed the Hindu Code Bill, which significantly reformed Hindu law, despite opposition from conservative Hindu groups. By contrast, he acquiesced to pressure from comparable Muslim groups and left Muslim law unreformed. In raising the issue of the uniform civil code, the BJP establishes a parallel between the Congress Party's capitulation to Muslim conservatives in the 1950s and then again in the 1980s around the Shah Bano case (Hasan, this volume).

By decrying the actions of successive Congress regimes on the issue of family law, the BJP seeks to demonstrate its own commitment to secularism and constitutional principles. "Personal law," Uma Bharati argues, "defies the spirit of the constitution."[5] Arun Jaitley, an additional solicitor general and important BJP functionary, argued that the BJP's support for a uniform civil code demonstrated that it alone among political parties respected the Constitution.[6]

More broadly, the BJP often seeks to define itself in relationship to Muslim "fundamentalism" both by asserting its own superiority and by presenting Hindus as beleaguered victims. Hindu women play a key role in both of these constructions. BJP members often express condescension toward Muslims for practicing *parda* (female seclusion) and extol the greater freedom of Hindu than of Muslim women. Mridula Sinha, the president of the all-India BJP women's organization, described the downfall of Hindu women in the aftermath of Muslim rule:

In the Vedic era, the status of women used to be much higher than it is today. You can see from the statue of *adhinarishvakar*, which is half Shiva and half Parvati, that the roles of men and women were considered interdependent and complementary. And women made important contributions to four domains: employment, religion, procreation, and the economy. After the Muslim invasion all of this changed: Hindus were forced to marry off their daughters at much younger ages, they adopted seclusion, and women's role in public life declined.[7]

Similarly, Atal Behari Vajpayee states, "Historically women were respected in this culture; indeed women wrote verses of the Vedas and Vedantas. . . . Later on because of foreign invasions various evils cropped up in our society."[8] Hindu nationalists claim that Muslim rule contributed to a decline in Hindu women's position both by force and example. Hindu men encouraged their wives to retreat into the domestic sphere to protect them from Muslim invaders.

In claiming that the subjugation of Muslim women reveals the backwardness of the Muslim community, the BJP ironically echoes the colonial view that the downtrodden Indian woman signifies the backwardness of Indians. The nineteenth-century social reform movement sought to "uplift" Hindu women in response to this very charge, to demonstrate Indians' fitness to govern themselves. Similarly for the BJP today, the lowly status of Muslim women signifies the inferiority of Muslims.

Joseph Alter (1994) finds in male celibacy an expression of cultural nationalism among Hindus. He argues that Hindus invest in celibacy notions of the fit body, disciplined according to a rigorous regimen that produces a citizen who embodies national integrity and strength. He further argues that the *brahmacharya*, who renounces sexuality, developed in opposition to colonial characterizations of upper-caste Hindu men as emasculated. In response to feelings of powerlessness amidst sociomoral change, Hindu men responded by demonstrating their capacity for self-discipline and self-restraint through celibacy.

In parallel fashion, Hindu "communalists" depict Muslim male sexuality as unrestrained, undisciplined, and antinational. They advocate rigorous measures to control Muslim family size, prohibit polygyny, and punish rapists. Indeed Hindu communalists' most vicious slogans, speeches, and graffiti allude to Muslims' sexual practices. Take, for example, a cassette recorded by Sādhvī Saraswati, whose hysterical tones mimic Sādhvī Rithambara and Uma Bharati. Saraswati begins by decrying polygyny, which she suggests is sanctioned by Muslim law. It turns Muslim women into sexual objects and breeders and results in large Muslim families. For every five children that Hindus have, Muslims have fifty. She continues:

> And who feeds these fifty children? Hindus do! After Muslims divorce, then the *waqf* (religious charity) boards support the children with taxes that we pay. . . . Within twenty-five years you will be living like a poor minority in this country. . . . Muslims have forty-six countries but Hindus have only one, Nepal! If you become a minority in this country then who will provide refugee status for you? None of the neighboring countries provide the kind of orphanage that India does.

By conjoining the backwardness of Muslims with the weakness of the Indian state, the BJP can extol the superiority of Hindus and the Hindu nation. Women, who figure in "fundamentalist" movements as symbols of tradition and continuity with the past, figure in "communal" movements as symbols of progress and modernity.

Dismantling "Communalism" and "Fundamentalism"

As I have argued elsewhere, one of the BJP's major strengths is its ability to speak in many voices (Basu, 1995b). Thus while in some contexts it may present itself as a champion of women's rights, elsewhere it defends conservative Hindu conceptions of women's place. An excellent example both of the BJP's doublespeak and of its selective conservatism concerns the issue of *satī* (widow immolation). In the aftermath of the Roop Kanwar satī in Rajasthan in 1987, the BJP was closely associated with the pro-satī lobby. In this context, it played the role that I have argued is often associated with "fundamentalist" positions: it sought justification for satī in Hindu scriptures, idealized women's roles as dutiful wives, and accused feminists of being *azād* (promiscuous) Westernized women.

Both the RSS and the Rashtra Sevika Samiti are also characterized by some of the features that are associated with "fundamentalism." In contrast to the BJP women's organization, the Rashtra Sevika Samiti possesses a coherent worldview and rashtra sevikas enjoy a distinctive lifestyle. Like many religious nationalist groups in the Middle East and South Asia, the Rashtra Sevika Samiti offers women the opportunity to remain unmarried and spend their lives in the company of other women.

Although the women's organizations of the RSS, BJP, and Durga Vahini are independent of one another in principle, they are closely affiliated in practice. At the leadership level, some of the most prominent women members of the BJP—Vijayraje Scindia, Uma Bharati, Mridula Sinha—are of Rashtra Sevika background. At the local level, these organizations seem to have overlapping memberships in that the same women participate in the activities that any one of these organizations sponsors.

Perhaps the issue that most reveals the BJP's affinity with "fundamentalist" movements is its anxiety about the moral corruption that modernity entails. For Hindu communalists, political and sexual morality are deeply intertwined. A central theme running through Rithambara's cassettes is the notion that India has lost its moral bearings. "Things have deteriorated to the point that everything is now bought and sold, minds, bodies, religion, and even the honor of our elders, sisters, mothers, and sons," she cries out. "We cannot auction our nation's honor in the market of party politics." In a sweeping gesture, Rithambara ingeniously links the corruption of the political process, capitalist development, and sexual objectification.

Another expression of the women's organization concern for sexual morality is around the issue of pornography. Purnima Sethi reported that the BJP women's organization for Delhi state, over which she presided, had organized a major campaign to ban "obscene" publications.[9] It had organized raids of three hundred establishments that were displaying "obscene" material and had pressured the press commissioner into confiscating this material. In Delhi, Lucknow, Bhopal, and other cities, BJP women organized direct-action campaigns that entailed blackening billboards that displayed women's bodies. The BJP has also demanded that the board of film certification censor vulgarity in Indian cinema. According to Shashi Ranjan, president of the BJP film cell, "Mainstream cinema is being shamelessly imbued with innuendo and vulgarity which is threatening to strike at the very core of our culture so steeped in decency and decorum" (*Indian Express*, 8 February 1994).

The Rām Janambhūmi movement and the events that surround it have given expression to some very conservative ideas that cloak themselves in religious garb. The Gita Press in Gorakhpur published a series of cheap, readable books on the proper roles of Hindu women. They are written in the form of treatises that draw upon the authority of religious scriptures. Portions are in Sanskrit, which are then translated into Hindi. Some chapters are written in question-and-answer format: a disciple poses questions to which he or she receives responses, presumably from religious authorities. The books lay out codes of conduct for women around minutiae of social life: how a woman should behave around her relatives, what she should eat while pregnant, what ornaments she should wear after marriage, and whether she should use birth control.

The series' central message for women is the importance of devotion to their families and the dangers that await those who refuse to conform. One book, *How to Lead a Householder's Life* (Ramsukhdas, 1992a), states that misery awaits the bride who chooses her own husband, and sisters who demand a share in their father's property. It counsels the daughter-in-law to accept the harsh treatment of her mother-in-law and "to pay attention to the comfort of her husband, even at the cost of her own comfort." "What should the wife do if her husband beats her and troubles her?" the disciple asks. The response: "The wife should think that she is paying her debt of her previous life and thus her sins are being destroyed and she is becoming pure" (Ramsukhdas, 1992a: 44–50). Another question raised is whether a widow should remarry. The response: it is "beastliness" for the family to remarry her when she is no longer a virgin and thus cannot be offered "as charity" to anyone else. The main point is that a woman's purity must be safeguarded after marriage, when there is the risk of her acting independently. *Nari Siksha* (Women's Education) (Poddar, 1992) voices the same theme in its open support for satī. In these texts the fear of the widow's attainment of economic independence echoes Muslim "fundamentalists'" worries about Shah Bano gaining maintenance payments from her husband.

Another book, *Disgrace of Mother's Prowess* (Ramsukhdas, 1992b), opposes abortion on grounds that it denies the unborn child the possibility of *mokshā* (liberation through rebirth) and thus constitutes a sin. Ramsukhdas argues that the sin of abortion is twice as great as the sin of killing a Brahman. Thus a man whose wife has an abortion must disown her. The only acceptable form of birth control, he continues, is celibacy.

These books echo many of the ideas that are associated with "fundamentalism." First, they juxtapose Indian values with Western values and emphasize the links between women's biological and social roles. *Nari Siksha* in particular engages in a diatribe against Western feminism for supposedly destroying the family and with it the moral backbone of society (Poddar, 1992). It insists upon the sanctity of motherhood for Hindu women and enjoins them to reject Western notions of liberation. *Nari Siksha* states that for a woman to become *satī* (revered as a devoted wife), she must possess *dharma* (faith) and treat her husband like a god. Among other things this entails cooking well for guests and in-laws, rising early to clean the house, and demonstrating deference to in-laws.

It is difficult to know whether the BJP combine has any direct connection to the authors or publishers of these books. But even if these new voices of Hindu conservatism have no direct link to the family of RSS organizations, the BJP and its affiliates have created a climate that promotes such views.

Although I have used the concepts of "communalism" and "fundamentalism" in hopes of achieving precision, the terms are imprecise and heavily laden with unintended meanings. First, both "fundamentalism" and "communalism" are pejorative terms. It is difficult to understand views that one assumes are irrational. It is also difficult to decouple the concepts of "communalism" and "fundamentalism" from religion, even though the growth of "fundamentalism" and "communalism" have more to do with conflicts over the distribution of power and wealth than with religion per se. Furthermore, the beliefs and practices to which "fundamentalists" and "communalists" refer are selectively filtered from religious doctrines that afford many interpretations.[10]

The connotations of the term "fundamentalism" are especially troublesome (Metcalf, this volume). Through habitual usage, "fundamentalism" has come to be identified almost exclusively with Islam, to the disregard of other religious fundamentalisms, among other places in the United States. A tendency to brand the entire Islamic world "fundamentalist" ignores the experiences of the Muslim countries that are not "fundamentalist." It is also erroneous to assume that "fundamentalists," unlike "communalists," are disinterested in political power. Indeed, they have often compromised their principled commitments to women's seclusion on grounds of political expediency. In Pakistan, for example, although the Jama'at-i-Islami had previously opposed the principle of a woman head of state, by 1965 it had supported a woman presidential candidate because of electoral considerations (Mumtaz, 1994: 232). Similarly, despite the decision of the Islamic state in Iran to remove women from public office in the 1980s, it organized four thousand *"basīj"* women into a militia to guard government ministries and banks (Moghadam, 1991: 278). Moreover it would be wrong to assume the absence of women's activism in "fundamentalist" movements. There are several accounts of women's active support for the Iranian revolution, including its veiling of women. Margot Badran (1994) describes a group of conservative women in Egypt who justify women's political participation on grounds of religious commitment. Khawar Mumtaz (1991) shows that in Pakistan in the 1980s and 1990s, "fundamentalist" women associated with the Jama'at-i-Islami opposed feminism for eroding the barriers between male and female worlds because their own activism was premised upon sexual segregation. We simply do not have the evidence to conclude that women's activism is greater in "communal" than in "fundamentalist" movements.

There is also a danger of implying that "communalism" represents a progressive force that encourages women's activism and empowerment, whereas "fundamentalism" does the opposite. This comparison draws on the assumption that Hinduism compares favorably with Islam in its views on women's place. Several scholars have noted that Hinduism rejects notions of women's inherent weakness and considers them powerful and thus potentially dangerous (Wadley, 1977). The varied personalities of female deities in Hinduism may inspire a range of female personas in political life. Ascetic women have the freedom to remain single, travel extensively, and engage in worldly pursuits (Denton, 1991). But even for "ordinary" Hindu women, religious devotion has always provided a culturally sanctioned escape from domestic drudgery and opportunity for self-realization. However, the qualities of Hinduism cannot explain women's activism in communal politics. The BJP has taken a decentered, pluralist religious tradition and rendered it more centralized. Given its willingness to transform Hinduism in such far-reaching ways, the BJP is hardly bound by religious doctrines on questions concerning women. Islam too can be interpreted in diverse ways: some Muslim feminists have emphasized its emancipatory features; fundamentalists have found within it justification for sexually repressive practices.

Both "communalism" and "fundamentalism" are responses to the strains of modernity: the erosion of state legitimacy, the integration of postcolonial economies into the global capitalist system, and the influx of Western cultural influences. But at the same time, both "communalism" and "fundamentalism" seek justification from the past. Both employ gendered images of motherhood to romanticize the past and suggest continuity with it. Hindu "communalism" also finds in motherhood imagery a basis in religion because of the ways in which Hinduism worships mother goddesses. But motherhood imagery is not confined to "communalism" or "fundamentalism"; it is a staple of nationalist movements. Both by virtue of its stated commitments and its actions, the BJP can best be described as a religious nationalist party. The BJP asserts a deep affinity between Hindus and the nation-state. This supposed affinity rests upon the notion that Hindus were the original and thus the most legitimate inhabitants of India. Just as the BJP employs an organic conception of citizenship, so too it assumes that the Muslim minority, and the Congress Party, which supposedly appeases it, are implicitly antinational.

In many respects the recent growth of majoritarian nationalism signals a response to the steady growth of minority nationalism in India. Historically, the BJP's predecessor, the Jan Sangh, often mobilized around Hindu issues like cow protection and mandatory use of Hindi following periods of minority linguistic and ethnic mobilization. In the recent past, the backdrop of secessionist movements in the Punjab and Kashmir seem to have played a key role in the BJP's renewed commitment to Hindu nationalism. The growth of minority nationalisms is vital to explaining how the BJP can convincingly present Hindus, who dominate economic and political life in India, as beleaguered victims.

This chapter opened by remarking on the unusual extent and nature of women's activism around the Rām Janambhūmi issue. I argued that women's activism may be partially explained by the BJP's expedient support for certain (Hindu) women's rights. However, expediency is by definition dual-faceted: it encourages the BJP to take up women's rights, and allows the BJP to ignore, disparage, and undermine them.

The BJP is ultimately less committed to women's rights than to the denial of Muslim rights. While it highlights the inequities of Muslim law, it is remarkably silent about the discriminatory traits of Hindu law.[11] Thus Arun Jaitley defended differences in inheritance rights of sons and daughters on grounds that women's equal rights to inheritance would fragment family landholdings. There are many indications that the BJP's interpretation of a uniform civil code would be modeled on Hindu law. Furthermore, the BJP has championed women's rights in only a narrowly legalistic fashion. Its women's organization has issued statements condemning violence against women but has not campaigned to oppose it. For example, it accepts the dowry system and avoids the issue of dowry deaths.

At this stage it is important to refine the concept of women's activism. Many of the women who took part in processions, campaigns, and riots seemed exhilarated by the opportunity for activism that this provided: leaving their homes, putting aside domestic work, and devoting themselves to a cause. Particularly for lower-middle-class housewives, who form an important part of the BJP's constituency, Hindu nationalist mobilization offered a rare opportunity for self-realization.

But Hindu women's activism has not necessarily challenged patterns of sexual inequality within the home and the world. Nor are women necessarily drawn to the BJP simply because it advocates their rights. Mridula Sinha stated emphatically, "For Indian women, liberation means liberation from atrocities. It doesn't mean that women should be relieved of their duties as wives and mothers. Women should stop demanding their rights all the time and think instead in terms of their responsibilities to the family."[12] Mohini Garg, the all-India secretary of the BJP women's organization, echoed this point: "We want to encourage our members not to think in terms of individual rights but in terms of responsibility to the nation."[13]

Indeed, a striking feature of women's participation in the activities of the BJP's women's organization is women's reenactment of conventional sex-linked roles within the broader public arena. Nirupuma Gour, the organization's secretary in Uttar Pradesh, reported that in preparation for the BJP procession to Ayodhya in October 1990 (the dress rehearsal for 1992), women had developed an elaborate ritual for sending the "*kar sevaks*" (volunteer workers) like warriors to the battlefield.[14] They would congregate at designated spots at the train stations with food, portable stoves, and other paraphernalia. As the men boarded the trains, the women would garland them, place *tilaks* (vermilion marks) on their foreheads, and give them freshly prepared hot food. She said that women were instructed to prepare up to fifty thousand food packets each day. Gour estimates that five to six thousand women arrived in Lucknow from all over the country. Many others could not travel to Ayodhya because transportation was inadequate, but those who reached Lucknow assumed responsibility for protecting men from repression. Thus, for example, when trains approached Ayodhya, the women would sound the alarms to stop them; the men would disembark immediately while the women would confront the train conductors. At Ayodhya, the women would encircle the men to prevent the police from wielding their *lāthīs* (bamboo sticks). When the *kar sevaks* broke through the police cordons and climbed atop the Babari Masjid, however, the women were absent. I asked Mala Rustogi, a member of the Durga Vahini in Lucknow, why the women had not participated in the culmination of their actions. She responded that it would have been undignified for Hindu women to be climbing a mosque in their *sārīs*.[15]

The particular roles that the BJP assigned to women in its very expensive, elaborate electoral campaigns are also significant. Whereas men had primary responsibility for addressing large public gatherings, women engaged in door-to-door campaigning that brought them into contact with housewives who might have been less willing to speak with men.

Women's reenactment of their private roles in the public arena may also play a particularly important place in the context of Hindu nationalism, which has sought to challenge the public/private divide in other ways. The BJP's central platform during the period of its ascendance to power in the late 1980s was its demand that the Congress government demolish the Babari Masjid in Ayodhya and build a Rām temple in its place. Implicit in this demand was the BJP's attempt to accord centrality in political life to questions of religious faith. This proves especially difficult in a democratic context such as India, where the state may intervene to prevent political parties from bringing religious matters into politics. Women are well positioned to further the BJP's project. During the 1991 elections when the election commissioner had prohibited the BJP from shouting religious slogans, I marched with processions of women who appeared to be observing these dictates on the streets. But as soon as they entered the courtyards of people's homes, cries of *"Jāī Shrī Rām!"* (Victory to the Lord Rām!) and *"Mandir vahān banāyenge!"* (We will build a temple there!) filled the air. In this vital phase of Hindu nationalism, women served as emissaries of private-domain religion into the public sphere and of the BJP's supposed religious commitments into the home and family. BJP leaders felt that women's electoral support would affirm the party's religious commitment because, they claimed, women were more devout than men.

What of women themselves? What did they gain from being assigned a role that enabled them to venture out of their homes without challenging norms of sexual subordination? The experiences of Mala Rustogi are instructive. Rustogi said that when she first began working with the Durga Vahini in Lucknow in 1989, she feared the opposition of her husband and in-laws, for her daughter was only three years old at the time. To her surprise, they supported her. She described a newfound sense of pleasure in serving others: "Serving one's husband is expected of women and of course it is important. But serving a third person whom you don't know and aren't expected to serve is much more exciting—for just that reason." Her comment captures some of the traits that were mirrored in women's activism: their experience of self-affirmation through self-sacrifice, and their empowerment through public-sphere activism, which ultimately renewed their commitment to their domestic roles.

Some of the changes under way in Indian society might help explain Hindu women's acceptance of their ambiguous placement between public and private domains. The growth of the BJP coincides with unprecedented economic liberalization, which has truncated the public sphere and redefined the private arena. Women have access to larger markets than ever before, stocked with a range of goods that convey the allure of freedom: ready-made clothes, prepared foods, and gadgets to simplify housework. The Indian women who appear in advertisements for these products have light hair and skin, wear Western or Westernized clothing, and convey a sexy demeanor. Release from domesticity also comes from women's increased employment, particularly among the middle classes in the service sector. Consumerism and employment both lend support to women's growing involvement in the political domain.

The BJP and its women's wing give voice to profound middle-class ambivalence about these social and economic changes. While embracing the modernist project of capitalist expansion, they worry incessantly about the excessive individual freedom that it enables. Indeed, the BJP's changing economic policy is an excellent indicator of this ambivalence. Under the influence of the RSS, it has sought to promote *svadeshī*, a nationalist response to globalization that encourages self-sufficiency in certain areas of the economy. But it does so without repudiating economic liberalization altogether.

Many of the forms of women's activism that have been identified with Hindu nationalism are mirrored within anticolonial nationalism in India. Within the anticolonial movement we find very similar patterns of women's entering the public sphere without challenging the norms of sexual segregation and seclusion. Although the most exalted images are Gandhian depictions of women's pacifism, there are many instances of women's complicity in violence: in collaborating with the Punjabi revolutionary Bhagat Singh; in the Chatri Sangh in Calcutta in the late 1920s; and in the Chittagong Armoury Raid in the early 1930s. The nationalist revolutionary Subhash Chander Bose formed a women's militia called the Rani of Jhansi Regiment, which trained women in the use of arms and ammunition. Women were also active in revolutionary violence in the Telengana movement in Andhra Pradesh.

Situating Hindu women's activism within a broader context of nationalist mobilization reveals parallels with a range of political movements that make ascribed identity the basis for political mobilization (Moghadam, 1994). There are striking resemblances between Hindu nationalism and some right-wing and fascist movements that harness women's activism around racist and anti-Semitic campaigns.[16] The extent of women's participation in Islamic movements in the Middle East and North Africa is also striking. Sondra Hale (1994) finds that women have been extremely active in the Islamist party in the Sudan; these women find in the Sharī'a justification for their activism and for asserting their rights as women. Similarly the Muslim Sisters in Egypt justify their activism by reference to Islamic principles. Aisha Abd al-Rahman, a well-known Qur'anic scholar, argues that the "truly Islamic" and the "truly feminist" option is neither immodest dress nor identical roles for the sexes in the name of Islam. "The right path is the one that combines modesty, responsibility and integration into public life with the Qur'anic and naturally enjoined distinctions between the sexes" (Hoffman-Ladd, 1987: 37). Muslim women were active in the "turban movement" in Turkey, which opposed the legal prohibition of the Islamic head scarf for women students; this movement played a vital role in radicalizing the Islamic cause (Toprak, 1994). In all these cases religious idioms provided women with the means of opposing the denigrating forces of Western modernity.

The global dimensions of religious nationalism are striking. The BJP's anti-Muslim propaganda is legitimated by the role of the United States in the Gulf War and the anti-Muslim sentiment that predated and succeeds it, just as Islamic "fundamentalism" finds justification in the U.S. exertion of cultural superiority, political control, and economic dominance in the Middle East. In countries like Iran, leaders can mobilize Muslim sentiment in opposition to Western economic and cultural domination.

In its emphasis on the transnational character of Islamic "fundamentalism," Hindu nationalism finds justification for its own transnational ambitions. The Rām Janambhūmi movement provided the occasion for the development of far-reaching networks among Indians in North America, Africa, Europe, and other regions. These networks can build upon the growth of two groups within the expatriate Indian community: business people who seek ways of demonstrating their nationalist commitments, and self-employed business people for whom Hindu nationalism is a response to racism and discrimination abroad.

Conclusion

Certain features of "communalism," such as its support for a uniform civil code, encourage women's activism, but women do not achieve lasting gains from these spurts of activism. Their intense identification with "communal movements" is likely to be short-lived.

The contrasts between "communalism" and "fundamentalism" diminish when we explore the ways in which both are influenced by the economic and political context. Of particular importance are electoral influences. The more committed groups are to exercising power, the more expedient they are likely to be in interpreting religion. This in turn has extremely significant implications for women. The more a group believes itself to be the authentic voice of religion, the more likely it is to treat women as symbols of tradition. Conversely, the more committed a group is to exercising power democratically, the more women count numerically as a means of demonstrating popular support and winning elections. This in turn might entail appealing to women's gender interests.

Furthermore, "communalism" and "fundamentalism" are both essentialist concepts: they infer from religious identities a stable set of values and beliefs.

In India, "fundamentalism" is an even more pejorative concept than "communalism." This in turn is partly a reflection of the very influence of Hindu nationalism. The term "fundamentalism" denotes the beliefs and practices of Muslims; "communalism," those of Hindus. The BJP has strengthened the assumption that Muslims compare particularly unfavorably with Hindus in the treatment of women. Thus the use of the concepts of "fundamentalism" and "communalism" effectively pits Islam against Hinduism. Both terms are so premised on assumptions of primordialism that no amount of creative reinterpretation can sufficiently launder them of it.

In highlighting the modern political ambitions of Hindu "communalism," it is impossible to ignore the complicated ways in which this modernizing project restores, utilizes, and reinterprets traditional forces. Even though the BJP's ambitions are wholly modern—a powerful, expansionist state, integration with the global capitalist system—it also strengthens antimodernist impulses. Thus Vijayraje Scindia at one moment supports a uniform civil code that will accord women legal rights and at another moment suggests that *satī* provides the normative ideal to which Hindu women should aspire.

Hindu nationalists have turned to women as exemplifications of the contradictory qualities they seek to project: a rootedness in the past and a commitment to a modern India in the future. But Hindu women can exemplify these two very different qualities only by taking on another quality: a willingness to render Muslims into dehumanized Others.

Notes

I received valuable comments on an earlier draft of this chapter from participants at the conference Appropriating Gender: Women and Religious Nationalism in South Asia, held at Rockefeller Conference and Study Center in Bellagio, August 1994; the conference Gender, Nation and the Politics of Culture in India, at Cornell University, 1 April 1995; and at the Peace and World Security Studies workshop at Hampshire College on 3 April 1995. I am particularly grateful to Mary Katzenstein for her encouragement and advice, and to Barbara Metcalf for her forceful denunciation of the concept of fundamentalism. I received research and writing support from the Amherst College Research Award and the John D. and Catherine T. MacArthur Foundation.

1. See Bhaktal (1993: 12–13). Kishwar (1993) describes similar forms of women's violence in the Bombay riots in December 1992 and February 1993, and Shah et al. (1993) describe the complicity of Hindu women in the Surat riots in December 1992.

2. As I indicate later in my paper, I find the terms "communalism" and "fundamentalism" of limited analytic utility because of their pejorative connotations. I much prefer the terms religious nationalism, or Keddie's "new religious politics" or "religiopolitics" (see Keddie, 1997). However while I use the concept "religious nationalism" whenever possible, I must

use the terms communalism and fundamentalism when I seek to compare the two phenomena.

3. Interview with Kusum Mehdre, Bhopal, 14 June 1991.
4. Interview with Uma Bharati, New Delhi, 17 December 1991.
5. Ibid.
6. Interview with Arun Jaitley, New Delhi, 11 April 1991.
7. Interview with Mridula Sinha, New Delhi, 7 February 1991.
8. Speech delivered at the BJP plenary meeting, Jaipur, December 1991.
9. Interview with Purnima Sethi, New Delhi, 27 March 1991.
10. On this question, see Ahmed (1992). On the Pakistani context, see Gardezi (1990); Mumtaz and Shaheed (1987); Rouse (1986); and Shaheed and Mumtaz (1990).
11. Agnes (1995) similarly points to the failures of the Indian women's movement to redress some of the sexist aspects of Hindu law. If two Hindus marry under the Special Marriages Act, according to a 1954 amendment, the secular code that grants equal rights to men and women—the Indian Succession Act of 1925—does not apply. Instead, the couple is governed by the Hindu Succession Act, which grants men coparcenary rights (the rights to the family's ancestral property). Under the Hindu Adoption and Maintenance Act, a Hindu wife can neither adopt nor give a child in adoption. In reformed Hindu law, although marriages are in principle monogamous, in practice they may be polygynous, and co-wives are denied the protection that they are afforded in Hindu customary law.
12. Interview with Mridula Sinha, New Delhi, 7 February 1991.
13. Interview with Mohini Garg, New Delhi, 11 April 1991.
14. Interview with Nirupuma Gour, Lucknow, 5 January 1992.
15. Interview with Mala Rustogi (pseudonym), Lucknow, 28 December 1992. Other references to Rustogi's views are drawn from the same interview.
16. There are many parallels between women's activism in Hindu nationalism and in German fascism; see Koonz (1987); Bridenthal, Grossman, and Kaplan (1984). See Blee (1991) and Klatch (1987) for parallels with women's activism in racist and right-wing organizations in the United States.

Chapter Eleven

Motherhood as a Space of Protest

Women's Political Participation in Contemporary Sri Lanka

MALATHI DE ALWIS

DURING THE YEARS 1987 TO 1991, Sri Lanka witnessed an uprising by nationalist Sinhala youth (the JVP or Janata Vimukhti Party) and reprisals by the state that gripped the country in a stranglehold of terror. The militants randomly terrorized or assassinated anyone who criticized them or supposedly collaborated with the state. The state similarly, but on a much larger scale, murdered or "disappeared" anyone it suspected of being a "subversive," which included thousands of young men, some young women, and a number of left-wing activists, playwrights, lawyers, and journalists who were either monitoring or protesting the state's violation of human rights. Bodies rotting on beaches, smoldering in grotesque heaps by the roadsides, and floating down rivers were a daily sight during the height of state repression from 1988 to 1990. It was in such a context that the Mothers' Front, a grassroots women's organization with an estimated membership of more than twenty-five thousand women, was formed in July 1990 to protest the "disappearance" of approximately sixty thousand young and middle-aged men. Its only demand was for "a climate where we can raise our sons to manhood, have our husbands with us and lead normal women's lives" (*Island*, 9 February 1991). The seemingly unquestionable authenticity of their grief and espousal of "traditional" family values provided the Mothers' Front with an important space for protest unavailable to other organizations critical of state practices.[1]

The Mothers' Front phrased its protest in the vocabulary that was most available to it through its primary positioning within a patriarchally structured society—that of motherhood, which I define here as encompassing women's biological reproduction as well as women's signification as moral guardians, care givers, and nurturers. I fully agree with the argument that maternalist women's peace groups project essentialist views of women that reinforce the notion of biology as destiny and legitimize a sex-role system that, in assigning responsibility for nurture and survival to women alone, encourages masculinized violence and destruction (Enloe, 1989; Hartsock, 1982; Houseman, 1982; Lloyd, 1986). Nevertheless, I think we need to consider carefully the reasons that "motherist movements" (Schirmer, 1993) adopt the strategies they do, and what effects they have. In light of such a project, I would like to consider here the contingent usefulness of maternalized protest at a particular moment in Sri Lankan history. However, such an attempt at a positive reading cannot ignore the complex interplay of power within this space that also reinscribed gender and class hierarchies and reinforced majoritarian ethnic identities while those of minorities were erased.

Though the Mothers' Front's agenda remained very limited, its few, brief, and spectacular appearances on the Sri Lankan political stage nevertheless placed a government on the defensive, awoke a nation from a terrorized stupor, and indelibly gendered the discourses of human rights and dissent. It also created a space in which a much larger, nonracist, and more radical protest movement could be launched to overthrow in the general elections of August 1994 an extremely repressive and corrupt government that had been in power for seventeen years.

This chapter will concentrate only on exploring how the Mothers' Front created a space for itself within a predominantly patriarchal political landscape by articulating its protest through the available, familiar, and emotive discourse of motherhood. This space was mediated by a powerful political party that was predominantly male, Sinhala, and middle class. Yet the repertoire of protest employed by these women, albeit under the sign of the mother and mainly limited to tears and curses, was the most crucial component in an assault on a government that had until then held an entire nation at ransom on the pretext of safeguarding the lives of its citizens. It is in this sense that I assert the contingent value of the Mothers' Front's repertoire of protest.

The Mothers' Front

Tears . . . are common to all. Yet, there is nothing more powerful
on earth that can wring tears from others than a mother's tears.

—*Lankadeepa*, 28 June 1992

The first branch of the Mothers' Front was formed on 15 July 1990 in the southern district of Matara, a region severely affected by "disappearances."[2] The meeting was held under the auspices of Mangala Samaraweera and Mahinda Rajapakse, members of Parliament and of the main opposition party, the Sri Lanka Freedom Party (SLFP), from Matara and Hambantota, respectively. Fifteen hundred women from the district elected officers to coordinate the group's activities. They decided to work out of Mr. Samaraweera's home because the climate of violence warranted some protective measures.[3] A majority of the women were severely traumatized: "At that time we were like children constantly needing to be told what to do. Sometimes I would come away from one of our meetings not remembering a single matter that was discussed," commented one officer.[4] Within six months, branches of the Mothers' Front had been set up in ten other Districts (often under the aegis of an SLFP MP). By 1992, Front members numbered twenty-five thousand, most of whom were from rural and semirural areas and of the lower and lower-middle classes, women well acquainted with poverty and hardship.

Initially, the Front's focus was mainly regional and it made little headway, except in compiling systematic and extensive documentation about the "disappeared." Visiting police stations, army camps, and local government offices with lists of the missing and petitioning various state institutions and officials for information produced few results. The women often viewed their reception at such places with a certain resignation and cynicism, tolerating politicians who promised the earth when campaigning but became dismissive when elected, and accepting that the everyday provision of state services was often contingent upon one's wealth and status. Yet, what fueled their pursuance of such activities and their increasing anger at being thwarted was an overriding confidence that their "disappeared" were alive and should be sought before trails grew cold. As one mother eloquently pointed out to me, "I gave birth to that boy. Surely, won't *I* sense it if he dies?" The first seeds of protest were sown in such moments of stubborn refusal to give up hope, to concede failure. The "absence of bodies," noted Jennifer Schirmer (1989: 5), creates a "presence of protest." In early 1991 the Mothers' Front showed "its muscles" (*Island*, 27 January 1991) by targeting the epicenter of power—the capital Colombo—and capturing the attention of the entire country.

A 19 February rally in a Colombo suburb at which thousands of these "chronic mourners" (Schirmer, 1989: 25), clad in white and holding mementos of their "disappeared," demanded that the nation not forget them or their "disappeared." The rally also commemorated the death of well-known actor, newscaster, and journalist Richard de Zoysa, who had been abducted, tortured, murdered, and dumped upon a beach by a paramilitary squad the year before. His mother, Dr. Manorani Saravanamuttu, who had publicly accused senior police officers of being involved in her son's abduction, had returned from self-exile at this time and was invited to serve as the president of the National Committee of the Mothers' Front. The nature of the Front, its seemingly conservative and apolitical rhetoric, and the unorthodox avenues of protest it subsequently employed made a counterattack by the state especially difficult and complicated. Unable to contain the Front through its usual authoritarian practices, the state was constantly on the defensive, dealing in counterrhetoric, counterrallies, and counterritual.

Counterrhetoric

As in the case of the Madres of Argentina or the GAM (Mutual Support Group for the Reappearance of our Sons, Fathers, Husbands, and Brothers) of Guatemala, the rhetoric of protest used by the Mothers' Front can be read as confronting a repressive state by revealing the contradictions between the state's own rhetoric and practices. By appealing for a return to the "natural" order of family and motherhood, the women were openly embracing patriarchal stereotypes that primarily defined them through familial/domestic subject positions such as wife and mother. However, by accepting the responsibility to nurture and preserve life, which is also valorized by the state (de Alwis, 1994), they revealed the ultimate transgression of the state: it was denying women the opportunity to mother by its resort to clandestine tactics (cf. Schirmer, 1989: 28).

The Sri Lankan state's major rhetorical counter to the Front's implicit accusation is very interesting. On the day of the Mothers' Front's first rally in Colombo, President Premadasa expressed sympathy "with the mothers whose children have been led astray by designing elements." He continued, "Many now in custody are being rehabilitated" (*Daily News*, 19 February 1991). In a similar vein, Minister of State for Defence Ranjan Wijeratne pontificated: "Mothers are not expected to stage demonstrations. Mothers should have looked after their children. They failed to do that. They did not know what their children were doing. They did not do that and now they are crying" (*Daily News*, 15 February 1991). Both men were suggesting that the women had not been good mothers, but the president was also suggesting that because of their deficiencies the state had taken on their responsibilities by rehabilitating their children. By bringing in notions of rehabilitation, the president was deflecting the women's accusations of the state's complicity in the "disappearances" and killings.

Government officials used various rhetorical ploys to slander the Mothers' Front. The most vociferous was Ranjan Wijeratne, who denounced the Front as "subversive" and "anti-government" (*Daily News*, 14 March 1991); characterized it as "against the security forces who saved democracy" (*Daily News*, 23

February 1991); threatened to "get at the necks of those using the Mothers' Front" (*Island*, 20 February 1991); and stepped up police surveillance of its leaders (*Sunday Times*, 29 March 1991).[5] The SLFP was also consistently accused by government-owned media and various government ministers of trying to use the Mothers' Front to further its power (*Daily News*, 19 February, 23 March 1991; *Sunday Observer*, 24 February 1991). The state's central thrust was (1) to undermine the primary subject position of the women by suggesting that they had been "inadequate" mothers and (2) to undermine their credibility by insinuating that their organization was a puppet of a political party.

Counterrallies

The state attempted to disrupt the first Mothers' Front rally by banning demonstrations and creating an atmosphere of distrust and panic with suggestions of possible bomb explosions and an LTTE (Liberation Tigers of Tamil Eelam) infiltration of Colombo. At the second rally in Colombo a month later to commemorate International Women's Day, the state implemented a different countertactic under the aegis of First Lady Hema Premadasa: a rally in another part of the city to which women were bussed in from various Sēvā Vanithā units affiliated to government departments, especially the armed forces.[6] While the Mothers' Front mourned the "disappeared," the women at the state counterrally mourned the deaths of male relatives who had been killed by the JVP in the south and by Tamil militants in the north and east. The state-owned *Daily News* (9 March 1991) carried an entire page of photographs of the state rally but no mention of the Mothers' Front rally.

In July 1992, the United National Party (UNP) government even inaugurated a UNP Mothers' Front in the Gampaha District, the stronghold of the Bandaranaike clan and thus synonymous with the SLFP. At its first meeting, the only female minister in the cabinet, Health and Women's Affairs Minister Renuka Herath, categorically declared, "It was the children of those mothers who slung photographs and marched who killed the children of you innocent mothers" (*Divaina*, 27 July 1992). She promised financial support for the members of the Gampaha District Mother's Front and to erect memorials to their children's bravery. The women were still waiting to have their promises fulfilled when the government was overthrown two years later.

Religious Rituals as Resistance

The tactic of the Mothers' Front that most unnerved the government, especially the president, who was known to be extremely superstitious, was the skillful use of religious ritual as resistance. As Marx has so perceptively pointed out, "Religious distress is at the same time the expression of real distress and the *protest* against real distress" (quoted in Comaroff, 1985: 252). Most families of the "disappeared" were intimate with such manifestations of religious distress, which included beseeching gods and goddesses, saints, and holy spirits with special novenas (Catholic masses), penances, offerings, donations, and the chanting of religious verses over a period of months; taking vows, making pilgrimages, and performing *bodhi pūjās* (offerings to the Bo tree); and resorting to sorcery and the placement of charms and curses on those deemed responsible.

The SLFP first realized the powerful potential of publicized religious practices when members of the Mothers' Front participated in the SLFP-organized 180-mile *pāda yātrā* (march) to protest government policies and human rights violations, in March and April 1992. The absolute abandon and passion that the mothers displayed at the Devinuwara and Kataragama *dēvālés* (temples), as they broke coconuts and beseeched the deities to return their sons and husbands, and heaped curses on those who had taken them away, surprised the SLFP organizers and provided tremendous photo opportunities for the media (e.g., *Divaina*, 4 April 1992). The president apparently took this collective and ritualized display personally; on the advice of his Malayalee swami, he immediately participated in a counterritual in which he was bathed by seven virgins. Sirimavo Bandaranaike (the leader of the SLFP) publicly linked the two events at the second national convention of the Mothers' Front on 23 June 1992, and her daughter Chandrika Kumaratunga suggested at the convention that the mothers' curses during the march had effected the sudden and much-publicized disclosures of former deputy inspector general of police Premadasa Udugampola, who had masterminded the paramilitary hit squads that terrorized the southern and central provinces of Sri Lanka at the height of the JVP uprising in 1989–1991.

The ritual of religious resistance that received the most publicity and generated much comment was the Dēva Kaññalawwa (the beseeching of the gods), which took place in the afternoon of 23 June 1992. The Mothers' Front had picked the date because it was President Premadasa's birthday and coincided with the commencement of his extravagant brainchild: the *Gam Udāwa* (village reawakening) celebrations. Not surprisingly, therefore, many of the wrathful speeches at the convention focused on his autocratic style of governance and megalomania. Afterward, the SLFP provided lunch to the mothers and bused them to the Kaliamman *kōvil* (temple) at Modera, where they were greeted by locked gates and a battalion of police standing guard. SLFP MP Alavi Moulana instructed the first group of mothers to break their coconuts outside the gates. Almost simultaneous with this and the loud chanting of "sādhu, sādhu" that rent the air, the gates were hastily opened by a somewhat chagrined senior police officer, though access to the inner sanctum was still denied. The small premises soon became packed with weeping and wailing women, many of whom boldly cursed Premadasa and his government. Asilin, one of the mothers and my neighbor at the time, chanted over and over, "Premadasa, see this coconut all smashed into bits. May your head too be splintered into a hundred bits, so heinous are the crimes you have perpetrated on my child." Another mother wept, saying, "Premadasa, I bore this child in my womb for ten months. May you and your family be cursed not for ten days or ten weeks or ten months or ten years or ten decades but for ten eons."

The passion, the pathos, the power of these weeping, cursing, imploring mothers riveted the entire nation. Not only did the mothers make front-page news the next day and for much of that week but their display of grief was a topic of discussion for several months. Some alternative as well as mainstream Sinhala dailies and Sunday editions began series of articles that focused on individual families of the "disappeared." An editorial warning issued when the Front was founded now seemed prescient: "When mothers emerge as a political force it means that our political institutions and society as a whole have reached a critical moment—the danger to our way of life has surely come closer home" (*Island*, 20 February 1991).

Counterrituals

To ward off the mothers' curses, President Premadasa sought refuge in an elaborate counterritual—the Kiriammāwarungé Dāné (the feeding of milk mothers), an archaic ceremony now connected with the Goddess Pattini.[7] On his birthday, 23 June 1992, the day of the commencement of Gam Udāwa (and the day of the Mothers' Front's Dēva Kaññalawwa at Modera), the president offered alms to sixty-eight (grand)mothers (*Silumina*, 28 June 1992). At the conclusion of Gam Udāwa and another Dēva Kaññalawwa organized by the Mothers' Front on a smaller scale at Kalutara, south of Colombo, on 3 July 1992, he offered alms to ten thousand (grand)mothers while North Central Provincial Council Minister for Health and Women's Affairs Rani Adikari chanted the Pattini Kaññalawwa to bring blessings on the president, the armed forces, and the country (*Daily News*, 7 June 1992).[8] Though the commonly held belief is that Pattini is predominantly a guardian against infectious diseases, she is also the "good mother" and ideal wife whose chief aim is to maintain "a just and rationally grounded society" and can thus be read as a counterpoint to the goddess that the Mothers' Front appealed to: the "bad mother" and evil demoness Kali, who deals with sorcery and personal and familial conflicts (Gombrich and Obeyesekere, 1988: 158–60).

It was not only Premadasa who was disturbed by such rituals. The urbane minister of industries, science, and technology Ranil Wickremasinghe, warned, "If your children have disappeared, it is all right to beseech the gods. After all, if there is no one else to give you succor it is fitting to look to one's gods. But if one conducts such Dēva Kaññalawwas with thoughts of hate and revenge, it could turn into a *hūniyam* (black magic) and backfire on you" (*Divaina*, 13 July 1992). Ironically, despite such dire warnings and counter-rituals, Premadasa was the victim of a suicide bomber before a year was out. A few days after his death, a beaming Asilin came to see me with a comb of plantains (considered to be an auspicious gift). "He died just like the way I cursed him," she said triumphantly.

Tears and Curses

The complicated interplay between the Mothers' Front and the state operated on a common terrain that took for granted the authenticity and efficacy of a mother's tears and curses. Though the state could retaliate that these women were not "good" mothers and that they were the pawns of a political party, it could not deny the mothers' right to weep or to curse because, after all, that was what was expected of women. Rather, when these women wept or cursed en masse and in public, it became an embarrassment for the state, which then organized its own "Fronts" to engage in counterrituals. In a context of violence and terror, the tears and curses of the mothers finally stirred a nation and shamed a government.

It is important to bear in mind that tears and curses differed in significa-tion. A mother's tears are a familiar, emotive trope in the arts and a part of the public practices of grieving, such as at funerals. A mother's curses are a famil-iar yet less discussed practice mostly restricted to the private, religious domain. The SLFP had manipulated the emotive power of tears at the Moth-ers' Front rallies it had organized, but it was the spontaneity of the women themselves, during the *pāda yātrā*, that had suggested an alternative avenue of protest that was not merely emotive but powerful—in its staging as well as in the ferocity of its call for revenge. The presumption inherent in a curse—that it could bring about change through the intercession of a deity—complicates efforts (for a believer such as the president) to stall such change, for the curse now transcends the human. The use of curses as public protest and the use of religious ritual as resistance not only had no precedent in Sri Lanka but could circumvent emergency laws that were applicable to standard forms of political protest such as demonstrations and rallies.[9] To ban the right to religious worship was something an autocratic government that repeatedly defined itself as a protector of the people's interests would not dare to do. Not that the government did not toy with the idea. After all, the gates of the Kaliamman *kōvil* were locked when the Mothers' Front arrived, and the alternative media were quick to highlight such blatant violations of human rights (*Aththa*, 24 June 1992; *Divaina*, 6 July 1992).

For the members of the Mothers' Front, weeping and cursing were nothing new. What was new was that the gaze of an entire nation was upon them and that their cause had achieved national prominence. One could also point out that despite their participation in a mass movement, their activism continued to be limited to tears and curses. It was quite common for politicians at the Mothers' Front rallies to exhort the mothers that it was "time to stop weeping and move beyond," while at the same time congratulating them for having brought about the sudden disclosures by the former deputy inspector general of police, Udugampola, the unnerving of Premadasa, and even the death of Wijeratne. This circumscribing of the mothers can be chiefly attributed to the fact that they had merely exchanged one structure of power riven with gender and class inequalities for another. Socialized within a society that defines women primarily through familial subject positions such as wives and mothers, these women might nevertheless have managed both to mobilize and transcend these categories had they chosen to organize themselves as the Mothers' Fronts in the north and east had done (see below) and as the Madres in Argentina continue to do. Mobilized and funded by a group of men who were representatives of a powerful political party, these women were never pushed to break out of gender and class stereotypes or to form links with other women's groups.

The Sri Lanka Freedom Party and Male Orchestration

On an everyday level and in organizing rallies and rituals, the financial backing and infrastructural support of the SLFP were crucial. Mothers' Front members elected their own officers and ran their regional offices relatively autonomously but remained under the control of their respective SLFP MPs, who provided much of their funding and office space. The SLFP coordinators (such as Mangala Samaraweera) set the agenda for rallies planned in Colombo, handled the advertising, sent out invitations, and hired buses to transport women from various regions of the country. A couturier, Samaraweera was central in designing the Mothers' Front logo: the Sinhala letter *M* containing a mother cradling a baby. He acknowledged that he was instrumental in identifying the Front with the color yellow because yellow was not associated with any Sri Lankan political party and because it echoed the ribbons displayed in the United States that symbolized hope for the return of the American hostages held in Iran. His office drafted petitions for the Front—demanding an independent commission to inquire into "disappearances," and calling for the state to issue death certificates and to compensate the families of the "disappeared"—and organized the lobbying to bring these demands into effect.

It was the events held in Colombo, however, that made the SLFP/male dominance of the Mothers' Front the most visible. The following account of the 19 February rally in Nugegoda (a suburb of Colombo) is especially telling:

Most of the people on the stage, in the shade, are men, with perhaps two or three women visible. Most of the mothers, dressed in white, are seated at the foot of the stage in the sun. As the meeting starts, the press, cameras, videos spill onto the stage ... sometimes even blocking the microphone and the speaker ... the disrespect for the speakers is more apparent when a "mother" is speaking. ... About twenty women's testimonies were interspersed among the politicians' speeches, which often took over fifteen minutes, to the five minutes the women seemed to use. (Confidential report, INFORM, 1991)

Though representatives of other opposition parties had been invited to speak, they were a mere "smattering" compared to the SLFP MPs "jostling on the stage," who in their speeches "were hell bent on making it a party political rally" (Confidential report, INFORM, 1991).[10] Even the two leading women in the SLFP, party leader Sirimavo Bandaranaike and her widowed daughter, Chandrika Kumaratunga, were obviously not committed to the Mothers' Front; their late arrivals and early exits annoyed many mothers who had hoped that these powerful women would be more approachable.

No attempt was made to rectify the errors of the previous year at the second national convention, which was held indoors and drew a more modest crowd on 23 June 1992. Once again, the stage was dominated by males mainly representing the SLFP. Of the twenty speakers, only eight were women, of whom four represented the SLFP. This gender imbalance created a marked spatial hierarchy that was completely contradictory to the goal of a national convention, where one would have thought that at least once a year, these mothers would have an opportunity to come to Colombo—the seat of power—and speak, and the politicians and concerned citizens would listen. On the contrary, what occurred was that the politicians on the stage were listened to by thousands of women seated below them who listened, wept, and wailed almost on cue. However, there were a few instances when women exceeded their roles as listeners: when their wailing drowned out a speaker; when a woman was so moved by a speaker that she insisted on sharing her own story; and when another demanded that she be allowed to hand a petition to Chandrika Kumaratunga while she was giving her speech. Yet, the majority of the women felt that at least this part of the meeting had been a useless exercise. One woman commented cynically, "At least this year they gave us a free lunch packet." The women's disillusionment with the SLFP-organized meetings and rallies stemmed not only from frustration at being marginalized but also from impatience with orthodox forms of political protest, such as when one politician after another either tried to absolve himself of blame for having participated in similar kinds of repression in the past or attempted to blame the state for all ills (views of some Mothers' Front members from the Matara District).

While the SLFP went to great lengths to build an antigovernment coalition by incorporating the participation of various political parties, progressive religious dignitaries, and specific interest groups, such as those representing the Organization of Parents and Families of the Disappeared and the Organization for the Disappeared Soldiers in the north-east, the majority of the mothers viewed the attempts as mere political ploys. The only worthwhile participation they were involved in, they felt, was when they were able collectively to beseech the deities on behalf of their "disappeared" and call for the punishment of those at fault. For someone like Asilin, who may never see her son again, the knowledge that she may have had a hand in the death of the president was indeed a powerful weapon in the hands of the weak.

Class Domination

The only woman who rose to national prominence as a Mothers' Front spokesperson was Dr. Manorani Saravanamuttu. The reasons for this hinged on her class position and social status. Dr. Saravanamuttu, a scion of a prominent Tamil family in Colombo, had married into an equally prominent Sinhala family, the de Zoysas. Her only child, Richard, was a popular actor, broadcaster, and journalist. Divorced for many years, she had an extensive medical practice. Her ancestry, professional status, and dignified bearing afforded her much respect among all ethnic groups in middle-class Sri Lankan society. She was transformed into a public personality when she courageously pressed charges against senior police officers for murdering her son, and an entire nation's sympathy was aroused when newspapers published photographs of her as she watched her son's burning pyre. When she had to flee the country because of threats to her life, she was also embraced by an international human rights community.

Dr. Saravanamuttu's main link with the women in the Mothers' Front was the shared pain of loss and grief. Yet, she counted herself more fortunate than they: "I am the luckiest woman in Sri Lanka—I got my son's body back" (*Amnesty Action*, November/December 1990). She was conscious from the outset of the chasm of inequality that divided her from the other mothers: they could not afford to leave Sri Lanka when their lives were threatened; they were not fluent in English or literate enough to file habeas corpus writs; the list was endless. But what the mothers appreciated was that Dr. Saravanamuttu made it clear that she genuinely cared about them and constantly tried to form bridges of friendship and support. Her speeches, often in faltering Sinhalese or simple English, always directly addressed the concerns of the mothers present—cautioning them to be "watch dogs" in regard to political parties, including the SLFP; reminding them that they were not alone in their grief, that Tamil women in the north and east were also suffering as were women in faraway Latin America; and sharing the news that women around the globe had pledged their support to the Mothers' Front. When Dr. Saravanamuttu realized that the mothers had been sidelined at the 19 February rally, she quietly left the stage and mingled with the women below (Confidential report, INFORM, 1991). Her individual mission to fight her son's murderers in court was articulated as a battle waged for all mothers: "Most of them don't have the means to obtain justice. But I have the means and the social position. I'm doing this for every mother in Sri Lanka who has lost a son" (*Amnesty Action*, November/December 1990).

Dr. Saravanamuttu's overtures and actions were not sufficient to shatter an entrenched class and patronage structure. When the mothers sought the help of their MPs, they were following a familiar route of patronage between politicians and constituents: the people elect an MP and then expect him or her to look after them. Even if the quid pro quo arrangement does not often work in practice, it is a last resort in the face of despair. MP Mangala Samaraweera noted that in his father's day, people would line up outside his office requesting jobs; in his day, people lined up outside his house asking him to find their sons and husbands (*Lankadeepa*, 28 June 1992).

Erasing Tamil Women's Agency

It was extremely unfortunate that the SLFP, in its efforts to build an oppositional coalition against the government through the Mothers' Front rallies in Colombo, did not make a sustained effort to forge links with minority ethnic parties or organizations, except for a token representation from the Eelam Peoples' Revolutionary Liberation Front (EPRLF). The most glaring absence was that no member of the original Mothers' Front—which began in the north of Sri Lanka in 1984 and later spread to the eastern part of the island—was invited to speak or even mentioned as providing inspiration for the Mothers' Front in the south at any of its meetings. In fact, when I questioned Mangala Samaraweera on that Front's antecedents, he promptly mentioned the Madres of Plaza de Mayo in Argentina, whose strategy of marching with photographs of their "disappeared" he had introduced among the Sri Lankan women. I found it quite astonishing that he did not think it worth mentioning that there had been an earlier parallel in his own country. Thus, in a seeming move to internationalize the southern Mothers' Front, its organizers were completely erasing the agency of Tamil women not just from their own memory, but from the memory of an entire population in the south. In fact, it was Gamini Navaratne, the former editor of an important English-language weekly in Jaffna, the *Saturday Review*, and one of the few Sinhalese civilians who chose to remain in the north during the height of the Civil War in the 1980s, who attempted to set the record straight, albeit in a somewhat skewed fashion. He disputed the claims made by the organizers of the southern Mothers' Front that it was "the first of its kind in Sri Lanka" and reproduced an article he had written in 1984 reporting on the first march organized by the northern Mothers' Front to protest the arrest of more than five hundred Tamil youths by the Sri Lankan state. It is dismaying that he trivialized the agency of Tamil women by portraying himself as the instigator and ultimate hero of that protest campaign (*Island*, 3 March 1991).

The northern Mothers' Front, like its southern counterpart, was active only for about two years.[11] However, unlike the newer Mothers' Front, it was controlled by and consisted of women from all classes who "mobilized mass rallies, and picketed public officials demanding the removal of military occupation and protesting against arrests. Not only the spirit, but also the enormous numbers that they were able to mobilize, spoke loudly of the high point to which such mass organizations, especially of women [could] rise" (Hoole et al., 1990: 324). The northern Mothers' Front also inspired Tamil women in the east to begin their own branch, which in 1986 took to the streets with rice pounders to prevent a massacre of members of the Tamil Eelam Liberation Organization (TELO) by the LTTE (Hensman, 1992: 503). In 1987, one of its members, Annai Pupathi, fasted to death to protest the presence of the Indian Peace Keeping Forces (IPKF). She was subsequently immortalized by the LTTE (it was common knowledge that the LTTE had forced her to keep at her fast), which now offers a scholarship in her memory. It was finally the increasing hegemony of the LTTE and its suppression of all independent, democratic organizations that did not toe the line that pushed the Mothers' Front in the north and east into political conformism, thereby losing its wide appeal and militancy. "It became another Y.W.C.A"; its central structure, mainly made up of middle-class women finally confined itself to works of charity (Hoole et al., 1990: 324). Many members also migrated abroad or to Colombo. Several in Colombo now work with southern feminist organizations with which they had had close ties. These women were an available resource that the organizers of the southern Mothers' Front chose to ignore, with one exception: Ms. S. Sujeewardhanam, from Batticoloa, who had been invited to be part of the presidium at the first national convention of the Mothers' Front on 19 February 1991, along with Dr. Manorani Saravanamuttu (Colombo) and Ms. D. G. Seelawathi (Matara). In contrast to the huge open-air public rally held later on that day and attended by more than fifteen thousand people (one of the country's biggest public gatherings in recent years), the convention of the Mothers' Front was much more focused on procuring international support and was attended by more than one hundred foreign invitees representing embassies, NGOs, and the press. It was in the organizers' interest to create an image that proclaimed that the Mothers' Front was not antigovernment but propeace and, more important, that it was being run by women from different ethnic groups and classes. Much concern was expressed about the plight of the mothers in the north and east and the need to form branches in those regions (Confidential report, INFORM, 1991).

The organizers had dispensed with such rhetoric, however, by the time of the second national convention in 1992. Only two of the twenty speakers mentioned the suffering of Tamil mothers, and, with the exception of Dr. Saravanamuttu, no Tamils were given an opportunity to address the gathering. The absence of Tamil or other minority participation in the Mothers' Front meetings reduced the possibilities of launching a more integrated, national protest campaign that could have also gained much from the experiences of Tamil women in the north and east of the island.

Conclusion

The members of the Mothers' Front were motivated not by ideology but by circumstance to participate in a protest campaign against the state. Despite repeated assertions that it was not political or antigovernment, the Front generally identified representatives of the state as perpetrators of "disappearances"; the president, the supreme repository of state power, was its key target. Yet, the fact that the main opposition party, the SLFP, was coordinating the organization justifies doubt about its nature. However, the political participation of so many women articulating a specific subjectivity, that is, motherhood, had been unheard of until the Mothers' Fronts in the north and east took to the streets in 1984 and 1986 and the southern Mothers' Front demonstrated despair and anger through public, collective, ritualized curses. Despite the limitations inherent in the identification with the familial and the nurturant, and the mobilization of feminized repertoires of protest such as tears and curses, these women did manage to create a space for protest in a context of terror and violence. In fact, the contingent power of their protest stemmed from their invocation of "traditional" sensibilities and the engendering of emotional responses by presenting themselves before a government and a nation as grief-stricken, chronic mourners for their "disappeared" whose only resort now was to beseech the deities for justice. Ironically, in a time when the protesting voices of several left-wing feminist and human rights activists had been silenced with death, it was the mothers' sorrowful and seemingly apolitical rhetoric and practices that alerted a nation to the hypocrisy of the state.

The Front's politicization of motherhood by frequently linking it to a discourse of rights and dissent (cf. Schirmer, 1989: 26) was continued to its full realization through the campaign strategies of SLFP politicians and, in the 1994 general elections, prime ministerial candidate Chandrika Bandaranaike Kumaratunga. Herself a grieving widow and mother, she cleverly articulated the mothers' suffering as both a personal and national experience. She too "sorrowed and wept" with them but also made it clear that she was capable of translating her grief into action, of building a new land where "other mothers will not suffer what we suffer."[12] Ironically, Ms. Kumaratunga's embodiment of these grassroots women's suffering also usurped their space of protest; the materiality of their lives was sacrificed for an election slogan.

What has become of the thousands of women in the Mothers' Front? Have their lives changed significantly with a more progressive government in power? The new government has appointed three Commissions of Inquiry to look into the "disappearances" and killings that occurred during 1988–1991.[13] We cannot yet predict what will result. Maybe the women will receive individual hearings, another chance to demand that the perpetrators of violence be brought to justice. Maybe their "disappeared" will be restored to them. Perhaps they will receive financial compensation, although that would pale in comparison to all that they have lost, sometimes even their sanity.

It also remains to be seen how the women's involvement, however marginal, in a protest campaign has changed their lives. Although the majority of women who were part of the movement had been relegated to their homes and to the margins of an increasingly militarized society throughout much of their lives, the Mothers' Front did provide some opportunities to air their grievances and anger in public and to create strong networks among themselves. Several groups of these women have now formed links with feminist groups and other nongovernmental organizations that are providing them with trauma counseling and help with establishing self-employment projects. Yet the numbers are minuscule relative to the thousands of women and their families across the country who continue to grieve and to bear the livid scars of a nation-state that has blood on its hands.

Notes

The research on which this chapter is based was made possible by grants from the John D. and Catherine T. MacArthur Foundation (administered by the Committee for the Advancement of the Study of Peace and International Cooperation, CASPIC); the Committee on Southern Asian Studies (University of Chicago); Class of 1905 Fellowship (Mount Holyoke College); and infrastructural support from the International Centre for Ethnic Studies, Colombo, for which I am most grateful. An earlier version was presented at the Senior Research Colloquium on Violence, Suffering, and Healing in south Asia, held at the Department of Sociology, Delhi University, in August 1993 and at the conference Appropriating Gender: Women's Activism and the Politicization of Religion in south Asia, held at the Bellagio Study and Conference Center in September 1994. The comments and suggestions that I received at both venues have been invaluable, and I extend my sincere thanks to the participants and most specially to my Patricia Uberoi and Patricia Jeffery, the latter being a most sensitive and patient editor as well. My thanks also to Uma Chakravarti, Mary Hancock, Pradeep Jeganathan, and David Scott for their critical comments on various versions. Mangala Samaraweera, SLFP MP for Matara made time to speak with me on many occasions, and Sunila Abeysekere and Kumi Samuel of INFORM shared their confidential files and filled in many details of the early days of the Mothers' Front.

I am especially indebted to Dr. Manorani Saravanamuttu and to many other women who wish to remain anonymous, who willingly shared their tales of despair and anger and whose courage has been an inspiration to me. I dedicate this chapter to them.

1. The Mothers' Front was inspired by and shares much with similar organizations in Latin America, but I want to highlight here the importance of historical and material specificities rather than make comparisons of different movements.

2. On 20 May 1990, the Organization of Parents and Family Members of the Disappeared (OPFMD) was formed to do similar work among the families of "disappeared" trade union workers and left-wing activists. It was closely aligned with Vasudeva Nanayakkara, opposition MP and politburo member of the left-wing NSSP (Nava Sama Samāja Pakshaya). The OPFMD rarely received as much publicity as the Mothers' Front, but it supported the Front and joined in its rallies, and members of the Front often participated in OPFMD rallies (see n. 9).

3. Mr. Samaraweera reports that a branch office set up independently in Weligama (in the southern Province) was attacked by thugs.

4. The event of "disappearance" not only inscribed the minds of family members with anguish but also turned their bodies into ciphers of agony. Most seemed to suffer from trauma-related neuroses: children who stopped speaking; old and young women who complained of memory loss, fainting spells, seizures, weight loss, severe chest pains, and the like; and fathers who died of sudden heart attacks.

5. When Wijeratne was killed in a bomb blast in late March 1991, many Front members and SLFP organizers directly connected his death to the efficacy of their collective protest.

6. All wives of government officials and all female officials had to join this national social service organization, Sēva Vanithā, which replicated the hierarchical structure of the government in that the president's wife was the leader, cabinet ministers' wives were below her, and so on.

7. For a brief description and analysis of this ritual, see Gombrich (1971); for a discussion of its origins, see Obeyesekere (1984), especially 293–96.

8. However, this was not the first time the president publicly participated in this ritual (e.g., *Lankadeepa*, 13 January 1992; *Island*, 22 March 1992). Nevertheless, the repetition of this ritual within such a short period and on such a grand scale suggests it was not mere coincidence. The ritual is usually performed with just seven (grand)mothers, and the chief (grand)mother, rather than a politician, leads the chanting.

9. Besides its efforts to ban demonstrations in February 1991, the state also attempted to ban and later curtailed a protest march of the Mothers' Front organized in Kalutara on 3 July 1992 (to coincide with the end of the Gam Udāwa) by forbidding the Front to carry its banner and insisting that the women walk in single file. As a news report pointed out, there were as many policemen as there were mothers (*Divaina*, 4 July 1992). On World Human Rights Day, 11 November 1992, a sit-down protest coordinated by the Organization of Parents and Family Members of the Disappeared (OPFMD) and joined by some Mothers' Front organizers like Mahinda Rajapakse was teargassed and baton charged by the Riot Squad, leaving several of the leaders injured (*Island*, 12 November 1992).

10. Mahinda Rajapakse did make an effort to rectify this gender imbalance halfway through the meeting, but since the stage was already very crowded, few women took up his offer (Confidential report, INFORM,1991).

11. I gratefully acknowledge the help of R. Cheran, Sarvam Kailasapathy, and Chitra Maunaguru in connection with the following material.

12. Excerpted from Ms. Kumaratunga's final advertisement before the elections that was published in both Sinhala and English newspapers.

13. While the previous government did appoint a commission to investigate "disappearances" due to intense pressure exerted by the Mothers' Front as well as international human rights organizations, it empowered the commission to look only into "disappearances" that occurred from the commission's date of appointment, 11 January 1991, rather than during the height of the repression in the south, January 1988. The commissions appointed under the new regime, although rectifying this error, continue to ignore the atrocities that were perpetrated in the north and east by the previous regime because it is not empowered to investigate "disappearances" of Tamil youth as far back as 1979, under the guise of the Prevention of Terrorism Act (cf. *Pravada*, 1/2 1995).

Chapter Twelve

Women and Islamic Revivalism in a Bangladeshi Community

KATY GARDNER

This chapter explores various meanings and effects of Islamic revivalism in a village in Sylhet, northeast Bangladesh, where I carried out fieldwork in 1987 and 1988.[1] This community, which I shall call Talukpur, has been heavily involved in overseas migration since the 1960s. It is colloquially termed a *Londoni-grām*; many of its inhabitants have kin in Newcastle, Manchester, and London, as well as in various countries in the Middle East. Partly—although by no means wholly—because of this, local interpretations of Islam are becoming increasingly "purist," with the most powerful villagers advocating a return to what they regard as the fundamentals of the Islamic creed.[2] One way in which this is expressed is through the behavior of household women. In wealthier households women tend to be in stricter *parda* (seclusion or veiling) than women in poorer and nonmigrant households. As women and their male relatives frequently reminded me, certain signs of modesty—covering one's head, particular postures and utterances, invisibility to nonrelated men—were unavoidable for a good Muslim woman. Indeed, *parda* and various other formal ritual observances were the only ways for women to express their religiosity "properly."

Countervailing forces, however, contradict and undermine purism. For instance, although rapid economic change has enabled more households to seclude their women, women in poorer households are increasingly being propelled into the labor market (see Feldman and Shaheed, both in this volume). Other discourses, of modernity, education, and "progressiveness" coexist with those of the new traditionalism. Islamic revivalism is experienced by different women in different ways and to varying extents, depending in part upon structural determinants of class and age. While in certain contexts all women express adherence to Islamic revivalism, some also participate in alternative discourses—songs and particular rituals—that subtly subvert dominant notions of correct female behavior and modesty. Through these we can see that women are not wholly muted and passive in the face of religious revivalism but express themselves and their situation in diverse ways and with multiple voices. In opposing purist Islam, however, these cultural alternatives are not ideologically or politically neutral. Whether or not participation in them amounts to resistance, or merely serves to reinforce women's subordination, is thus of central importance.

Sylhet, the National Context, and International Migration

Like other villages in Sylhet, Talukpur has been profoundly altered by its involvement with global labor markets over the past thirty or so years. International migration is, of course, of huge importance nationally as well as regionally. Since the 1970s remittances have been an increasingly central source of foreign revenue to Bangladesh: from 1976 to 1983, more than U.S.$2 billion; as a proportion of the gross national product, rising from 0.7 percent in 1976 to 4.1 percent in 1981 (Hossain, 1985). Most Bangladeshi remittances come from the Middle East: 78.12 percent in 1983 (Islam et al., 1987: 9). The rest are largely from Britain. Although migrants to the Middle East come from all over Bangladesh, those to Britain originate largely from Sylhet. A House of Commons survey in 1986, for example, indicated that of the estimated 200,000 Bangladeshis living in Britain, more than 95 percent of them were Sylheti. This *Londoni* migration from Sylhet originates in particular regions— Beani Bazar, Maulvi Bazar, Golapganj, and Nobiganj are among the most well known. Within these small pockets not every village is a *Londoni-grām,* and within such villages not every household has a member abroad. There is little doubt, however, that even though migration is not spread homogeneously throughout the region, it has had a profound effect upon local economic and political structures.

As elsewhere in South Asia, Bengali migration to Britain is closely tied to colonialism and to the changing demands of the global labor market (Ballard, 1989; Bhachu, 1985; Visram, 1986). As in many villages in Sylhet, men have been leaving Talukpur since the beginning of the twentieth century, initially to work as lascars (sailors) on British ships docked in Calcutta. Originally, the Calcutta docks attracted men from other areas of East Bengal, such as Noakhali and Chittagong. By the 1950s, however, Sylhet appears to have been increasingly gaining a monopoly for reasons that are both complex and not entirely clear (Gardner, 1995: 36–40). The British created a large number of independent tenants, who paid rents direct to the British rather than to *zamīndārs* (landlords), a factor that has been used to explain the reputed independence of Sylhetis, as well as their economic ability to risk migration. Chance factors, such as the success and subsequent patronage of certain key individuals, were also probably important.

Before 1947, many lascars jumped ship in Britain and New York, usually finding work in the hotel and restaurant trade (Adams, 1987). During the first part of the twentieth century, a small community of single men began to be established in London. After World War II, labor shortages in Britain led to a vast increase in opportunities for migrant workers—many of them recruited from South Asia—who provided both cheap and plentiful labor. Many villages in Sylhet already had contacts in London, so the networks that served to increase Sylhet's monopoly over British migration were already established and the number of Bengali migrants to Britain rose dramatically in this period (Peach, 1990). Villages such as Talukpur may have originally had only a few men in Britain, but many now began to make the journey to *Bilhātī* (from *vilāyat* (abroad), or more specifically Britain, or "Old Blighty"). Since most migrants were recruited through kinship ties, the benefits of migration began to be concentrated in particular lineages and households.

By the late 1960s, British industry had declined and immigrant labor was no longer desirable to the British. Indeed, from 1962 onward, increasingly restrictive immigration legislation radically curtailed labor migration to Britain. Rather than stopping the flow, however, the legislation precipitated a new form of migration from South Asia (Ballard, 1990). Alarmed by the increasing insecurity of their situation, most migrants responded by applying for British passports and sending for their wives and children. And as factory work became less available, many Bengalis switched to private businesses, most commonly restaurants. Meanwhile, as in much of Bangladesh, another route to overseas incomes opened up for Sylhetis. Since the early 1970s, oil-rich but sparsely populated states in the Middle East have been recruiting foreign workers, mainly for laboring jobs. At the bottom of the pile, in terms of working conditions, security, and pay, are workers from South Asia (Owens, 1985). Although low by the standards of the wealthy Gulf, wages have been sufficient to persuade many Bangladeshis to migrate. As in the early days of migration to Britain, remittances are often enough to support a whole family.

Villages in Sylhet that have experienced high levels of *Londoni* migration are startlingly distinct. Rather than the usual adobe and thatch houses, they have numerous stone buildings, sometimes two or three stories high. Such villages seem prosperous, with extensive material evidence of their overseas success—a far cry from the impoverishment of the rest of rural Bangladesh. In local terms, most migrant families have enjoyed considerable success and seen their economic positions transformed. Many were originally small landowners. Usually, the initial costs of migration were very low and migrants had enough capital to meet them or could borrow from kin or neighbors. These men returned home comparatively rich, investing their earnings in land, the vital commodity upon which the well-being and position of all households in rural Bangladesh depends. Most became moderate or very large landowners (Gardner, 1992, 1995).

During the 1960s, the period of most intense migration, migrants struggled to buy as many fields as possible and local land prices rose quickly. Today an acre of land in Sylhet is three or four times more expensive than in other, nonmigrant districts. Sylhetis without access to foreign wages have found it increasingly difficult to compete for local resources, and there has been increasing polarization between migrants and nonmigrants. In Talukpur, for example, twenty-five households are landless and fifteen are in the lowest landholding category. Seventeen households have more than eight acres, and six have more than sixteen. The biggest landowner in the village has more than forty. These divisions in landholding are closely linked to households' migration histories. Households without migration are far more likely to be landless. Only one landless household has links with Britain, whereas all larger landowning families have members in Britain or the United States.

The economic transformations in Talukpur and other similar villages need also to be understood in terms of the wider national context. Over recent decades, the political economy of Bangladesh has experienced substantial restructuring. Manufacturing industries in urban areas have become increasingly important, and the capitalization of agriculture has contributed to growing rural poverty, landlessness, and underemployment (see Feldman, this volume). The economic polarization of households in Talukpur is thus similar to rural polarization taking place throughout Bangladesh. Here, however, overseas migration is the crucial factor that influences people's access to land. Recent studies suggest that these wider changes are also associated with the entrance into the labor market of women from poor households that can no longer rely on traditional forms of security (Feldman, 1993). Thus, while ideologies of female modesty and seclusion are increasingly articulated in Bangladesh, economic pressures are forcing some women into the public domain. This contradiction is just one of those structuring gender relations in Talukpur today.

Islamic Revivalism

In Sylhet, the increasing importance of international migration and foreign revenue has been accompanied by increased religious fervor. Indeed, return-migrants are often the most keen to assert traditionalism (in this case, in the form of religious doctrine). Like all religious ideology, growing "purism" in Sylhet should be interpreted as the product of historically distinct processes (Asad, 1983: 251). As Eickelman (1982: 1) suggests: "The main challenge for the study of Islam in local contexts is to describe and analyse how the universalistic principals of Islam have been realised in various social and historical contexts without representing Islam as a seamless essence on the one hand or as plastic congeries of beliefs and practices on the other."

Revivalist trends in Sylhet must first and foremost be placed within their specific political context in Bangladesh. Nationally, during the rule of both General Ziaur Rahman (1975–1981) and President Ershad (1982–1990), Islam increasingly appeared in state discourse. This is a significant departure from earlier phases of Bangladesh's short national history, and can be partly explained in terms of the country's changing relationship to Pakistan and India. In the years immediately surrounding the war of independence from West Pakistan in 1971, Bengali nationalism was notably secular. India was an ally during the war, and subsequent state discourse stressed Bengali rather than Muslim identity. After Sheikh Mujib's assassination in 1975, however, relations with India began to deteriorate and the Bangladeshi state grew more friendly with Pakistan. During his rule, General Ziaur Rahman introduced a formal commitment to fostering international Islamic brotherhood into the state Constitution (Jahangir, 1986: 80). Of General Ziaur's policy, Jahangir writes: "He defined Muslims as one unit against non-Muslims. This unity through religion . . . was for him the essence of the Bangladesh situation" (79). Similar comments might be made of Ershad, who increasingly presented himself and his legitimacy in Islamic terms. In 1988, during my fieldwork, Ershad declared Islam the state religion. Secular Bengali nationalism, then, has been largely replaced by the ideal of the national community of Islam (Eade, 1990; Feldman, this volume).

This shift also reflects the increased role of Saudi Arabian aid to Bangladesh, as well as wider global trends. Missionary movements such as Tablīghī Jama'at (the north Indian movement of spiritual renewal; see Metcalf, this volume) and political parties such as Jama'at-i-Islami, for example, have both grown hugely over recent decades. Since 1987, other national and regional developments have affected local understandings of Islam. Increasingly, it seems, religious identity in South Asia has become central to political struggle. Events at Ayodhya, the Gulf War, and the Salman Rushdie affair have all, in different ways, played a key symbolic role in creating pan-national Muslim identities. In Bangladesh, Islam remains an important part of state discourse and legitimacy, and mass communications (newspapers, radio, and battery-run televisions) reach villages such as Talukpur and aid the spread of ideas both from Dhaka and overseas. Similar processes have been at work all over

South Asia. Indeed, there is a growing tendency for purist networks to spread across national boundaries (Caplan (ed.), 1987: 3).

Combined with these forces, Islamic purism in Sylhet is also linked to overseas migration and the relative prosperity of the region. Although it would be misleading to suggest a clear-cut polarization of beliefs and practices, the economic differences structured by migration are also reflected by those of ideology. Within villages like Talukpur, the new discourses of purism are dominated by the most economically powerful men, many of whom are or have been migrants, or whose close kin have migrated. It is they who are most keen to present themselves as Islamic purists. This association of doctrinal purity with wealth is not new, and there has always been religious heterogeneity among Bengali Muslims. Roy (1982), for example, writes of the presence of a small Ashraf elite that claims descent from the original Muslim invaders, since the first days of Islam. A minority of wealthy and educated people probably always leaned toward the higher-status textual tradition. The differences in Islamic practices in Talukpur do not wholly depend upon class, but the most purist of the men tend to be the most wealthy. Remittances have meant that many higher-status activities have now become accessible to migrant households in Sylhet. Such families can pay for sons to learn Arabic, and they can perform *hajj* (pilgrimage to Mecca), pay for sacrifices on holy days, follow fasts rigorously, and hold *milād* (events based on group prayer) in their households. For the vast majority with little or no property, such practices are out of their financial grasp: they cannot read Arabic or afford activities such as *hajj* or *milād*. It is not surprising that the wealthy villagers should seek to differentiate themselves from their poorer, illiterate neighbors and their religious activities.

Combined with this, migrants to Britain and the Middle East moved from an Islam based on localized cults and molded to the culture of the homelands (what has been termed "syncretism" by Roy, 1982) to foreign countries where Muslim migrants from many different countries and cultures together created an international version of Islam, an Islam of universals in which the holy texts are the only common language and Mecca is the only commonly accepted core (Metcalf, 1982: 12). Travel to a foreign culture may also prompt a heightened sense of "being a Muslim" (Eickelman and Piscatori, 1990: 16). Thus, although not all migrants are fundamentalists, many have been forced to define themselves first and foremost as Muslim. In their religious institutions—their mosques, *madrasās* (Islamic academies), and festivals—they increasingly join with other Muslims to create a universalistic Islam (Eade, 1990).

Within Talukpur, the Tablīghī Jamaʿat has also been important. The village *madrasā* is run by it, as is the *waʿz* (preaching). The Tablīghī Jamaʿat also has a missionary role and several village families give board and lodgings to these young men. One explained to me that his family lived in Sylhet town, where there are many *madrasās*, and he had been sent to Talukpur to spread "correct" Islam in the rural areas. As part of this missionary activity, the students help organize a *wa'z* in the village each year. This involves twenty-four hours of preaching, recitation of the Qur'an Sharif, and prayer by eminent *mullās* from outside the area. All the village men attend—but on this special day, when everyone is more aware than usual of the importance of piety, women do not even venture outside their households. Village men told me later that the Tablīghī *mullās* instructed them on how to lead more pure lives: keeping women in stricter *pardā*, and rejecting charismatic *pīr* (Muslim saints) and "un-Islamic" behavior, such as dancing, drumming, gambling, or smoking ganja.

Revivalism and *Pardā* in Talukpur

The increase of Islamic purism in Talukpur has brought increasing emphasis on seclusion and female modesty (*sharm*).[3] These discourses find physical expression in the practice of *pardā* (seclusion or veiling). One woman, the widowed head of a large and prosperous household, explained this to me in the following terms: "Allah offered us two paths: one is the path of Heaven and the other is the path of Hell. One path is covered in thorns, and the other is white.... If you walk the thorny way, they'll pierce the flesh of your feet. You know that if you don't cover your head or body, people will see you. If you wear a skirt, then there'll be fire." Other women told me that *pardā* means "being covered," physically expressed through a *burqā* (overgarment with veil), or covering the head with a *sārī*. Seclusion is also expressed through various shifting physical dividers that separate women from the "outside." The bamboo fences that wall off the inner yards of homesteads, verandas around houses, and umbrellas that shield women moving outside their homesteads from the gaze of nonrelated men are all signs that *pardā* is being observed.

Pardā is an internal spiritual state of modesty and respect toward God, and often is presented in explicitly religious terms (for example, "We do it because it is Allah's order"). But women also acknowledged it to be a set of social rules controlled by village elders, a part of social organization separating men and women and preventing the development of illicit relationships between them. This blurring of boundaries between the "religious" and the "social" is, of course, very much part of Muslim ideology that conflates the "religious" and social orders through Islamic law. As Farida Shaheed (this volume) observes, in Pakistan, *pardā*, like other religious practices, is integrated into women's "everyday experience." In Talukpur, too, women tend not to separate religious ritual from their everyday lives and practices; it is male ritual domains, such as shared prayer at the mosque, or *milād* that do this. Covering one's head at particular times, lowering one's eyes, and wearing garments such as the *burqā* when taking trips outside are all ways in which religiosity is informally integrated into women's daily activity. This is perhaps one reason that women tended to tell me that they know nothing of (formal) religion because that is men's concern.

In general, *pardā* is explained in terms of women's need for male protection, and the sinfulness of strange men's seeing them. The actual rules (*niyam*) of *pardā* and notions of respectable behavior vary according to context, but considerable consensus on certain cultural givens exists in Talukpur. No women explicitly challenged the notion that men were placed above them; all outwardly accepted that they were barred from various male spaces and should follow, unquestioningly, the laws of the male household head and of male elders of their lineage. This, they told me, was Allah's *ni-yam*. When asked why men should have such power over their lives, women frequently quoted a local saying: "Women's heaven is at their husbands' feet."

Most academic observers agree that although articulations of *pardā* differ, it is both ideologically and economically linked to the subordination of women and their dependency on men. It restricts women's movement, and thus radically affects their access to production and economic autonomy (Jeffery, 1979; Sharma, 1980; White, 1992). It emphasizes both the physical separation of women and men and women's need for male shelter (Papanek, 1973; Jeffery, 1979). This in turn organizes work and the separation of male and female worlds. Men are denied access to women's domains, and women are banned from male areas such as the fields, the mosque, and the market, all domains where substantial economic and political power can be gained. As Sharma (1980: 215) puts it, *pardā* "is one way, among others, of controlling women and the domestic sphere, ensuring that they step outside it only with difficulty." *Pardā* thus enforces and validates the dependency of women upon men. By separating male and female spheres of production, it ensures their interdependency. Notions of female modesty also mean that women need men to protect and shelter them (Jeffery, 1979).

Pardā has to do not solely with economic and political relations of this kind, however; it is also linked to a wider cultural construction of femininity, sexuality, and biology. As several Muslim writers have pointed out, the threat of female sexuality is a central concern of Islam, which must balance human sexual needs with man's sacred relationship with God (Mernissi, 1975b; El Saadawi, 1980). The seclusion of women in Islam, as symbolized by the veil, therefore involves ambivalent notions of femininity. Women's sexuality is threatening to the male order, and therefore to be controlled, but at the same time women are weak and vulnerable, and must be protected from men by means of their seclusion. Such interpretations take us some way toward understanding *pardā*. Taken out of context, however, there is a danger of collapsing into an essentialism that constructs veiling and Islam as objective, predetermined entities. In many ways, *pardā* does function to subordinate and exclude women from important arenas of power, but its effects cannot be understood homogeneously. Women from richer households are not simply "oppressed" by *pardā*. We need also to recognize how women observing *pardā* gain public status within the dominant discourse. Further, *pardā* is not fixed but negotiable, especially for women who already have some economic and social status. For women who lack such power, the growing stress on modesty and seclusion further underwrites their subordination, both practically and symbolically. The economic and social position of individual women is therefore key to their relationship to revivalist discourse, which (while hegemonic) is not homogeneous. In addition, *pardā* is not the only way in which female identity is constructed, and the "alternative" discourses in which women participate express very different images of female experience and behavior.

Pardā and Class in Talukpur

The outward signs of *pardā* are undoubtedly increasing in Talukpur. Landowning households now generally have houses with verandas and walls to conceal the women inside, and separate guest rooms (*bangla ghar*) for male visitors. Their women use *burqās*, cars or *rikshās* are hired to carry women from place to place rather than their walking through male domains, and labor is hired to run errands and do work that might otherwise have forced women to leave the homestead. Previously, women told me, they could not afford *burqās*, and were too poor for cars or *rikshās*. These changes are linked with remittances and growing prosperity, and are by no means enjoyed by all households.

The changes experienced by women in more prosperous households should not, however, be exaggerated. Ideologies of *pardā* have long been present to some degree among rural Bengali Muslims. Older village women recollected that they spent large amounts of their lives within the confines of their homesteads in the 1960s and 1970s. It is therefore the *degree* to which *pardā* is stressed as essential to correct Muslim female behavior that has changed. At the same time, other forms of behavior and beliefs, which once were apparently acceptable, are now presented as oppositional to "correct" Islam. I therefore suggest that the new purism has more profound effects on the women who cannot afford to participate in it, than on those who can.

Although *pardā* can be analytically linked to female dependency and exclusion from key political and economic domains, it also carries meanings of virtue, purity, and status for women whose households can afford its outward signs. There may be huge hidden costs, but there are also benefits to be gained from "buying in" to the discourse (Kandiyoti, 1988). For many women in Talukpur, adherence to cultural codes of modesty is a sign of status and is central to their Muslim identity. Given that the dominant discourse stresses female seclusion, women who participate are more likely to gain public status and male approval. Thus, women are not simply the passive victims of the honor building of family men. Those who are demonstrably in *pardā* enjoy far more public prestige than others who are not, and I do not know any women in Talukpur for whom this is not important.[4] Village women often visit their neighbors and kin, and all are aware of one another's relative status. Even if they do not regularly exchange visits, local women hear news of, and place each other on, the continually shifting social hierarchy. This area of influence extends outside Talukpur to nearby villages and even Sylhet or Nobiganj towns. *Pardā* implies male protection and economic security. Going outside the homestead without a *burqā* or being exposed to the gaze of strange men is seen as undesirable by all women. Being carried from place to place in a *rikshā* or wearing a fashionable pastel-colored *burqā* is a sign of individual virtue and one's family's status.

Women's spirituality, expressed through being covered and through prayer, fasting, and study of the Qur'an Sharif, also adds to their prestige within households. The religious behavior of new brides may enhance their standing with their in-laws, and older women who are highly religious command almost as much respect as their male counterparts, especially if they have performed hajj. Besides enhancing social status, then, *pardā*-related behavior is also central to many women's spirituality (although, of course, this has been originally defined and constructed through the discourse of elite men). Many women in Talukpur said that *pardā* helps them grow closer to Allah. The *sharm* (in this context, the "shame") of poverty-stricken women forced to seek waged employment in strangers' households has partly to do with their relationship to God, but also with the censure of their fellow human beings.

Writing of the Awlad 'Ali Beduins, Abu-Lughod (1986: 159) comments, "Veiling is both voluntary and situational." Can we come to similar conclusions in Talukpur? If *pardā* helps to give women from higher status and wealthier households public status, and is also spoken of approvingly by them, can we say that they are participating voluntarily in Islamic purism? I would argue that it is important to acknowledge the agency of individual women and the benefits that adherence to *pardā* may offer them, but we must also acknowledge that these "choices" take place within a context where the dominant discourse, and the economic and political relations that support it, are controlled by elite men—usually the heads of their households. Moreover, women's partial participation in other, alternative discourses also indicates considerable ambiguity in many women's feelings about seclusion. Centrally, too, we must ask what happens to women who are not secluded.

In Talukpur, women who must leave their households in search of employment face public censure and their lowly status and vulnerability is reinforced. This has been described elsewhere in Bangladesh, where the growing public acceptance of Islamic purism coexists with increasing poverty and the concomitant appearance of women on the labor market (McCarthy, 1993: 337). In Talukpur, nearly all women from landless households found employment as domestic workers outside their homesteads. Some labored in the households of their kin, a situation seen by all as the most preferable and that tended to be described in terms of reciprocal "helping" (Gardner, 1995: 152–56). Many others were forced to seek more formal employment in nonrelated households. This was presented to me as highly shameful, for not only the individual women but also their whole lineage, and it was often kept secret. One woman, for example, walked many miles a day in order to find employment in an area where she would not be recognized. Such women are extremely vulnerable to male harassment and economic exploitation.

In her analysis of female garment workers in Dhaka, Feldman (1993: 231) suggested that the contradictions of ideology and material need have given rise to new forms of appropriate female behavior; the *burqā*, for example, is used by women wishing to travel to and from work. In Talukpur, however, *burqās* are not affordable for the poorest women. As they say, "How can I bother with *pardā* when my belly's empty?" When asking working women about *pardā*, I was frequently told, "It's an internal state." At one level encompassed by dominant ideologies of *sharm* and seclusion, these comments also indicate both that *pardā* is far from fixed and that there are alternatives.

Context and Interaction

We can list the outward manifestations of *sharm* (covering the head or face, avoidance of certain categories of men, downcast eyes, silence, etc.), but these external signs do not carry homogeneous meanings and they are not the only discourses affecting women's identity in Talukpur. Writing of another part of Bangladesh, Jitka Kotalova (1993) uses the concept of "encompassment" to describe how her female informants moved between various positions regarding dominant cultural codes. Although encompassed by "official" rules, they can express dissidence without overtly questioning them (3). In some situations, rules of veiling are rigidly imposed; in others, they are broken with relative ease. On first arrival in her fieldwork village, Kotalova was sternly exhorted to cover her head and wear her *sarī* correctly. Once she had demonstrated her literacy in the official rules, however, she could deviate substantially without exciting adverse comment. Kotalova concludes that although the structural models organizing the world of her informants are presented as homogeneous and self-contained, the norms can also be strategically played, according to context. To understand culture we must therefore focus on interaction and process, rather than structure per se (Kotalova, 1993: 53). In Talukpur, too, the rules that women recited to me were clearly far more flexible in everyday use, and the malleability was very much dependent upon particular contexts and the positioning of individual women.

As is widely noted in South Asia, codes of modesty and veiling are structured by a woman's life cycle. Young brides in their husbands' homes are the most rigorously subject to seclusion, and the least able to manipulate its interpretation. Older women, especially those who have passed their menopause, are able to move around with relative freedom, participate in lineage meetings, and even enter sacred spaces. One matron in Talukpur who frequently went inside the mosque her lineage had built within their homestead told me that this was because she was now "like a man." Likewise, spatial location is important. On annual visits to their fathers' homesteads, for example, married daughters rarely cover their heads, and they can talk openly with village men, for it is only with certain categories of men that modesty is important.

Class also influences the degree to which a woman can negotiate the definitions of what is and what is not acceptable behavior. So long as women participate in formal activities that generate status and spirituality (such as prayer or the use of a *burqā)* and avoid others associated with low status and sin (such as non-Islamic ritual), older women from the wealthier households have considerable room for maneuver without damaging their reputation. Those who cannot operate within these boundaries because they seek public employment, have no males to chaperon them, and cannot afford a *burqā*, may be regarded as shameless or even sinful. Some women can therefore negotiate and redefine the rules, at least to some degree. Indeed, while condemning the "non-Islamic" practices of other women, and perhaps enforcing strict seclusion on their young daughters-in-law, older women from high-status families continually demonstrate the flexibility of *pardā.* If an older woman wishes to speak with a male guest, then she will. Likewise, if she wishes to visit another household or village, she can do so without damaging her reputation, so long as she wears a *burqā.* Whenever they were questioned about behavior that (I perceived) infringed their *pardā,* such women would reply that *pardā* was an internal state.

Women may also hold apparently contradictory beliefs. While explaining for me the importance of seclusion, many also seemed to value personal freedom. Usually, only the richer women could visit or move to Sylhet town. Women from poorer households generally do not have middle-class urban kin to visit. In town, I was told, women have more freedoms. They can travel unaccompanied by *rikshā,* visit the shops filled with Western consumer goods, and become friendly with unrelated households. The town gives them an anonymity that means they need worry less about seclusion. Some urban women even attend college or have salaried jobs. No woman from Talukpur is yet in this position, but *parda* is unlikely to be a constraint if the opportunity were to arise and the rewards were sufficiently large. Likewise, in urban areas women are more likely to be exposed to Hindi and Bengali films whose female characters so often have love marriages, work outside the household, and go around with their heads uncovered. This behavior is not necessarily viewed as oppositional to Islam, for it is part of the "progressive" and hence prestigious nature of the city. The value of modernity (within certain boundaries) is as great as that of religious piety. Without compromising their modesty, women can attend college, have salaried work, and enter public spaces, so long as they are involved in respectable and prestigious activities (such as shopping for *saris*, or visiting a relative in hospital).

Thus, not only are official rules of seclusion and modesty more flexible than originally presented to anthropologists, but they are not the only discourse that structures women's behavior. Islamic revivalism has to be contextually placed alongside other ideologies and codes in which different women participate in a variety of ways. Some, for example those of modernity and development *(un-nati)*, coexist harmoniously with Islamic purism. Others are constructed in more conflictual terms.

Alternative Discourses

Raheja and Gold (1994) argue that north Indian women's songs and rituals are forms of "poetic resistance" that can furnish women with a positive self-image and a means for subverting dominant discourses of gender and kinship, and provide a powerful alternative discourse of female identity. Although their informants sometimes spoke within the dominant discourse, Raheja and Gold suggest that by recognizing the multiplicity and discontinuity of those voices, their analysis reveals the agency and power of individual women, as well as the negotiated and contested nature of culture:

> If we begin to view culture not as a single totalizing discourse but as a universe of discourse and practice in which competing discourses may contend and play off each other . . . we might then be able to interpret experience and subjectivity not in terms of a single incarcerating mode of thought, but in terms of multiply voiced, contextually shifting and often strategically deployed readings of the social practices we seek to explicate (3).

In Sylhet, too, songs and rituals are an important alternative domain in which women construct their identities and express their experience. Women do not, however, participate in them equally. Indeed, as notions of purist Islam become increasingly dominant, songs are becoming associated with poorer, low-status women. Whether they can be interpreted as domains of resistance to the dominant order or simply as part of the process whereby the low status of certain groups is reaffirmed is highly debatable.

Songs are conventionally sung by women at weddings or when working together at home. Some female servants have a reputation for their knowledge of songs, and will sing while the household women gather around, laughing and teasing them. Such activities are generally treated by women in more prosperous households as rather risqué, for the songs are often about passionate love and illicit affairs, or the Hindu deity Krishna and his various lovers. Certainly, they do not conform to what the dominant discourse deems to be correct Islamic behavior. Here are two examples:

> Lover, come in the night, I forbid you to come in the day.
> If you come in the day, people will see.
> You are mine, and I am yours, Lover.
> I always think of you.
> If I don't see you for just a moment, I want to die.
> How many people talk badly of me, because of you.
> Being in love with you, my love, I have lost my reputation.

> Woman: Friend, at which *ghāt* (bathing place) shall I fill my water pot?
> Man: The pond to the east has a golden *ghāt*.
>   At that ghat you can fill your pot.
> Woman: If you were truly my friend you would give me a golden pot.
>   If you were truly my friend you would take my pot and make waves to fill it.

In these songs, women are constructed as sensual, passionate, and in the second (a traditional Bengali wedding song) able to make sexual demands of men. Similar images are reflected in Bengali and Hindi films, which those with access to television watch: heroines are often presented as highly emotional, volatile, and sensual. More traditionally, the Hindu Bengali cult of Kali, the female destroyer, is of huge importance, and in village lore *bhūt* (evil spirits) have a female counterpart in *porī*, marauding female spirits with a penchant for seducing (and possessing) unwary men. Other songs detail the emotions felt by a bride on her wedding day. Again, these express impermissible sentiments, for a virtuous woman must acquiesce to the marriage arranged for her by her family:

> I am going to a new country today as a bride.
> My father-in-law's home is full of darkness.
> Riding on the bamboo casket, four men will carry me on their shoulders.

In front and behind will be the decorated bridal party.
They will read the *kalima* [confess the faith at a funeral procession].
Wife, son, daughter, sister and brother—all will become my enemy.
Ah, new bride, I will leave my own country.
I will wear a white *sārī* [funeral shroud]. [And so on.]

Women presented all these songs as oppositional to correct, modest behavior; they must therefore be sung behind the backs of senior men, especially the particularly pious ones. When I asked to tape the songs, recording sessions were arranged within my household in an air of secrecy, and we had to wait until the very religious household head had gone to the *bazār* before the recitations could start.

The only men I ever heard singing songs were laborers, often at the tops of their voices as they worked in the fields. Many of their songs are also devoted to Sufi saints, again something generally disapproved of by those intent on seeing a more "pure" form of Islam locally (Gardner, 1993). In one instance, household women joined the homestead laborers to listen to their singing, an unusual alliance between two different categories of people—women and low-status men—who are subordinated and largely excluded by purist Islam.

Even more oppositional to norms of female modesty is dancing. Many people termed it "mistaken" *(dushī)* and a sin *(gunāh)*. In many households, people claimed that dancing never took place, yet some of the lowest-status and poorest women showed me traditional Bengali dances that, they told me, were once performed at weddings. This was, however, behind locked doors, and under an oath of secrecy on my part not to tell my higher-status hosts. Unlike songs, which women from all social classes seem to enjoy, dancing is—at least, as far as I am aware—largely confined to women from landless households, and is presented by others as actively "anti-Islamic" and impure *(napāk)*.

Particular rituals, perhaps because of their similarity to Hindu practice, are also vehemently condemned by women and men from higher-status households. One example of this is rituals performed by women for Ghar Lokī, a local version of Lakshmi, the Hindu goddess of wealth. Lokī is said to reside in village homes, so long as women keep them clean and light lamps at dusk. Lokī ensures household prosperity. Far more than any man, she controls the domestic economy. Lokī, and rituals to appease her, are just one domain in which the symbolic power and autonomy of women is expressed in Talukpur. This, and various other rituals and beliefs all support an essentially multidimensional image of women as nurturers and providers, and also, when embodied by porīs, as powerful, dangerous, and potentially destructive. Beliefs in Lokī are, however, dismissed by the more educated and the Islamically pious as superstitious nonsense.

Another example of the disputed nature of female ritual domains is the practice of giving *shinni* (ritual distribution). As Fruzzetti (1981) has shown, Bengali women have traditionally been responsible for the reproduction of their households through various private rituals; these contrast with the public nature of male ritual, which aims at ensuring the reproduction of the wider society. The importance of such female rituals is decreasing in Talukpur. Some women make and distribute sweetmeats to mark particular household events, but the regular donation of *shinni* by women to characters such as Kwaz (the *pīr*, or Muslim saint, of water) or Lokī is gradually being eroded. Women from predominantly lower-status landless families told me that these latter rituals are the responsibility of women and ensure the well-being of household members. Other women, however, condemned them as *dush* (mistakes, sin), arguing that only men should perform sacrifice, and never to a character such as Lokī or Kwaz. Many landless women described how they gave *shinni* to the river, but women from landed and educated households tended to deny such activities. Although many agreed that Kwaz existed or was a figure from the Qur'an Sharif, they told me that giving *shinni* to Kwaz was at best the result of ignorance, and at worst, sinful. Within purist discourse, all these activities appear suspiciously close to Hinduism. The participation of predominantly landless and illiterate women in them thus reaffirms their low status and perceived ignorance.

These alternative discourses certainly demonstrate the heterogeneity and contested nature of local culture, but it is important not to underestimate how all discourses are weighted according to the power of those who produce and participate in them. Discourse cannot be separated from power, and as revivalist discourse becomes increasingly hegemonic, alternative "languages" become subordinate (see Banerjee, 1989; Minault, 1994; Jeffery and Jeffery, this volume). Although traditional wedding songs are still largely tolerated—in their appropriate contexts at weddings—other activities, such as dancing and "syncretic" rituals aimed at saints or spirits shared with Bengali Hindus, are increasingly placed outside the locally constructed boundaries of correct Muslim behavior. Women from higher-status, orthodox households are thus unlikely to participate in them, for their personal status and power within their households depends in part upon largely adhering to the dominant codes of their husbands, fathers, and brothers.

Resistance or Subordination?

Rather than being wholly passive in the construction of ideology, women in Talukpur construct and reconstruct particular identities and ideas, some of which appear to contradict purist notions of correct behavior. But are such alternative discourses politically loaded, and are these songs and alternative rituals "everyday forms of resistance" (Scott, 1985)? This would concur with Raheja and Gold's (1994: 186) conclusion that even if the expressive forms of resistance that they found in north India did not directly change systems of domination, tradition and resistance are not antithetical; tradition can, in particular circumstances, slide into protest. Of course, interpreting women's songs and rituals in Talukpur as forms of resistance depends upon how resistance is defined. As Raheja and Gold show, resistance is not necessarily the same as deliberate activism growing from full-fledged political consciousness. Indeed, in rural Bangladesh, women may have (limited) agency, but political activism is rare. As Florence McCarthy (1993: 324) comments: "Given the structures of domination and subordination which characterize women's lives, it is not surprising to consider that the active awareness of women in their condition remains largely unexpressed."

Yet, at less explicit levels, women are conscious of their situations. McCarthy goes on to suggest that resistance grows out of the contradictions and exploitation facing women. Their increasing involvement in once-forbidden social institutions or new forms of participation, such as the women's credit or literacy groups set up by many nongovernmental organizations (NGOs), are an important arena for generating new forms of resistance (McCarthy, 1993: 325).

I would not wish to suggest that women in Talukpur never resist the dominant male order. Much of what I describe in this chapter suggests that in various subtle ways, they indeed do. In Talukpur, however, it is less that women are participating in once-forbidden social practices or institutions, and more that various domains that used to be encompassed within the dominant ideology and were largely acceptable are now increasingly being constructed by those who control the dominant discourse as improper or even sinful. These have not become domains in which women might potentially come together for deliberate activism of the sort outlined in McCarthy's (1993) case studies of women involved in NGO activities. On the contrary, women's participation in these alternative domains in Talukpur is increasingly individualized and fragmented, as well as polarized between landed, migrant and landless, nonmigrant households.

There are therefore certain problems in labeling women's alternative discourses resistant. First, local women would not agree with such a label. Second, the discourses are very far from generating activism. Last, as purist Islam is increasingly accepted as the mainstream in rural Sylhet, these alternatives are increasingly relegated to low-status women with little negotiating power, who are largely denied access to "correct" Islamic activities. Their participation in alternative discourses is not simply a voluntary choice. Indeed, since many women from landless households have little contact with elite purist men, they may not even be aware that giving *shinni* to Kwaz is "sinful." Rather than being politically threatening to the dominant order, these activities are seen by those who now insist upon Islamic purity as one sign among many of the ignorance and impurity of women from low-status land-less households. Resistance is thus not absolute but relative and can be under-stood only contextually. According to the particular contexts in which they operate, these alternative discourses may assert notions of female power and subvert dominant ideologies, but they may also reinforce the low status and subordination of those who participate in them.

Notes

1. I revisited the village in 1990, 1993, and 1994. My research was funded by the Economic and Social Research Council (U.K.).
2. Of seventy households in Talukpur, only five are Hindu, the rest Muslim. All migrant households are Muslim.
3. For an important discussion of the meaning of this term, see Abu-Lughod, 1986: 107ff.
4. The suggestion by some writers that power and status in the public arena is irrelevant to secluded Muslim women is, in the Talukpuri context, quite incorrect. Indeed, it is predicated upon a male-defined notion of "public" (i.e., the *bazār* and mosque).

Chapter Thirteen

Agency, Activism, and Agendas

PATRICIA JEFFERY

THE ORIGINAL KERNEL OF THIS VOLUME was women's activism in South Asia. *Feminist* activism in South Asia has contributed both to raising people's awareness of gender injustices and to directly combating them. In part, politicized religion may be a response to the challenges posed by feminist activism and by secular changes in the wider economy (Chhachhi, 1991). More certainly, politicized religion has often been implicated in developments that are potentially deeply inimical to women's interests—and yet many women's energies have been successfully engaged in their support. Feminists can surely derive little satisfaction, for instance, from the BJP's ability to mobilize women in defense of Rām's birthplace, often in far greater numbers than feminist organizations have managed to mobilize women to protest dowry murder.

Women's groups in South Asia have generally been deeply disquieted by the challenges that politicized religion poses for feminist activism and for women's rights in the region.[1] Such issues were crucial throughout our deliberations in Bellagio and are explored more or less explicitly in this volume. Here, I want to highlight some dilemmas facing feminists in South Asia—not, of course, that I have the audacity to claim to resolve them. Indeed, I am profoundly aware of treading a very fine line between excessive pessimism (that belittles the achievements of South Asian feminists) and undue optimism (that underestimates the difficulties and dangers they face).

Women's Agency

On the world stage and within South Asia, stereotypes of the South Asian woman have been dominated by her supposed passivity in the face of victimhood. In the nineteenth and early twentieth centuries, this might be epitomized by the child bride, the widow who committed or was made to commit *satê* (widow immolation), or the illiterate woman doomed to ignorance and superstition. More recently, the South Asian woman as victim has been embodied in victims of dowry murders, women subjected to "eve-teasing" [sexual harassment in public] and rape, or the (perhaps ultimate) innocent victim, the female fetus aborted after sex-determination tests (Balakrishnan, 1994; Das, 1995; Dube, 1983; Kishwar and Vanita (eds), 1984; Kumar, 1993; Mani, 1989, 1990; Qadeer and Hasan, 1987; Rajan, 1993; Ramanamma and Bhambawala, 1980; see also Mohanty, 1988).

Yet any truth in such tropes must be balanced by other equally compelling evidence. Women in South Asia have long been involved in various types of social and political movements. Many thousands were activists in the independence movements. Others engaged in class- or caste-based political activities, in which gender issues were generally not the primary orientation. Yet others joined movements to improve women's situation, and by the 1970s, many explicitly feminist organizations were active.[2]

But agency is not wholly encompassed by political activism. Women outside the ambit of high-profile activist organizations—whether feminist or not—are by no means passive victims, so successfully socialized into obedience that they cannot discern gender inequalities (Jeffery and Jeffery, Shaheed, this volume). In various low-profile ways, women critique their subordination and resist the controls over them—in personal reminiscences or songs, in sabotage and cheating. The husband treated like a lord or deity to his face may be derided behind his back or given excessively salty meals.[3] Such everyday resistance may seem tame in comparison with the ambitious agendas typical of feminism, but they confirm that South Asian women have a capacity for agency. Women's actions reflect their intentions and goals, even if other people's power forecloses some opportunities for their agency and even if the outcomes are sometimes unintended or even counterproductive (Gardner, Menon, this volume).

While we can celebrate women's everyday resistance and demonstrate that women are not wholly subdued by their situations, we must beware of overoptimism about the efficacy of such resistance and of conflating women's resistance with their agency (P. Jeffery and R. Jeffery, 1996a: introduction). If women do not use their agency in collaboration with others, individual women might ameliorate their own situations, but systemic gender inequalities will be untouched. Further, women do engage in oppositional agency aimed at resisting their situations, but women's agency is often deployed toward ends that give feminists much less cause for celebration. Women may make "patriarchal bargains" in expectation of rewards for good behavior (Kandiyoti, 1988). Women may consent to patriarchal authority rather than critique it, endure and comply rather than overtly challenge, or practice the bodily modesty and verbal reticence appropriate for a "good woman." Women may also oppress other women—as when a mother-in-law informs on her daughter-in-law while knowing that marital violence will ensue, or when a mother sends her daughter back to the marital home where she is being harassed about her dowry. And women may demarcate themselves from others, as when a housewife abuses her domestic servant, or when veiling is a crucial status marker of Muslim respectability (Gardner, this volume).

How women's agency is read, of course, depends on who is reading. Resistances applauded by feminists might provoke horror in family members. A woman's agency that upholds the status quo may be considered profoundly problematic and of questionable benefit for herself or others—or appropriate and entirely uncontroversial. How should feminists respond when women's agency fulfills their duties as elders protecting family honor? Should a mother-in-law check her son's wife? Should the mother try to ensure that her family's honor is undisturbed by her daughter's marital problems? And what of agency that foregrounds hierarchy and difference rather than egalitarian sisterhood and common humanity? In brief, the question is not whether women are victims or agents but, rather, what sorts of agents women can be despite their subordination. We need to explore the distinctive ways and diverse arenas in which women deploy their agency, the different people over whom they may exercise it, and the agendas that orient and direct it (Sangari, 1996). Only then can we determine what is key to *feminist* agency and imagine how women's agency might translate into feminist political activism.

The growth of politicized religion renders it urgent for those concerned about women's rights to grapple with such issues of women's agency and activism. As the chapters in this volume indicate, the diverse choreographies of politicized religion and feminist politics within South Asia necessitate a comparative framework. In Pakistan, the Islamization program included legislation that can perhaps be characterized as attempts to *immobilize* women and focus their agency within the home, as good Muslim wives and mothers. Yet these efforts fueled the *mobilization* of women to resist such developments, and changes in the economy drew more women into paid employment (Gardezi, 1990; Mumtaz and Shaheed, 1987; Shaheed and Mumtaz, 1990; Mumtaz 1991; Rouse, Shaheed, this volume). In India, especially since the mid-1980s, Hindu Right movements have *mobilized* women beyond their homes, while also sustaining images of the demure, self-sacrificing, and vulnerable Hindu woman (Bacchetta, 1993; Basu (ed.), 1993; Mazumdar,

1995; Sarkar, 1991, 1995; Thapar, 1993; Basu, Sarkar, this volume). Moreover, developments beyond South Asia indicate that the connections between politicized religion, nationalist politics, and gender issues have widespread salience. This volume, then, is exploring local variations on global themes (Anthias and Yuval-Davis, 1992; Kandiyoti (ed.), 1991; Moghadam (ed.), 1994a, 1994b; Parker et al. (eds.), 1992; *Feminist Review*, 1993a, 1993b).

Captivating Idioms

The far-reaching social changes visualized in feminist agendas require more than everyday forms of resistance. The prospects are bleak, though, unless women (despite their differences) are captivated and mobilized by idioms and programs that assert their unity on the basis of womanhood. But how might this be achieved?

Politicized religious movements are generally overtly antagonistic to feminist activism. For this reason alone, they cannot be ignored. It is also worth considering what feminists might learn from the accounts in this volume of women galvanized into activism of different kinds (Basu, de Alwis, Metcalf, Sarkar, this volume). How can feminists interpret such involvement of women with politicized religion? Why and how have such organizations recruited women as activists? And what are the implications for women's agency and for the furtherance of women's rights?

Politicized religious organizations represent the idioms used to mobilize adherents as founded on natural primordial loyalties. Yet such idioms are socially constructed frameworks for thinking about peoplehood and identity, despite often being "naturalized" by reference to genetic and racial purity or to claims that a people's culture, language, and religion are in their bones, blood, or genes. Hindutva or Islam are imagined communities (Anderson, 1991) in direct competition with "woman" as idioms for laying claim to people's primary allegiances. And politicized religious organizations assert a truth and authenticity that they refuse to concede to countervailing feminist claims.

The successes of politicized religion in mobilizing women necessitate being clear about what "success" means. Powerful female deities or pious role models clearly have considerable potency (Basu, de Alwis, Gardner, Metcalf, Sarkar, Shaheed, this volume). The trope of the good wife and mother is redolent with moral affirmation through which women can derive a sense of social worth. Involvement in politicized religion may also enable women to work with others beyond the immediate family, and to develop self-confidence and a sense of empowerment. By imagining the standpoint of women mobilized like this, it is not difficult to see the attraction of appeals that endorse and elaborate—rather than challenge and dismantle—assumptions about worthy behavior and noble womanhood.

Politicized Motherhood

On the face of it, appealing to women as mothers might facilitate their mobilization across community (and class) lines. Indeed, motherhood has sometimes been a very effective vehicle for women's political mobilization (de Alwis, this volume). The familiarity (in the sense both of family-based and known) of "motherhood" might suggest this is an avenue for feminists to follow.

Yet feminists surely need to be cautious, for the roles and images bound up in motherhood are ambiguous. Legitimate power embodied in motherhood can frame women's activism (Basu, this volume). But devotion to duty, self-sacrifice, and ennobling activity on others' behalf cannot easily mesh with feminist activism and demanding women's rights. Similarly, motherhood embeds women in families and derives their identity from relationships and duties to others. This gives little space for images of women freely making decisions about their own lives, and it tends to put women's agency into doubt. For instance, Menon (this volume) analyzes how women as sexual property (of men or the state) are regarded as victims of abduction (or someone's stolen property who must be returned to the rightful owner) rather than as agents capable of freely selecting their own sexual partners. Moreover, mobilizing women around motherhood restricts the space for negotiating the conditions under which women become (or choose not to become) mothers.

An even more intractable issue is that the terrain of politicized motherhood has been extremely well colonized by politicized religious movements in South Asia (and elsewhere). The iconized mother is often imbued with religious overtones and with textual and doctrinal legitimacy (framed, of course, in locally distinctive ways). By bearing legitimate children for their husbands and their community, mothers preserve the "racial" purity of the community. Through child rearing, mothers may hold prime responsibility for the crucial ideological role of transmitting the community's "authentic" culture. The glorification of women's selflessness in the home may be paralleled by the iconized mother serving the nation, aggressively defending national honor as she would her children, or released from domestic duties to become an activist for the nation (Basu, Metcalf, Sarkar, this volume). And motherhood may be turned against women, whether backsliders within the community or women of other communities, when domestic mismanagement and social chaos are blamed on "bad" mothers (de Alwis, this volume).[4]

Far from providing a point of unity for women of all classes and communities, then, the idiom of motherhood can be another source of separation. And, crucially, if feminists adopt motherhood as a route to mobilizing women, it may be impossible to keep a safe distance from politicized religion.

Women's Divided Loyalties

Women's positive experiences of mobilization within politicized religious movements present other dilemmas for feminists. Refusing to adopt religious imagery to mobilize women—and perhaps even critiquing religion's role in women's lives—can damage the feminist cause (as I suggest below). But, compellingly powerful as religious idioms seem on first glance, they would be a very problematic means of creating a common identity among women.

Women may not experience their religious identifications as oppressive, but in heightening awareness of religious allegiances, politicized religion drives wedges between women. Indeed, women's movements in South Asia have generally been alert to women's divided loyalties (Omvedt, 1980).[5] Within a religion, sectarian and class differences in doctrine or practice tend to exclude or devalue some people. Efforts to purify Islam, whether government-sponsored (as in Pakistan) or not (Gardner, Metcalf, this volume) establish firmer boundaries between "true believers" and the rest. In Pakistan, indeed, feminists argue over the wisdom of seeking inspiration in religion. And, in India, Muslim women took diverse stances in relation to the Shah Bano case (Hasan, this volume).

The potential for divisiveness is even more conspicuous where several communities coexist. In India, appealing to women in terms of the Hindu goddesses Kali or Durga or by reference to *shakti* (energy associated with female consorts of Hindu gods) clearly signals a Hindu core, and minority women are likely to be alienated and marginalized. Feminist organizations using such idioms found them usurped by Hindu organizations and deployed for precisely such divisive ends (Agnes, 1995; Mazumdar, 1995). Indeed, women mobilized by organizations of the Hindu Right have been closely implicated in activities directed against Muslim women and men (Bacchetta, 1993; Basu, forthcoming; Basu, Sarkar, this volume).

Appeals based on essentialist religious images, then, may unite and mobilize some women—by heightening their sense of "them and us" distinctions. Activism in politicized religious movements does not necessarily *create* divisions among women of different communities and religious persuasions. Without doubt, though, it exacerbates them and undermines women's identification with women en masse. Adopting explicitly religious idioms is likely to make transcending the barriers between women even more difficult than it has already proved to be.

An Imagined Community of Womanhood?

To improve women's situations in South Asia, the political imperative is to find some rallying call to mobilize women qua women. If appealing to religious identities or to motherhood is problematic, though, on what basis could an imagined community of South Asian womanhood be created? Despite women's divided loyalties, they are generally differentiated from men on the basis of essentialized (and often stigmatized) identities. Could women appropriate such identities in their own favor? Could a common sense of victimhood and of being othered provide an effective focus for women's mobilization? It might be tempting to think so—but feminists would confront several dangers if they adopted some form of essentialism as a riposte to politicized religion.

There is considerable awareness nowadays of how people's multiple sources of social identity crosscut and overlap one another in complex, shifting, and contradictory ways. People cannot be neatly boxed in by one identity alone (Hall, 1992; Rushdie, 1991). This, of course, has not inhibited politicized religion from making claims on people's supposedly primordial allegiances. Indeed, such essentialism has often enabled politicized religion to heighten people's sense of distinctiveness: simple messages about a common history or religious traditions can be compelling, even though they are demonstrably fabricated and invented (Hobsbawn and Ranger (eds.), 1983). Majoritarian movements, such as the Hindu Right, may develop agendas that represent themselves as victimized (even in the face of contrary evidence) in order to justify oppressing others. Essentialist appeals, then, entail perilously simple diagnoses of complex social and political issues. They would leave feminists open to charges of bad history from antagonists and sympathizers alike—even if women's claims to victimhood could quite readily be sustained.

Some feminists, of course, focus on women's biology when trying to transcend women's social differences. But appealing to apparent commonalities in women's biological capacities (e.g., childbearing), or their psychological characteristics (e.g., gentleness, pacifism), or their closeness to nature (e.g., nurturing children, caring for the environment) is an extremely problematic route (Segal, 1987). Contrasting women's "inherent" virtue with men's "inherent" wickedness or destructiveness rests on distinctions that cannot withstand critique, and on successfully asserting a higher value to "women's" characteristics. For one thing, the categories of biology and nature are themselves social constructions, varying in what they comprise and how they are evaluated (MacCormack and Strathern (eds.), 1980). A universally acceptable model of women's and men's inherent qualities is probably unattainable. Even within one place and time, indeed, women's experiences of their biology (however that is defined) are not homogeneous. Second, biological determinism generally implies political conservatism and the deployment of "nature" and "biology" to *oppress* women. If ideas about women's and men's qualities are already integral to cultural repertoires in which men's qualities are the more highly valued, can feminists simply revalorize women's qualities by inverting the conventional hierarchy? How can they convince others, whether other women or women's opponents, of the validity of their claims?[6]

In any case, images of women are generally open to positive and negative readings. On the one hand, religious texts and practices in South Asia are implicated in comparisons between women and goddesses, or the iconization of women as mother—but both these forms of imagery have already been deployed by politicized religious movements (as well as the independence movements). Equally, images that reflect the *devaluation* of women—such as notions of menstrual and childbirth pollution—would be unpromising tropes through which to enhance women's self-respect, whether individually or collectively (Blanchet, 1984; Jeffery, Jeffery, and Lyon, 1989; McGilvray, 1982; Thompson, 1985). If grounding appeals to women on biology seems inadvisable, though, do other idioms suggest themselves?

If "motherhood" is problematic, "wife" and "daughter" connote obedience, unassertiveness, and self-sacrifice, which are hardly encouraging in relation to feminist activism. "Mother-in-law" and "stepmother" imply evil female power, often wielded over younger females, while "co-wife" is a term of abuse associated with competitiveness. "Sister" comes to mind, not primarily because of Western feminist rhetoric but because the sister-sister bond can be used in South Asia to express fictive kinship, even across caste and other boundaries. And it implies mutuality, relative equality, and a capacity to collaborate that other kinship-based images do not. Yet how effective could it be in mobilizing women? In the northern parts of the region, real sisters usually find their bond is eroded (though not completely broken) after they move to their husbands' homes. In the south, and in many northern Muslim communities, this might be less of a problem—although, even then, bonds between sisters give way to the loyalties and duties of wife and mother. Equally, assertiveness is not a defining characteristic of "sisters."

Outside kinship-based idioms and apart from Hindu goddesses such as Kali and Durga, the impact of images of assertive womanhood is restricted by regional languages. But, in any case, their connotations of wayward disruptiveness make them rather implausible means of mobilizing women en masse.[7] Could *churail* (witch, or angry ghost of a woman who died in pregnancy or childbirth, linked to vulva) or *dākinī* (demoness, shrew) rally women in South Asia? In Pakistan, even the relatively unthreatening name for the feminist organization *Simorgh* (a magical androgynous bird) was derisively turned into *murgê* (hen) by detractors.

Just as in the West, pinpointing an effective way of appealing to women is very taxing for feminists in South Asia. Real women (as distinct from the iconized "woman") do not have identical histories and problems (see note 4).

Once we appreciate women's crosscutting allegiances and distinctive stand-points, it becomes hard to visualize an idiom that could appeal across the board—without alienating women for whom it fails to resonate. How, in other words, can feminism avoid riding roughshod over women's differing experiences (Basu (ed.), 1995; Marchand and Parpart (eds.), 1995; Mohanty, Russo, and Torres (eds.), 1991)? And yet feminist theories and agendas raise crucial social and political issues, and surely the political imperative of creating some basis for the category "woman" remains, problematic though that is.

Iconoclasm and Authenticity

Aside from these difficulties over the idiom through which women might be mobilized, women en masse will not be drawn into the ambit of feminist politics without meaningful political agendas. Feminist organizations in South Asia—as elsewhere—have been greatly exercised by debates over strategic priorities. Generally, though, politicized religious movements are considered such a crucial part of the context within which feminist politics must operate today that they cannot be disregarded. And countering the often explicitly antifeminist programs of politicized religion (in which, moreover, women have been mobilized), and mobilizing women around agendas to protect or advance their own rights are no easy tasks.

Sometimes feminists (and others) have responded to politicized religion by challenging its doctrinal interpretations. In Pakistan, for instance, feminists developed readings of the Qur'an Sharif and other textual sources to critique the Islamization program (Mumtaz and Shaheed, 1987). In India, this tactic has been less common, possibly because the Hindu Right has not explicitly drawn inspiration from a single holy book of Hinduism. Male ideologues, however, can readily discredit their female or feminist critics' theological credentials. In any case, religious texts are contradictory and ambiguous. Quite convincing feminist exegeses can generally be countered by antifeminist interpretations based on judiciously selected sources.

Mindful of these difficulties, feminists sometimes try to shift the debate off the terrain of politicized religion, with its reliance on texts and traditions that starkly differentiate women from men. Rather than attempting to invert conventional gender hierarchies by asserting women's special virtues, some feminists try to demolish the dichotomy on which gender differentiation rests. In doing so, they emphasize women's and men's common humanity (rather than their inherent differences) and move the discourse toward human rights issues. This tactic, however, is also problematic.

Globalization processes have spread Western universalistic frameworks that tend to devalue and oust local ones. In South Asia, critics of feminism generally see it as an instance of such processes. When feminists critique the family (and also the religious community) as a key site of women's subordination, their assaults on local values and identities generate a backlash that decenters their universalistic claims by pointing to their ethnocentrism, that asserts the equal (or even superior) validity of locally produced frameworks, and that insists on the contextual specificity of morality (Miller, 1995; K. Kumar, 1995). United Nations documents, for instance, display a gradual but very tentative widening of the notion of human rights to include gender-specific rights and the abuses perpetrated by private individuals as well as the state. Yet, significantly, the UN Convention on the Elimination of Discrimination against Women permits noncompliance on grounds of cultural relativism (which does not apply to men's rights), and the UN Declaration on the Elimination of Violence against Women is not legally binding and leaves governments free not to interfere in "tradition" (United Nations, 1979, 1993; Ashworth, 1993; Bunch, 1994; Coomaraswamy, 1994; James, 1994).

Crucially, one objective of politicized religious movements is to sustain the family and heighten women's identification with the domestic sphere. Not surprisingly, feminists' appeals to gender equality and their critiques of the family are widely dismissed as iconoclastic. Feminists stand accused of disloyalty and inauthenticity; of wanting to create chaos by driving wedges between women and men; of undermining the family and the community; of destroying traditional values; of being Westernized secularists detached from their cultural roots; and of being yet another sign of the pernicious and destabilizing influence of the foreign hand in South Asia (Basu, Rouse, Sarkar, this volume).[8] People's loyalties to what they believe to be indigenous seem immensely potent, but loyalties that transcend local boundaries tend to be viewed as despicably treacherous.

Of course, the authentically indigenous credentials of politicized religious organizations are unconvincing. Colonialism played an important role in the development of politicized religion (Pandey, 1990; van der Veer, 1993). And more recently, politicized religion itself is clearly a transnational phenomenon, heavily reliant on monies remitted from North America, Europe, and the Gulf states, whether for mosque building or for the activities of the Hindu Right. Yet such organizations often try to discredit feminists with accusations of foreign influence and inauthenticity, although the foreign hand in feminism is mainly evidenced in ideas, not economic resources (with the possible exception of development agencies that target gender issues).

Recently, postmodernist skepticism about the authority of metanarratives has been associated with ambivalence about Western feminism (or more correctly, Western feminisms) among South Asian feminists themselves. They cannot deny foreign influences on their ideas and priorities—but their relationships with Western feminisms are often brittle. Do Western feminisms deal in universal truths about justice and gender inequality—or are their agendas and understandings irredeemably beset by ethnocentrism? Should the influence of feminists in development agencies be applauded or not? Do Western feminisms (and Western feminists) misunderstand the culturally specific practices that affect South Asian women? Do they ignore the racism and poverty that influence the priorities of South Asian women—and in whose origins and perpetuation (white) women in the West are directly implicated? Are Western feminisms, in brief, simply another form of cultural imperialism, dominating women in the Third World?[9]

South Asian feminists are in a complex position, as Agarwal (1994c) neatly indicates in outlining her own identities: a woman confronting patriarchy, a Third World woman confronting Western feminist agendas, and an educated Indian woman confronting her own position of privilege within India. Can South Asian feminists combine respect for the local with a belief in universal standards for women's rights? Is it possible to draw selectively on Western feminist agendas without mimicking the inappropriate? Could such a hybrid feminism effectively counter politicized religion? Or would any whiff of universalism be dismissed as disloyalty to the nation? Can South Asian feminists be reflexive about their stances yet avoid a postmodernist relativism that denies them any criteria on which to base their judgments? The taint of foreign influence will probably be impossible to shake off—but can (or should) the allegations simply be brazened out?

Local Agendas

Since feminist activists in South Asia have predominately been urban, educated women, the accusation that they are deculturated and out of touch with the mass of South Asian women can easily put them on the defensive (Feldman, Shaheed, this volume). Suggestions that feminists should focus on understanding and incorporating the locally generated priorities of village or urban slum women rather than impose feminist agendas from outside strike a sympathetic chord—but may also generate intractable dilemmas.[10] Most women are embedded in family and community, their major (though not necessarily exclusive) sources of security and sense of worth. This is a boon for politicized religious movements but a problem for feminists. Might not critiquing the family outrage more women than it inspires? Can feminists challenge controls over women's sexuality, such as arranged marriages, veiling, and seclusion? Dare women distance themselves from the family, where the difficulties they face are offset by the support it provides? Without the provisions of a welfare state, most women probably cannot visualize realistic alternatives to family life.[11]

On the other hand, recent feminist scholarship might offer some opportunities to counter the accusation that South Asian feminists are out of touch with local realities and are the only malcontents (see note 2). One vital message in the voices of unlettered village women, unaware of feminism as conventionally understood, is that they do critique their situations. My research assistants in rural Bijnor—women from Bijnor town, but not feminist activists—were repeatedly astonished both by village women's experiences and by their responses. Moreover, the village men generally had little clue about the women's complaints. Why, then, should we imagine that the male ideologues of politicized religion, for the most part educated urbanites, are any the wiser?[12] Feminists might profitably target such grassroots critiques, both to mobilize women and to construct a dossier of "local feminisms" with which to dismiss charges of their own inauthenticity (Basu (ed.), 1995). Women's critiques also suggest—as I elaborate below—that a lack of activism is not readily explained away as a need for consciousness-raising.

Nevertheless, local feminisms cannot be expected to solve the "inauthentic" feminist's difficulties. Local feminisms arise out of women's everyday problems (their "practical" needs and interests) and do not necessarily develop long-term and broad-ranging frameworks (their "strategic" needs and interests) (Moser, 1993). Some aspects of local feminisms may be antithetical to principles held dear by feminist activists, who, of course, do not necessarily have a privileged capacity for feminist analysis (contra the assumption inherent in the contrast between practical and strategic needs and interests) (Marchand, 1995). Local feminist critiques may seem rather limited or they may coexist with disdainful views of women that undermine women's sense of self-worth. Moreover, women's interests are not homogeneous, and local feminisms may reflect power differentials among women at the local level. Some demands may be more easily squared than others with the views of feminist activists. So can feminist activists respect local understandings and incorporate their insights into feminist programs and yet avoid romanticizing and homogenizing local feminisms?[13]

For instance, many women's social worlds are premised on religious and doctrinal differences and class or caste snobberies (Gardner, Jeffery and Jeffery, this volume). Feminist agendas that explicitly assault such locally significant social divisions might antagonize grassroots women. Yet, pragmatically tempting as it might be to remain in tune with grassroots opinion, accepting women's community-based identities could easily locate women even more firmly within their religious community (Shaheed, this volume). And self-regulated, male-dominated communities may not be the best place to ensure the enhancement and protection of women's rights. Moreover, locally fragmented (and maybe also mutually hostile) feminisms could seriously compromise the ability of feminist programs to challenge what happens within the community. They would also inhibit effective engagement beyond the community with institutions such as the state. Thus links surely must be developed across the limiting boundaries of community, whether local or imagined.

States of Uncertainty

Women's involvement in the independence movements was based on opposition to the colonial state—and on faith in the newly independent states. Yet, as several papers here attest, the national states in South Asia have themselves been important contributors to women's problems. What optimism can women—and other relatively powerless sectors of society—entertain when states introduce legislation with detrimental effects on women or allow progressive legislation to lie moribund and unenforced; when they leave gender injustices in civil society unchecked or sacrifice women's interests to political expediencies; or when agents of the state fail to prevent violence against women, or themselves perpetrate it, apparently without redress (Chhachhi, 1991; Kabeer, 1991; Jalal, 1991)? Feminist organizations within South Asia have taken stances ranging from ambivalence to outright hostility toward the state, seeing the state as an uncertain and dilatory ally (at best) and a powerful adversary (at worst).[14]

Some feminists advocate disengagement from the state. This apparently apolitical stance, however, is profoundly political, for it suggests that women should act locally to tackle social injustices rather than make demands on the state. This position, perhaps, parallels the Tablīghī Jama'at avoidance of confrontation and its emphasis on personal reform, which may enhance self-respect but do little to alter the wider parameters of Muslims' lives in the region (Metcalf, this volume). Yet from apparently gender-neutral economic policies to health and population policies that overtly focus on women, from regional geopolitics to environmental agendas, the state impacts on people's daily lives. Much as some feminists might like to wish the state away, it is inescapable. And to disengage would leave carte blanche on the national stage for pressure groups unlikely to have women's interests at heart.

If South Asian states can be trusted in nothing else, however, they will surely respond somehow to pressure from interest groups within the nation-state (as well as beyond). In India, this responsiveness is often called "vote bank politics," when governments calculate the electoral implications of pleasing some groups (or alienating others). The assumption that such groups vote en bloc may be false—as witness the belief in the single-mindedness of Muslims in India—but it has been influential (Hasan, this volume). In such politics of expediency, a consistently prowomen orientation is unlikely, unless governments become convinced that enhancing women's interests is a vote winner.

Further, postcolonial states are not monoliths consistently developing and applying policy but a series of somewhat separate branches with their different levels often acting in contradictory and inconsistent ways (Jeffery and Jeffery, this volume). The South Asian states have indeed been ambiguous about gender issues. In Sri Lanka, women have benefited considerably from health- and education-sector provision. In Pakistan and Bangladesh, the requirements of Islamization have been contradicted by some government-endorsed social and economic changes—for instance, female employment outside the home, or literacy programs and credit facilities for women. The impact is not always as positive for women as proponents claim, but neither is it likely to be wholly negative (Feldman, 1993).[15] Some state sectors, then, might be hostile to women's interests and others more amenable. The most promising pressure points might be at the center or in the District town, they might be in education or agriculture, they might be in respect to new policy or the implementation of existing laws. Perhaps some spaces can be opened up, although local and national differences make it impossible to generalize about where they will be found (Kapur and Cossman, 1996).

But can the visions of feminism be preserved in the midst of entanglements with the politics of expediency? Would long-term agendas be sacrificed in favor of short-term gains? Would success entail being neutralized and co-opted? Might the state purloin feminist rhetorics and distort their meanings? There are several cautionary tales from within South Asia: the tardy and problematic legislation prompted by the Roop Kanwar satê in Rajasthan (which could make a women rescued from the pyre vulnerable to the charge of attempted suicide); or the outlawing of amniocentesis for sex-selection purposes in Maharashtra (which has pushed such facilities underground, where they are monopolized by the wealthy).

Furthermore, the very centrality of gender issues in politicized religion creates difficulties for feminists relating to the state. Indian feminists might prefer family matters to be governed by secular rather than religious law, but the positioning of the Hindu Right during the Shah Bano affair makes it difficult for feminists to support a uniform civil code without offending Muslims (Hasan, this volume; see also Parashar, 1992). High-profile feminist activities also tend to generate a backlash, such as sexual harassment in the workplace or public places or attacks on NGOs (like the Bangladesh Rural Advancement Committee [BRAC]), because they seem to enhance women's self-confidence and economic skills too successfully (Feldman, Rouse, this volume). Indeed, the state itself may deal repressively with feminist pressure, as during protests over the law of evidence in Pakistan (Mumtaz and Shaheed, 1987).

Thus, even if engaging in dialogue with the state is strategically appropriate, it may be very difficult to do effectively. Can feminists, though, perhaps learn from women activists involved in politicized religious movements? Does their activism provide an experience of empowerment? And can they work effectively for their own agendas?

Activism and Empowerment

In practice, the linkages between women's agency, activism, and empowerment seem very unclear (Hasan, this volume; Molyneux, 1985). Certainly, activist women may experience a considerable sense of empowerment through an enhanced awareness of their abilities (Basu, Metcalf, this volume). Yet this empowerment seems rather equivocal from other angles. Often women activists are circumscribed by virtue of the very idioms (e.g., motherhood, pious Muslim) through which they were mobilized (Metcalf, Sarkar, this volume; Sarkar, 1991). Women in the Mothers' Front in Sri Lanka wept and cursed, and participated in rallies and processions (de Alwis, this volume). The powerfulness implied in *shakti* is greatly feared by women and men when it is unbridled. The rumors of an affair used against Uma Bharati—to manage an unmarried woman seemingly out of control—are instructive here. But domesticated *shakti* (as wife or mother) opens the way for a contained activism, as when women mobilized to defend Rām were asked to cook for the *kar sevaks* (volunteers) rather than demolish the Babari Masjid in Ayodhya, or when they exhort their menfolk to acts of violence rather than commit such acts themselves (Basu, this volume and forthcoming). Many women's activism, though, is far less conspicuous and public than such examples (Basu, Metcalf, Sarkar, this volume). Often, it also seems to be rather short-lived (Basu, de Alwis, this volume).

Further, women's contained mobilization often (but not always) appears passive or responsive, with women being mobilized around agendas managed by others, rather than actively mobilizing around their own agendas. In Sri Lanka, women's individual losses became collective grieving under the orchestrations of male politicians, and their mobilization neither crossed class and ethnic boundaries nor created substantial links with feminist organizations; in the 1994 election campaign, too, the idiom of bereaved motherhood was usurped (de Alwis, this volume). In India, Hindu Right organizations mobilized women over the state's failure to protect Rām's birthplace—not its failure to further women's interests. Generally, indeed, politicized religious organizations are opposed to women's pressing for their rights (Basu, this volume). While activist women presumably do not believe their interests are being harmed, their responsive mobilization runs starkly counter to feminist dreams that women actively mobilize themselves, and develop their own parameters for activism, without being answerable to the caprices and agendas of others.

Women's capacity for activism is not in question, then, but the character of that activism most certainly is. We should not trivialize or be complacent about the contained and responsive activism of women mobilized around agendas that are not their own. Such women may not be greatly empowered by their activism. But their firmer identification as members of a particular community and their stronger sense of what issues are worth fighting for obstruct a transcendent sense of womanhood and the translation of their activism into *feminist* activism. Women's agency at home may be directed against the interests of other women. So, too, may their activism on behalf of the agendas of politicized religion.

Women as a Vote Bank?

No matter how much feminist idioms and agendas might be made to resonate with women's everyday experiences, ideas alone are not enough for putting effective pressure on the state. Empowerment entails more than thinking wayward and disruptive feminist thoughts. It involves being given or (better still) wresting power to bring about desired changes. In brief, the question of whether women could become a feminist vote bank also hinges on understanding why many women express their discontent through individualized forms of resistance rather than through feminist activism.

Women involved in male-dominated organizations may be *permitted* to engage in contained activism. But women mobilizing themselves around feminist agendas are unlikely to receive such indulgence. Images of benign and unified households have often been cornerstones of movements mobilizing people around religious as well as ethnic and class issues. For feminists, though, gender divisions within the household are simultaneously central to their critiques of gender inequalities and among the most powerful means by which women's mobilization can be thwarted. Women within households—most women in South Asia—are rather poorly placed to activate feminist visions. They may experience stiff opposition from their menfolk (and other women in the household) and be prevented from networking beyond their homes, even within the fairly immediate locality (Mandelbaum, 1986; Jeffery, Jeffery, and Lyon, 1989; Sharma, 1978). Women activists—whether in feminist organizations or those of politicized religion—often come from middle-class urban backgrounds. But most women complete their work unaided by servants and have little time for other activities. Unlettered women may certainly have feminist visions, but illiteracy hampers women's attempts to communicate and mobilize very far beyond their homes. And gender differences in access to economic resources mean that few women dare abandon the very institution that they might seek to critique. Most can challenge the family only from within, where their style is liable to be very cramped (Agarwal,

1994a). These considerations also have serious implications in electoral politics. Women are not congregated in localized constituencies but are dispersed in households separated by class, ethnic, or religious distinctions.

In brief, most women in South Asia face numerous barriers to activism and find it hard to make their voices heard. Clearly, though, regional and class differences in domestic organization and in women's access to education and income give some women more opportunities for mobilization than others. Grassroots women do mobilize in pursuit of their interests, sometimes translating the agendas around which they were originally mobilized into more feminist terms, sometimes highlighting the facilitating involvement of middle-class educated women. Such examples often expose the fragmentation—by locality, class, and so forth—likely to beset feminist organizations. But they also confirm the high levels of consciousness among women with no previous exposure to feminism as conventionally understood, and the tenacity and determination of women fighting for their rights even in the face of obstruction (see note 1).

Alliances

Male-dominated organizations, such as trades unions and political parties, are often unreliable champions of women's interests and are reluctant to concede that women have special interests and concerns in the domestic sphere and beyond, as well as in the intersection of these two arenas. Women pressing for their interests—whether on conditions of employment, citizenship rights, domestic violence, controls over their sexuality and fertility, or access to resources—may stand accused of dividing the movement by challenging not just an anonymous system but known individuals at home or in the organization itself. It often proves difficult (if not impossible) to generate enthusiasm for a feminist program among such organizations' male members. And women's domestic responsibilities generally prevent their participating on a par with men and ensuring that their priorities are heard (e.g., Rose, 1992, on the origins of the Self-Employed Women's Association). Not surprisingly, women's groups have debated the wisdom of allying with other groups when collaboration so often results in compromising women's interests. Given the difficulties inherent in mobilizing women and the considerable powers of institutions inimical to women's interests, however, alliances of some sort may need to be considered. Without them, the fragmentation of women's movements would limit their capacity to protect women from repression, whether by the state or their families.

Particularly pertinent here is the potential for feminist organizations to bridge international divisions in order to enhance their impact. The rather recent national boundaries in South Asia separate areas with many parallels in social organization, including gender relationships. Generating global feminist agendas is fraught with difficulties. But, without denying differences of subregion and class, regionally appropriate feminist agendas may be another matter. Feminist groups in the region, however, have generally found it difficult to link up with counterparts in other countries, although there are now several important examples of collaboration in research and publication (e.g., the activities carried out through the South Asian Women's Forum, the Women Living Under Muslim Laws regional research projects, and the International Centre for Ethnic Studies, Colombo), some of them linked into organizations beyond the region. Why such collaborations—until relatively recently—have been such a small part of feminist activism in South Asia is a crucial question.

Tension, war, and civil war have peppered the region since the mid-1940s and have often resulted in restrictions on travel. Othering, mutual demonizing, and diametrically opposed readings of history have made it difficult for people to detach themselves fully from nationalist sentiments. Just as families claim privacy or subnational groups demand self-rule, so, too, do nations generally resent interference from outside—and the intertwined histories of countries in South Asia have produced a special sensitivity to the "foreign hand." And feminists' credibility can be jeopardized just as much by questioning the loyalties of those who transcend the region's national boundaries as by damning feminist agendas as inauthentic symptoms of Western cultural imperialism.

In addition, although feminists may critique nationalism and the nation-state and there may be commonalities in women's everyday lives, women's movements are invariably situated within specific national contexts of state and economy. The countries of South Asia have had different experiences of state and civil society, electoral politics and military rule, theocracy and secularism. Their economies and their integration into the world economy have taken different trajectories. All these specificities must be integrated into feminist agendas. For instance, Bangladesh's aid-dominated economy leaves it vulnerable to internationally defined agendas, including population control programs directed primarily at women. By contrast, Pakistan—a crucial buffer in relation to Afghanistan—has been rather less subject to foreign influence in its internal affairs. The Islamization program was imposed despite international censure. Pressures from the international population lobby were resisted for many years, leaving Pakistani women ill-placed to control their own fertility. It would be difficult, then, to develop even a reproductive rights agenda appropriate throughout the region.

Of course, politicized religion is a crucial player here. Its entanglement with gender issues has made it hard enough for feminists to operate within a single country. But politicized religion also spills over national boundaries. Events in neighboring countries may be used to warrant animosities across borders and the othering of minorities within. In Pakistan and Bangladesh, the Indian Supreme Court's role in the Shah Bano controversy was seen as yet another example of India's disregard for Islam. The demolition of the Babari Masjid in Ayodhya and the associated attacks on Indian Muslims were followed by demolitions of Hindu temples and attacks on Hindus in Pakistan and Bangladesh. Yet how can feminists intervene? Taslima Nasrin (1993) wrote about the shame of such attacks in *Lajja*. In Bangladesh, her loyalty to the nation, her Muslim identity, and her sexual life were themselves publicly shamed (Feldman, this volume). In India, though, she became a trophy for the BJP, a symbol of Muslim maltreatment of women. And feminists there could either keep quiet and seem to condone her hounding or speak out and appear to be in the BJP camp—a dilemma that parallels the one they face over BJP support for the uniform civil code (Basu, Hasan, this volume). The debate about gender issues has been virtually indelibly overwritten by the agendas of politicized religion. Feminists within the religious community or the nation can be readily accused of inauthenticity, and feminists outside can be charged with intervening in other people's business.

Nevertheless, alliances and dialogue across national boundaries are vital. For instance, the Indian and Bangladeshi population programs have used family planning targets for state employees and incentives to achieve civilian compliance. Along with donor-controlled contraceptive methods (sterilization, intrauterine devices, or hormone implants and injections), such coercive methods have seriously compromised women's capacity to give informed consent to decisions about their fertility. Such cautionary tales could alert feminists in Pakistan, where family planning services are now being rapidly expanded. Parallels in women's experiences can also offer important insights. Dowry murders, marital violence, and son preferences, for instance, might be amenable to quite direct comparisons, particularly between Pakistan and northwestern India, or Bangladesh and West Bengal, or Sri Lanka and southern India.

Yet awareness of local specificities is also crucial. Feminists with differing experiences of the state—whether hostility and repression, or the co-opting of feminist agendas—might fruitfully learn from one another about the pitfalls and possibilities of engagement with the state. Comparing accounts of grassroots mobilization might also be instructive. Emphases and tactics successful in one place might entail high risk elsewhere. Sometimes, lobbying the central state to pass new legislation may be most constructive. Sometimes, empowering grassroots women may be more urgent so that legislation does not remain a dead letter.

As feminist activists in South Asia have already found, exchanging information about their diverse experiences can keep wider issues in view and help clarify which strategies might be successful and which counterproductive. Such dialogue does not imply unthinking aping of imported programs but learning from one another's mistakes as well as successes and collaborating in the search for ways forward.

Activism and Proactivism

The world does not stand still while feminists argue over strategic priorities. Of course there must be debate, but debate that allows reflexivity about the past to guide decisions for the future, not debate that dissipates energies and gives the opponents of women's rights a free hand. Certainly feminists must respond to the agendas of politicized religion, but is there room for more proactive feminist activism in South Asia?

The numerous examples of women's capacity for agency, whether activism or individual everyday resistance, perhaps provide some hope that women's energies might be channelled toward pressing for women's rights. Yet some women's energies have been deployed in ways that are deeply problematic (if not downright inimical) for women's rights, and many women have directly suffered from the effects of politicized religion. Feminists have learned many unpalatable lessons from the successes of politicized religious movements in pressurizing governments and mobilizing women.

In addition, important as local and regional contexts are, women's difficulties are generated in many sites besides the localities where they live. What is experienced locally and seems to be merely local may reflect much wider phenomena. Gendered processes operate everywhere, within households, in apparently gender-neutral macroeconomic policy and in income-generation schemes for women, in the state's inaction and action. In various and complex ways, all the countries of South Asia are linked into global processes, over which governments themselves may have little control. Thus, feminists in South Asia must also engage with the gender implications of the changing integration of national economies into the global economy; of structural adjustment programs and World Bank conditionalities on social sector spending; of liberalization policies and changing employment patterns that link some people directly into the global economy and encourage consumerism where many cannot afford to play the consumerism game; of foreign-financed development programs and the globalization of the media and communications technology.

In part, the localisms arising around the world are responses to such tendencies. Localisms often try to counter globalization with romanticized "authentic traditions" but following this fashion would give feminists little space for confronting gender biases in the local arena and wresting the initiative from politicized religion (whose local character is anyway in doubt). For instance, politicized religious organizations in South Asia have condemned the commodification of women's bodies—in terms with which some feminists might sympathize (Basu, this volume; Kapur, 1996), even though politicized religion normally sits very uneasily with feminist agendas.[16]

In sum, although women's experiences are locally specific, the magnitude of the processes confronting them and the fragmentation implied by "localisms" suggest that local (or even regional) feminist resistance could have only limited effect. Wherever they are, then, feminists cannot ignore the *global* dimensions of gender issues any more than their locally specific manifestations. Western feminisms, with their tendencies to universalism, are undoubtedly problematic. Yet, ironically, they may nevertheless be important allies for feminists in South Asia in critiquing and resisting the local effects of those Western governmental and business organizations from which so many globalizing processes emanate. In this, of course, South Asian feminists must guard against being parties to feminist agendas dominated by the parochial concerns of Western feminists.

The battle against gender injustices will not be easily won and will have to be fought at different levels and in different ways. Without constant vigilance, gains may be retrenched or apparent victories may turn out to be Pyrrhic. Individual women will undoubtedly need to struggle against their everyday situations. Yet, if women experience their oppressions at the local level and in locally specific ways, these experiences are by no means simply local in their origins and they cannot be effectively combated at the local level alone.

Notes

These thoughts have drawn upon discussions (formal and informal) at the Bellagio workshop and with the SSRC/ACLS Joint Committee on South Asia. Special thanks also go to Amrita Basu, Roger Jeffery, and the Edinburgh University Nationalism Study Group for numerous helpful comments. They must not be held responsible for the following discussion, of course.

1. Kapur and Cossman, 1995, discuss the discourses surrounding secularism and equality in India, and the entanglement of community membership and gender issues. See also Hasan (ed.), 1994; Jayawardena and de Alwis (eds.), 1996; Sarkar and Butalia (eds.), 1995.

2. The following is a selection of the now-considerable literature on such topics: Agarwal, 1994b; Basu, 1992; Calman, 1992; Gandhi and Shah, 1991; Gardezi, 1990; Jahan, 1995; Jayawardena, 1986; Kabeer, 1991; Kishwar and Vanita (eds.), 1984; R. Kumar, 1993, 1995; Liddle and Joshi, 1986; Mazumdar, 1992; Minault (ed.), 1980; Mumtaz and Shaheed, 1987; Omvedt, 1980, 1993; Palriwala and Agnihotri, 1996; Rose, 1992; I. Sen, 1990; Shaheed and Mumtaz, 1990; Shastri, 1993; Sobhan, 1994; Stree Shakti Sanghatana, 1987; Thapar, 1993.

3. Scott (1985) inspired much of the recent historical and anthropological literature on such topics. See also Appadorai et al. (eds.), 1991; Banerjee, 1989; Haynes and Prakash (eds.), 1991; Hossain, 1988; Jeffery, 1979; P. Jeffery and R. Jeffery, 1996a; Karlekar, 1991; McCarthy, 1993; Minault, 1994; O'Hanlon, 1991; Oldenberg, 1991; Raheja and Gold, 1994; Wadley, 1994; White, 1992.

4. The woman as victim of rape or as an image of the nation (as in Mother Earth) may be a powerful means of mobilizing *men* in the nation's defense.

5. Differences among women have been central in much recent feminist writing in the West. See Afshar and Maynard (eds.), 1994; Anthias and Yuval-Davis, 1992; hooks, 1981, 1984; Phillips, 1987; Ramzanoglu, 1989.

6. This has been addressed in several contexts, for instance, by Jackson (1993a, 1993b, 1995) and Nanda (1991) in relation to some ecofeminist writing (e.g., Shiva, 1988; Mies and Shiva, 1993).

7. Feminist publishing houses have sometimes adopted such images: Kali in India, and Virago (witch with uncontrolled sexuality or fearful powers) in Britain. My favorite was the Scottish feminist journal ironically entitled *Harpies and Quines*, from the Scots "harpy" (rapacious woman or a half bird–half woman monster), and "quine" (saucy woman of worthless character).

8. This is despite feminists' claims that they draw attention to existing gender divisions. Allegations that feminists *generate* division between men and women are also commonly leveled at women activists in "progressive" political movements. Note also that Metcalf emphasizes that spiritual equality between men and women is central to the Tablīghī position, but not economic and social sameness (Metcalf, 1994b, and this volume).

9. Quite different conclusions have been drawn on whether there are universal criteria for talking about women's rights. See, for example, Apfel-Marglin and Simon, 1994; Basu, 1995a; Bhasin and Khan, 1986; Brah, 1992; Çagatay, Grown, and Santiago, 1986; Kishwar, 1990; Marchand and Parpart (eds.), 1995; Mohanty, 1988; Mohanty, Russo, and Torres (eds.), 1991; Nicholson (ed.), 1990; Sen and Grown, 1987. Rather problematically, some writers stereotype Western feminism and Western feminist writing about Third World women, despite the diversity of Western feminisms.

10. Contrast this with "social uplift" organizations that impose ready-made—and often irrelevant and patronizing—agendas (e.g., Caplan, 1985). Many development agencies now appreciate that successful mobilization requires that people "own" the agendas around which they mobilize (Hobart (ed.), 1993).

11. See A. Sen (1990) on "cooperative conflicts" within the household, gendered entitlements, and women's problems in the event of marital breakdown.

12. Localisms or nativisms tend to deny or ignore inequalities and oppressions *within* the Third World while critiquing the oppressions—including the

discursive power of metanarratives—that emanate from the West (Kiely, 1995: chap. 7).

13. Parpart (1995), in a spirited defense of the "local," does not grapple with the problems created for locally acceptable development work by differences *within* the local. In addition to power differentials between development experts (whether foreign or national) and local women, class and other differences mean that local women's voices are not homogeneous. See P. Jeffery and R. Jeffery (1996a) for more on this.

14. This is not unique to South Asia; these issues have also been addressed in the West, China, and the erstwhile Soviet Bloc (for instance, Pateman, 1989; Showstack Sassoon (ed.), 1987). Similar dilemmas confront Western socialists, too (London Edinburgh Weekend Return Group, 1979).

15. Of course, Free Trade Zones and NGOs such as BRAC reflect Bangladesh's location in the global aid economy, in which population control is extremely significant and can adversely affect women (Hartmann and Standing, 1985; Hartmann, 1995).

16. The debate is complex. Some feminists would ban pornography but others object to censorship on grounds of freedom of speech. Yet others applaud literature celebrating female sensuality and argue that the boundaries between exploitative, male-centered pornography and celebratory representations of female sensuality would not be drawn to anyone's satisfaction, especially because censors would probably not have feminist agendas.

Bibliography

'Abdu'sh-Shakur Tirmizi, Sayyid. (1981) *Da'wat o tabligh ki shar'i haisiyyat* (The legal/moral situation of mission and invitation). Lahore: Idarah-yi Islamiyat.

Abul A'la Maududi, Saiyyid. (1972 [1939]) *Purdah and the Status of Woman in Islam.* Lahore: Islamic Publications.

Abu-Lughod, Lila. (1986) *Veiled Sentiments: Honor and Poetry in a Bedouin Society.* Berkeley: University of California Press.

Adams, C. (1987) *Across Seven Seas and Thirteen Rivers: Life Stories of Pioneer Sylheti Settlers in Britain.* London: Tower Hamlets Arts Project.

Afshar, Haleh, and Mary Maynard (eds.). (1994) *The Dynamics of "Race" and Gender: Some Feminist Interventions.* London: Taylor & Francis.

Agarwal, Bina. (1994a) *A Field of One's Own: Gender and Land Rights in South Asia.* Cambridge: Cambridge University Press.

———. (1994b) "Gender, Resistance and Land: Interlinked Struggles over Resources and Meanings in South Asia." *Journal of Peasant Studies* 22, 1: 81–125.

———. (1994c) "Positioning the Western Feminist Agenda: A Comment." *Indian Journal of Gender Studies* 1, 2: 249–56.

Agarwal, Purushottam. (1995) "Surat, Savarkar and Draupadi: Legitimising Rape as a Political Weapon." In Tanika Sarkar and Urvashi Butalia (eds.), *Women and the Hindu Right,* 29–57. London: Zed Books; New Delhi: Kali for Women.

Aggarwal, Partap C. (1971) *Caste, Religion and Power: An Indian Case Study.* New Delhi: Shri Ram Centre for Industrial Relations.

Agnes, Flavia. (1995) "Women's Movement Within a Secular Framework: Re-defining the Agenda." In Tanika Sarkar and Urvashi Butalia (eds.), *Women and the Hindu Right,* 136–57. London: Zed Books; New Delhi: Kali for Women.

Ahmed, Durre S. (1991) "Modernist Rationality, Religious Fundamentalism and the Struggle for Pakistan." Paper presented at Conference on the Eighth Five Year Plan, Islamabad.

Ahmed, Leila. (1992) *Women and Gender in Islam: Historical Roots of a Modern Debate.* New Haven and London: Yale University Press.

Ahmed, Rafiuddin (ed.). (1983) *Islam in Bangladesh: Society, Culture and Politics*. Dhaka: Bangladesh Itihas Samiti.

———. (ed.) (1990) *Religion, Nationalism and Politics in Bangladesh*. New Delhi: South Asian Publishers.

Akbar, M. A. (1988) *Riot After Riot: Reports on Caste and Communal Violence in India*. New Delhi: Penguin Books (India).

Akbarabadi, Maulana Said Ahmad. (1971) "Islam in India Today." In S. T. Lokhandwala (ed.), *India and Contemporary Islam: Proceedings of a Seminar*, 335–39. Simla: Indian Institute for Advanced Studies.

Akhtar, Rais, and Nilofer Izhar. (1986) "Spatial Distribution of Health Resources within Countries and Communities: Examples from India and Zambia." *Social Science and Medicine* 22, 11: 1115–29.

Alam, S. M. Shamsul. (1990) "The Military and the Crisis of Political Hegemony in Bangladesh." *South Asian Bulletin* 10, 2: 32–41.

———. (1993) "Islam, Ideology, and the State in Bangladesh." *Journal of Asian and African Studies* 28, 1–2: 88–106.

Altaf Husain Qasimi. (1968) *Safarnama-yi Haramain* (A travel account to the two holy places). Gorakhpur.

Alter, Joseph. (1994) "Celibacy, Sexuality and the Transformation of Gender into Nationalism in North India." *Journal of Asian Studies* 53, 1: 46–66.

Anderson, Benedict. (1991) *Imagined Communities*. London: Verso.

Anitha S., Manisha, Vasudha, and Kavitha. (1995) "Interviews with Women." In Tanika Sarkar and Urvashi Butalia (eds.), *Women and the Hindu Right*, 329–35. London: Zed Books; New Delhi: Kali for Woman.

Anthias, Floya, and Yuval-Davis Nira. (1989) *Women-Nation-State*. London: Macmillan.

———. (1992) *Racialized Boundaries: Race, Nation, Gender, Colour and Class and the Anti-Racist Struggle*. London: Routledge.

Apfel-Marglin, Frédérique, and Suzanne L. Simon. (1994) "Feminist Orientalism and Development." In Wendy Harcourt (ed.), *Feminist Perspectives on Sustainable Development*, 26–45. London: Zed Books.

Appadorai, Arjun, F. J. Korom, and M. A. Mills (eds.). (1991) *Gender, Genre and Power in South Asian Expressive Traditions*. Philadelphia: University of Pennsylvania Press.

Appleby, Scott, and Martin Marty (eds.). (1994) *Fundamentalists and the State*. Chicago: University of Chicago Press.

As'ad Gilani, Sayyid. (1982) *Tin aurteen, tin tahzibeen*. Lahore: Islami Akademi.

Asad, Talal. (1983) "Anthropological Conceptions of Religion: Reflections on Geertz." *Man* 18: 237–60.

———. (1993) *Genealogies of Religion: Discipline and Reasons of Power in Christianity and Islam*. Baltimore and London: Johns Hopkins University Press.

Ashworth, Georgina. (1993) *Changing the Discourse: A Guide to Women and Human Rights*. London: Change.

Aziz, K. K. (1993) *The Murder of History in Pakistan: A Critique of History Textbooks Used in Pakistan*. Lahore: Vanguard.

Bacchetta, Paola. (1993) "All Our Goddesses Are Armed: Religion, Resistance, and Revenge in the Life of a Militant Hindu Nationalist Woman." In Amrita Basu (ed.), *Women and Religious Nationalism in India*. Special issue, *Bulletin of Concerned Asian Scholars* 25, 4: 38–51.

———. (1994) "Communal Property/Sexual Property: On Representations of Muslim Women in a Hindu Nationalist Discourse." In Zoya Hasan (ed.), *Forging Identities: Gender, Communities and the State*, 188–255. New Delhi: Kali for Women.

———. (1996) "The Sangh, the Samiti and Differential Concepts of the Hindu Nation." In Kumari Jayawardena and Malathi de Alwis (eds.), *Embodied Violence: Communalising Women's Sexuality in South Asia*, 126–67. New Delhi: Kali for Women.

Badran, Margot. (1994) "Gender Activism: Feminists and Islamists in Egypt." In Valentine M. Moghadam (ed.), *Identity Politics and Women: Cultural Reassertions and Feminisms in International Perspective*, 202–28. Boulder: Westview Press.

———, and Miriam Cooke. (1990) *Opening the Gates: A Century of Arab Writings*. London: Virago.

Bagchi, Amiya Kumar. (1972) *Private Investment in India: 1900–1939*. Cambridge: Cambridge University Press.

Bagchi, Jasodhara. (1996) "Ethnicity and the Empowerment of Women." In Kumari Jayawardena and Malathi de Alwis (eds.), *Embodied Violence: Communalising Women's Sexuality in South Asia*, 113–25. New Delhi: Kali for Women.

Baird, Robert (ed.). (1993) *Religion and Law in Independent India*. Delhi: Manohar.

Baker, David. (1971) "The Rowlatt Satyagraha in the Central Provinces and Berar." In Ravindra Kumar (ed.), *Essays in Gandhian Politics: The Rowlatt Satyagraha of 1919*, 93–125. London: Oxford University Press.

Balakrishnan, Radhika. (1994) "The Social Context of Sex Selection and the Politics of Abortion in India." In Gita Sen and Rachel Snow (eds.), *Power and Decision: The Social Control of Reproduction*, 267–86. Boston: Harvard School of Public Health and Harvard University Press.

Balchin, Cassandra (ed.). (1996) *Women, Law and Society—An Action Manual for NGOs*. Lahore: Shirkat Gah and Women Living Under Muslim Laws.

Ballard, Roger. (1989) "Effects of Labour Migration from Pakistan." In Hamza Alavi and John Harriss (eds.), *Sociology of Developing Societies: South Asia*, 112–22. London: Macmillan Education.

———. (1990) "Migration and Kinship: The Differential Effect of Marriage Rules on the Processes of Punjabi Migration to Britain." In Colin Clarke, Ceri Peach, and Steven Vertovec (eds.), *South Asians Overseas*, 219–49. Cambridge: Cambridge University Press.

Bandopadhyaya, Sekhar. (1990) *Caste, Politics and the Raj in Bengal, 1872–1937.* Calcutta: K. P. Bagchi.

Banerjee, Ashish. (1990) "'Comparative Curfew': Changing Dimensions of Communal Politics in India." In Veena Das (ed.), *Mirrors of Violence: Communities, Riots and Survivors in South Asia,* 37–68. Delhi: Oxford University Press.

Banerjee, Sumanta. (1989) "Marginalization of Women's Popular Culture in Nineteenth Century Bengal." In Kumkum Sangari and Sudesh Vaid (eds.), *Recasting Women: Essays in Colonial History,* 127–79. New Delhi: Kali for Women.

Banerji, Debabar. (1972) "Health Behaviour of Rural Populations: Impact of Health Services." *Economic and Political Weekly* 8, 51: 2261–68.

Bardhan, Pranab. (1984) *The Political Economy of Development in India.* Oxford: Blackwell.

Barth, Fredrik (ed.). (1969) *Ethnic Groups and Boundaries.* Boston: Little, Brown.

Bastian, Sunil. (1990) "Political Economy of Ethnic Violence in Sri Lanka: The July 1983 Riots." In Veena Das (ed.), *Mirrors of Violence: Communities, Riots and Survivors in South Asia,* 286–320. Delhi: Oxford University Press.

Basu, Amrita. (1992) *Two Faces of Protest: Contrasting Modes of Women's Activism in India.* Berkeley: University of California Press.

———. (1995a) "Introduction" in Amrita Basu (ed.), *The Challenge of Local Feminisms: Women's Movements in Global Perspective,* 1–21. Boulder: Westview Press.

———. (1995b) "Feminism Inverted: The Real Women and Gendered Imagery of Hindu Nationalism." In Tanika Sarkar and Urvashi Butalia (eds.), *Women and the Hindu Right,* 158–80. London: Zed Books; New Delhi: Kali for Women.

———. (1995c) "When Local Riots Are Not Simply Local: Collective Violence and the State in Bijnor, India, 1988–93." *Theory and Society* 24: 35–78.

———. (1996) "Mass Movement or Elite Conspiracy: The Puzzle of Hindu Nationalism." In David Ludden (ed.), *Contesting the Nation: Religion, Community and the Politics of Democracy in India.* Philadelphia: University of Pennsylvania Press.

———. (forthcoming) "Communal Violence Engendered: Men as Victims, Women as Agents." In Julia Leslie (ed.), *Gender, Religion and Social Definition.* Delhi, Oxford University Press.

——— (ed.). (1993) *Women and Religious Nationalism in India.* Special Issue, *Bulletin of Concerned Asian Scholars* 25, 4, 3–52.

——— (ed.). (1995) *The Challenge of Local Feminisms: Women's Movements in Global Perspective.* Boulder: Westview Press.

Basu, Tapan, Pradip Datta, Sumit Sarkar, Tanika Sarkar, and Sambuddha Sen. (1993) *Khaki Shorts, Saffron Flags.* Delhi: Orient Longman.

Bhachu, Parminder. (1985) *Twice Migrants: East African Sikh Settlers in Britain.* London: Tavistock.

Bhaktal, Svati Shakravati. (1993) "Sisterhood and Strife." *Women's Review of Books*, 10–11 (July): 12–13.

Bhasin, Kamla, and Nighat Said Khan. (1986) *Some Questions on Feminism and Its Relevance in South Asia.* New Delhi: Kali for Women.

Bhasin, Kamla, Ritu Menon, and Nighat Said Khan (eds.). (1994) *Against All Odds: Essays on Women, Religion and Development from India and Pakistan.* New Delhi: Kali for Women.

Bilgrami, Akeel. (1993) "What Is a Muslim? Fundamental Commitment and Cultural Identity." In Gyanendra Pandey (ed.), *Hindus and Others: The Question of Identity in India Today*, 273–99. Delhi: Viking.

Billig, Michael. (1995) *Banal Nationalism.* London: Sage.

Blanchet, Thérèse. (1984) *Women, Pollution and Marginality: Meanings and Rituals of Birth in Bangladesh.* Dhaka: University Press.

Blee, Kathleen M. (1991) *Women of the Klan: Racism and Gender in the 1920s.* Berkeley: University of California Press.

Brah, Avtar. (1992) "Questions of Difference and International Feminism." In Jane Aaron and Sylvia Walby (eds.), *Out of the Margins.* London: Falmer.

Brass, Paul R. (1974) *Language, Religion and Politics in North India.* London: Cambridge University Press

———. (1979) "Elite Groups." In David Taylor and Malcolm Yapp (eds.), *Political Identity in South Asia*, 35–77. London and Dublin: Curzon Press.

Bridenthal, Renate, Atina Grossman, and Marion Kaplan. (1984) *When Biology Becomes Destiny.* New York: Monthly Review Press.

Bunch, Charlotte. (1994) *Women's Rights as Human Rights: Towards a Re-vision of Human Rights.* Colombo: Social Scientists' Association.

Çagatay, Nilüfer, Caren Grown, and Aida Santiago. (1986) "The Nairobi Women's Conference: Toward a Global Feminism?" *Feminist Studies* 12: 401–12.

Calman, Leslie. (1992) *Toward Empowerment: Women and Movement Politics in India.* Boulder: Westview Press.

Caplan, Lionel (ed.). (1987) *Studies in Religious Fundamentalism.* London: Macmillan.

Caplan, Patricia. (1985) *Class and Gender in India: Women and Their Organizations in a South Indian City.* London: Tavistock.

Chakravarti, Uma. (1989) "Whatever Happened to the Vedic Dasi? Orientalism, Nationalism and a Script for the Past." In Kumkum Sangari and Sudesh Vaid (eds.), *Recasting Women: Essays in Colonial History*, 27–87. New Delhi: Kali for Women.

———, Prem Choudhury, Pradip Dutta, Zoya Hasan, Kumkum Sangari, and Tanika Sarkar. (1992) "Khurja Riots, 1990–91: Understanding the Conjuncture." *Economic and Political Weekly* 27, 18: 951–65.

Chandra, Kanchan. (1994) Inside the Bharatiya Janata Party: Political Actors and Ideological Choices. Paper presented at the 46th Annual Meeting of the Association for Asian Studies, Boston, 26 March.

Chatterjee, Partha. (1989) "The Nationalist Resolution of the Women's Question." In Kumkum Sangari and Sudesh Vaid (eds.), *Recasting Women: Essays in Colonial History*, 233–53. New Delhi: Kali for Women.

———. (1994) "Secularism and Toleration." *Economic and Political Weekly* 29, 28: 1768–77.

Chhachhi, Amrita. (1989) "The State, Religious Fundamentalism and Women: Trends in South Asia." *Economic and Political Weekly* 24, 11: 567–78.

———. (1991) "Forced Identities: The State, Communalism, Fundamentalism and Women in India." In Deniz Kandiyoti (ed.), *Women, Islam and the State*, 144–75. London: Macmillan.

———. (1994) "Identity Politics, Secularism and Women: A South Asian Perspective." In Zoya Hasan (ed.), *Forging Identities: Gender, Communities and the State*, 74–95. New Delhi: Kali for Women.

Chowdhury, Benoy. (1967) "Agrarian Economy and Agrarian Relations in Bengal, 1859–1885." In N. K. Sinha (ed.), *The History of Bengal, 1757–1905*. Calcutta: Calcutta University Press.

Clark, Alice (ed.). (1993) *Gender and Political Economy: Explorations of South Asian Systems*. Delhi: Oxford University Press.

Cockburn, Cynthia. (1977) *The Local State*. London: Pluto Press.

Comaroff, Jean. (1985) *Body of Power, Spirit of Resistance*. Chicago: University of Chicago Press.

Coomaraswamy, Radhika. (1994) *Violence Against Women: Its Causes and Consequences*. Preliminary Report submitted by the UN Special Rapporteur in Accordance with Commission on Human Rights Resolution 1994/45. Special issue, *Thatched Patio* 7, 6: 1–116.

Das, Veena. (1990) "Introduction: Communities, Riots and Survivors." In Veena Das (ed.), *Mirrors of Violence: Communities, Riots and Survivors in South Asia*, 1–36. Delhi: Oxford University Press.

———. (1995) *Critical Events: An Anthropological Perspective on Contemporary India*. Delhi: Oxford University Press.

Datta, Pradip. (1993) "Dying Hindus: Production of Hindu Communal Common Sense in Early twentieth Century Bengal." *Economic and Political Weekly* 28, 25: 1305–19.

———. (1995) Hindu-Muslim Relations in Bengal in the Nineteen Twenties. Ph.D. diss., University of Delhi.

de Alwis, Malathi. (1994) "Towards a Feminist Historiography: Reading Gender in the Text of the Nation." In Radhika Coomaraswamy and Nira Wickramasinghe (eds.), *Introduction to Social Theory*, 86–107. Delhi: Konark.

Denton, Lynn Teskey. (1991) "Varieties of Hindu Female Asceticism." In Julia Leslie (ed.), *Roles and Rituals for Hindu Women*, 211–31. Rutherford, N.J.: Fairleigh Dickinson University Press.

Devi, Jyotirmoyee. (1995) *The River Churning*. New Delhi: Kali for Women.

Devji, Faisal Fatehali. (1991) "Gender and the Politics of Space: The Movement for Women's Reform in Muslim India, 1857–1900." *South Asia* 14, 1: 141–53.

Dhagamvar, Vasudha. (1993) "Women, Children and the Constitution: Hostages to Religion, Outcaste by Law." In Robert Baird (ed.), *Religion and Law in Independent India*. Delhi: Manohar.

Dube, Leela. (1983) "Misadventures in Amniocentesis." *Economic and Political Weekly* 18, 3: 279–80.

Dyson, Tim, and Mick Moore. (1983) "Kinship Structure, Female Autonomy and Demographic Behavior in India." *Population and Development Review* 9, 1: 35–60.

Eade, John. (1990) "Nationalism and the Quest for Authenticity: The Bangladeshis in Tower Hamlets." *New Community* 16, 4: 493–503.

Economist. (1995): 40.

Eickelman, Dale. (1982) "The Study of Islam in Local Contexts." *Contributions to Asian Studies* 12: 1–17.

———, and J. Piscatori. (1990) *Muslim Travellers: Pilgrimage, Migration, and Religious Imagination*. London: Routledge.

El Saadawi, N. (1980) *The Hidden Face of Eve: Women in the Arab World*. Translated by Sherif Hetata. London: Zed Press.

Engineer, Asghar Ali. (1991) "The Bloody Trail: Ramjanmabhoomi and Communal Violence in UP." *Economic and Political Weekly* 26, 4: 155–59.

———. (1992) *The Rights of Women in Islam*. New Delhi, Sterling.

——— (ed.). (1984) *Communal Riots in Post-Independence India*. Hyderabad: Sangam Books India.

——— (ed.). (1987) *The Shah Bano Controversy*. Hyderabad: Orient Longman.

Enloe, Cynthia. (1989) *Bananas, Beaches and Bases: Making Feminist Sense of International Politics*. Berkeley: University of California Press.

Far Eastern Economic Review, 25 September 1971.

Farouqui, Ather. (1994) "Urdu Education in India: Four Representative States." *Economic and Political Weekly* 29, 14: 782–85.

Faruqi, Ziya-ul Hasan. (1971) "The Tablighi Jama'at." In S. T. Lokhandwala (ed.), *India and Contemporary Islam: Proceedings of a Seminar*. Simla: Indian Institute for Advanced Studies.

Feldman, Shelley. (1992) Individualism Recast: Changing Relations Between the State and Labor in Rural Bangladesh. Paper presented at the Fourteenth Annual Middlebury College Conference on Economic Issues: Contributions to an Ongoing Agenda.

———. (1993) "Contradictions of Gender Inequality: Urban Class Formation in Contemporary Bangladesh." In Alice Clark (ed.), *Gender and Political Economy: Explorations of South Asian Systems*, 215–45. Delhi: Oxford University Press.

Feminist Review. (1993a) Thinking Through Ethnicities, 44.

———. (1993b) Nationalisms and National Identities, 45.

Forbes, Geraldine. (1996) *Women in Modern India.* The New Cambridge History of India, pt. 1, vol. 2. Cambridge: Cambridge University Press.

Fruzzetti, Lina. (1981) "Muslim Rituals: Household Rites versus Public Festivals in Rural India." In Imtiaz Ahmed (ed.), *Religion and Ritual Among Muslims in India,* 91–112. New Delhi: Manohar.

Gandhi, Nandita, and Nandita Shah. (1991) *The Issues at Stake: Theory and Practice in the Contemporary Women's Movement in India.* New Delhi: Kali for Women.

Gardezi, Fauzia. (1990) "Islam, Feminism, and the Women's Movement in Pakistan: 1981–1991." *South Asia Bulletin* 10, 2: 18–24

Gardner, Katy. (1992) "Migration and the Rural Context in Sylhet." *New Community* 18, 4: 579–90.

———. (1993) "Mullahs, Migrants, Miracles: Travel and Transformation in Rural Bangladesh." *Contributions to Indian Sociology* 27, 2: 213–35.

———. (1995) *Global Migrants, Local Lives: Travel and Transformation in Rural Bangladesh.* Oxford: Oxford University Press.

Geertz, Clifford. (1968) *Islam Observed: Religious Development in Morocco and Indonesia.* New Haven: Yale University Press.

Gladney, Dru. (1994) "Representing Nationality in China: Refiguring Majority-Minority Identities." *Journal of Asian Studies* 53, 1: 92–123.

Golwalkar, M. S. (1980) *Bunch of Thoughts.* Bangalore: Vikrama Prakashan.

Gombrich, Richard. (1971) "Food for Seven Grandmothers: Stages in the Universalization of a Sinhalese Ritual." *Man* 6, 1: 5–17.

———, and Gananath Obeyesekere. (1988) *Buddhism Transformed: Religious Change in Sri Lanka.* Princeton: Princeton University Press.

Government of Bangladesh. (1972) *Constitution of the People's Republic of Bangladesh.* Dhaka: Government of Bangladesh.

Guhathakurta, Meghna. (1994) "The Aid Discourse and the Politics of Gender." *Journal of Social Studies* 65: 101–14.

Gupta, Dipankar. (1991) "Communalism and Fundamentalism: Some Thoughts on the Nature of Ethnic Politics in India." *Economic and Political Weekly* 26, 11–12: 573–79.

Hale, Sondra. (1994) "Gender, Religious Identity and Political Mobilization in Sudan." In Valentine M. Moghadam (ed.), *Identity Politics and Women: Cultural Reassertions and Feminisms in International Perspective,* 145–66. Boulder: Westview Press.

Hall, Stuart. (1992) "The Question of Cultural Identity." In Stuart Hall, David Held, and Tony McGrew (eds.), *Modernity and Its Futures,* 273–325. Cambridge: Polity.

Haq, M. Anwarul. (1972) *The Faith Movement of Maulana Muhammad Ilyas.* London: George Allen & Unwin.

Hartmann, Betsy. (1995) *Reproductive Rights and Wrongs: The Global Politics of Population Control and Contraceptive Choice* (2nd ed.). New York: Harper & Row.

————, and Hilary Standing. (1985) *Food, Saris and Sterilization: Population Control in Bangladesh*. London: Bangladesh International Action Group.

Hartsock, Nancy. (1982) "Prologue to a Feminist Critique of War and Politics." In Judith Stiehm (ed.), *Women's Views of the Political World of Men*, 121–50. New York: Transnational.

Hasan, Mushirul. (1988) "Indian Muslims since Independence: In Search of Integration and Identity." *Third World Quarterly* 10, 4: 818–42.

————. (1996) "Minority Identity and its Discontents." In Praful Bidwai, Harbans Mukhia, and Achin Vanaik (eds.), *Religion, Religiosity and Communalism*, 167–204. Delhi: Manohar.

Hasan, Zoya. (1989) "Minority Identity, Muslim Women Bill Campaign and the Political Process." *Economic and Political Weekly* 24, 1: 44–50.

————. (1993) "Communalism, State Policy and the Question of Women's Rights in Contemporary India." In Amrita Basu (ed.), *Women and Religious Nationalism in India*. Special issue, *Bulletin of Concerned Asian Scholars* 25, 4: 5–15.

———— (ed.). (1994) *Forging Identities: Gender, Communities and the State*, New Delhi: Kali for Women.

Haynes, Douglas, and Gyan Prakash (eds.). (1991) *Contesting Power: Resistance and Everyday Social Relations in South Asia*. Delhi: Oxford University Press.

Hélie-Lucas, Marie-Aimée. (1994) "The Preferential Symbol for Islamic Identity: Women in Muslim Personal Laws." In Valentine M. Moghadam (ed.), *Identity Politics and Women: Cultural Reassertions and Feminisms in International Perspective*, 391–407. Boulder: Westview Press.

Hensman, Rohini. (1992) "Feminism and Ethnic Nationalism in Sri Lanka." *Journal of Gender Studies* 1, 4: 501–6.

Hobart, Mark (ed.). (1993) *An Anthropological Critique of Development: The Growth of Ignorance*. London: Routledge.

Hobsbawm, Eric, and Terence Ranger (eds.). (1983) *The Invention of Tradition*. Cambridge: Cambridge University Press.

Hoffman-Ladd, Valerie. (1987) "Polemics on the Modesty and Segregation of Women in Contemporary Egypt." *International Journal of Middle East Studies* 19: 23–50.

hooks, bell. (1981) *Ain't I a Woman: Black Women and Feminism*. Boston: South End Press.

————. (1984) *Feminist Theory: From Margin to Center*. Boston: South End Press.

Hoole, Rajan, Daya Somasunderam, K. Sritharan, and Rajani Thiranagama. (1990) *The Broken Palmyra: The Tamil Crisis in Sri Lanka—An Inside Account*. Claremont, Calif.: Sri Lanka Studies Institute.

Hossain, A. (1985) *Remittances from International Migration: A Case Study of Bangladesh*. Dhaka: Bangladesh Manpower Studies Centre.

Hossain, R. S. (1988) *"Sultana's Dream" and Selections from "The Secluded Ones."* Edited and translated by Roushan Jahan. New York: City University of New York, Feminist Press.

Houseman, Judy. (1982) "Mothering, the Unconscious and Feminism." *Radical America* 16: 47–62.

Human Rights Commission of Pakistan. (1994) *State of Human Rights in Pakistan 1993*. Lahore: Maktaba Jadeed Press.

Human Rights Watch/Asia. (1994) *Bangladesh: Violence and Discrimination in the Name of Religion*. New York: Human Rights Watch/Asia.

Huq, Maimuna. (1994) Old Boundaries, New Visions: Women's Islamic Activism in Bangladesh. Senior Fellowship Program thesis, Dartmouth College.

Huque, Ahmed S., and Muhammad Yeahia Akhter. (1987) "The Ubiquity of Islam: Religion and Society in Bangladesh." *Pacific Affairs* 60, 2: 200–25.

Imam, Jahanara. (1994) "From *Of Blood and Fire*" (Bengali diary, 1989). In Miriam Cooke and Roshini Rustomji-Kerns (eds.), *Blood into Ink: South Asian and Middle Eastern Women Write War*. Boulder: Westview Press.

Islam, Muinul, Hasanuzzaman Chowdhury, M. Salehuddin, Jyoti Prokesh Dutta, Muhammad Ali, and A. K. Enamul Hoque. (1987) *Overseas Migration from Bangladesh: A Micro-Study*. Chittagong: Chittagong University Press.

Jackson, Cecile. (1993a) "Women/Nature or Gender/History? A Critique of Ecofeminist 'Development.'" *Journal of Peasant Studies* 20: 389–419.

———. (1993b) "Doing What Comes Naturally? Women and the Environment Debate." *World Development* 21: 1947–63.

———. (1995) "Radical Environmental Myths: A Gender Perspective." *New Left Review* 210: 124–140.

Jahan, Rounaq. (1977) *Pakistan: Failure in National Integration*. New York: Columbia University Press.

Jahan, Roushan. (1995) "Men in Seclusion, Women in Public: Rokeya's Dream and Women's Struggles in Bangladesh." In Amrita Basu (ed.), *The Challenge of Local Feminisms: Women's Movements in Global Perspective*, 87–109. Boulder: Westview Press.

Jahangir, B. K. (1986) *Problematics of Nationalism in Bangladesh*. Dhaka: Centre for Social Studies.

Jalal, Ayesha. (1991) "The Convenience of Subservience: Women and the State in Pakistan." In Deniz Kandiyoti (ed.), *Women, Islam and the State*, 77–114. London: Macmillan.

James, S. M. (1994) "Challenging Patriarchal Privilege through the Development of International Human Rights." *Women's Studies International Forum* 17: 563–78.

Jayawardena, Kumari. (1986). *Feminism and Nationalism in the Third World*. London: Zed Books.

———, and Malathi de Alwis (eds.). (1996) *Embodied Violence: Communalising Women's Sexuality in South Asia*. New Delhi: Kali for Women.

Jeffery, Patricia. (1979) *Frogs in a Well: Indian Women in Purdah*. London: Zed Press.

———. (forthcoming) "Identifying Differences: Gender Politics and

Community in Rural Bijnor, UP." In Julia Leslie (ed.), *Gender, Religion and Social Definition.* Delhi: Oxford University Press.

Jeffery, Patricia, and Roger Jeffery. (1994a) "Killing My Heart's Desire: Education and Female Autonomy in Rural North India." In Nita Kumar (ed.), *Women as Subjects: South Asian Histories,* 125–171. Calcutta: Stree; Charlottesville: University of Virginia Press.

———. (1994b) Engendering Communalism: Everyday and Institutional Aspects of Gender and Community in Bijnor. Paper prepared for conference, Appropriating Gender: Women's Activism and the Politicization of Religion in South Asia, Bellagio Study and Conference Center, 30 August–1 September 1994.

———. (1996a) *Don't Marry Me to a Plowman: Women's Everyday Lives in Rural North India.* Boulder: Westview Press.

———. (1996b) "What's the Benefit of Being Educated? Girls' Schooling, Women's Autonomy and Fertility Outcomes in Bijnor." In Roger Jeffery and Alaka Basu (eds.), *Girls' Schooling, Women's Autonomy and Fertility Change in South Asia,* 150–83. New Delhi: Sage.

———, and Andrew Lyon. (1989) *Labour Pains and Labour Power: Women and Childbearing in India.* London: Zed Books.

Jeffery, Roger. (1988) *The Politics of Health in India.* Berkeley and London: University of California Press.

———, and Alaka Basu (eds.). (1996) *Girls' Schooling, Women's Autonomy and Fertility Change in South Asia.* New Delhi: Sage.

———, and Patricia Jeffery. (1993a) "Traditional Birth Attendants in Rural North India: The Social Organization of Childbearing." In Shirley Lindenbaum and Margaret Lock (eds.), *Knowledge Power and Practice: The Anthropology of Medicine and Everyday Life,* 7–31. Berkeley: University of California Press.

———. (1993b) "A Woman Belongs to Her Husband." In Alice Clark (ed.), *Gender and Political Economy: Explorations of South Asian Systems,* 66–114. Delhi: Oxford University Press.

———. (1994) "The Bijnor Riots, October 1990: Collapse of a Mythical Special Relationship?" *Economic and Political Weekly* 29, 10: 551–58.

———. (1997) *Population, Gender and Politics: Demographic Change in Rural North India.* Cambridge: Cambridge University Press.

Jehangir, Asma, and Hina Jilani. (1990) *The Hudood Ordinances: A Divine Sanction.* Lahore: Rhotas Books.

Jones, Kenneth. (1976) *Arya Dharm: Hindu Consciousness in nineteenth Century Punjab.* Berkeley: University of California Press.

Jordens, J. T. F. (1978) *Dayanand Saraswati: His Life and Ideas.* Delhi: Oxford University Press.

Joshi, Murali Manohar. (1995) "Western Feminism: Second among Equals?" *Asian Age* 8 (December).

Kabeer, Naila. (1991) "The Quest for National Identity: Women, Islam and the

State in Bangladesh." In Deniz Kandiyoti (ed.), *Women, Islam and the State*, 115–43. London: Macmillan.

Kamaluddin, S. (1988) "The Islamic Way." *Far Eastern Economic Review*, 23 June: 14–17.

———. (1989) "Pulpit Politics." *Far Eastern Economic Review*, 16 February: 30–31.

———. (1992) "People's Verdict." *Far Eastern Economic Review*, 15 April: 22–23.

Kandiyoti, Deniz. (1988) "Bargaining with Patriarchy." *Gender and Society* 2: 274–90.

———. (1989) "Women and Islam: What Are the Missing Terms?" *Dossier 5/6* (Grabels): 5–9.

———. (1991a) "Identity and Its Discontents: Women and the Nation." *Millennium, Journal of International Studies* 20, 3: 429–43.

———. (1991b) "Introduction" in Deniz Kandiyoti (ed.), *Women, Islam and the State*. London: Macmillan.

——— (ed.). (1991) *Women, Islam and the State*. London: Macmillan.

Kapur, Ratna. (1996) "Who Draws the Line: Feminist Reflections on Speech and Censorship." *Economic and Political Weekly*, 31, 14–15. Review of Women's Studies: WS 15–30.

———, and Brenda Cossman. (1995) "Communalising Gender/Engendering Community: Women, Legal Discourse and the Saffron Agenda." In Tanika Sarkar and Urvashi Butalia (eds.), *Women and the Hindu Right*, 82–120. London: Zed Books; New Delhi: Kali for Women.

———. (1996) *Subversive Sites: Feminist Engagements with Law in India*. New Delhi: Sage.

Karlekar, Malavika. (1991) *Voices from Within: Early Personal Narratives of Bengali Women*. Delhi: Oxford University Press.

Keddie, Nikki. (1997) *The New Religious Politics: Where, When and Why Do "Fundamentalisms" Appear?* Unpublished paper.

Kielmann, Arnfried, and associates. (1983) *Childhood and Maternal Health Services in Rural India: The Narangwal Experiment*. Baltimore: Johns Hopkins University Press.

Kiely, Ray. (1995) *Sociology and Development*. London: UCL Press.

King, Christopher. (1989) "Forging a New Linguistic Identity: The Hindi Movement in Banaras, 1868–1914." In Sandria B. Freitag (ed.), *Culture and Power in Banaras: Community, Performance and Environment, 1800–1980*, 179–203. Delhi: Oxford University Press.

Kishwar, Madhu. (1990) "A Horror of Isms." *Manushi* 61: 2–8.

———. (1991) "The Daughters of Aryavarta." In J. Krishnamurty (ed.), *Women in Colonial India: Essays on Survival, Work and the State*, 78–113. Delhi: Oxford University Press.

———. (1993) "Safety Is Indivisible: The Warning from Bombay Riots." *Manushi* 74–75: 2–8, 24–29, 33–49.

———. (1994) "Codified Hindu Law: Myth and Reality." *Economic and Political Weekly* 29, 33: 2145–61.

————, and Ruth Vanita (eds). (1984) *In Search of Answers: Indian Women's Voices from Manushi*. London: Zed Books.

Klatch, Rebecca E. (1987) *Women of the New Right*. Philadelphia: Temple University Press.

Kohli, Atul. (1987) *The State and Poverty in India*. Cambridge: Cambridge University Press.

Koonz, Claudia. (1987) *Mothers in the Fatherland*. New York: St. Martin's Press.

Kotalova, Jiri. (1993) *Belonging to Others: Cultural Constructions of Womanhood among Muslims in a Village in Bangladesh*. Uppsala Studies in Cultural Anthropology, no. 19. Sweden: Uppsala.

Kozlowski, Gregory. (1993) "Muslim Personal Law and Political Identity in Independent India." In Robert Baird (ed.), *Religion and Law in Independent India*. Delhi: Manohar.

Kristeva, Julia. (1993) *Nations Without Nationalism*. Translated by Leon S. Roudiez. New York: Columbia University Press.

Kumar, Krishan. (1995) *Post-industrial to Post-modern Society: New Theories of the Contemporary World*. Oxford: Blackwell.

Kumar, Radha. (1993) *The History of Doing: An Illustrated Account of Movements for Women's Rights and Feminism in India, 1800–1990*. New Delhi: Kali for Women.

————. (1994) "Identity Politics and the Contemporary Indian Feminist Movement." In Valentine M. Moghadam (ed.), *Identity Politics and Women: Cultural Reassertions and Feminisms in International Perspective*, 274–92. Boulder: Westview Press.

————. (1995) "From Chipko to Sati: The Contemporary Indian Women's Movement." In Amrita Basu (ed.), *The Challenge of Local Feminisms: Women's Movements in Global Perspective*, 58–86. Boulder: Westview Press.

Lâm, Maivan C. (1994) "Feeling Foreign in Feminism." *Signs* 19, 4: 865–93.

Lateef, Shahida. (1990) *Muslim Women in India—Political and Private Realities: 1890s–1980s*. New Delhi: Kali for Women.

Lelyveld, David S. (1978) *Aligarh's First Generation: Muslim Solidarity in British India*. Princeton: Princeton University Press.

Liddle, Joanna, and Rama Joshi. (1986) *Daughters of Independence: Gender, Caste and Class in India*. London: Zed Books.

Lloyd, Genevieve. (1986) "Selfhood, War and Masculinity." In Carole Pateman and Elizabeth Gross (eds.), *Feminist Challenges*, 63–76. Boston: Northeastern University Press.

Lokhandwala, S. T. (ed.) (1971) *India and Contemporary Islam: Proceedings of a Seminar*. Simla: Indian Institute of Advanced Studies.

London Edinburgh Weekend Return Group. (1979) *In and Against the State: Discussion Notes for Socialists*. London: London Edinburgh Weekend Return Group/Conference of Socialist Economists.

MacCormack, Carol, and Marilyn Strathern (eds.). (1980) *Nature, Culture and Gender*. Cambridge: Cambridge University Press.

Madan, Triloki N. (1987) "Secularism in Its Place." *Journal of Asian Studies* 46, 4: 747–59.

Mandelbaum, David. (1986) "Sex Roles and Gender Relations in North India." *Economic and Political Weekly* 21, 46: 1999–2004.

———. (1988) *Women's Seclusion and Men's Honor*. Tucson: University of Arizona Press.

Mani, Lata. (1989) "Contentious Traditions: The Debate on Sati in Colonial India." In Kumkum Sangari and Sudesh Vaid (eds.), *Recasting Women: Essays in Colonial History*. New Delhi: Kali for Women.

———. (1990) "Multiple Mediations: Feminist Scholarship in the Age of Multinational Reception." *Feminist Review* 35: 24–41.

Maniruzzaman, Talukdar. (1982) "The Future of Bangladesh." In A. Jeyaratnam Wilson and Dennis Dalton (eds.), *The States of South Asia: Problems of National Integration*, 265–94. Honolulu: University Press of Hawaii.

———. (1983) "Bangladesh Politics: Secular and Islamic Trends." In Rafiuddin Ahmed (ed.), *Islam in Bangladesh: Society, Culture and Politics*, 184–219. Dhaka: Bangladesh Itihas Samiti.

Mann, Elizabeth. (1994) "Education, Money and the Role of Women in Maintaining Minority Identity." In Zoya Hasan (ed.), *Forging Identities: Gender, Communities and the State*, 130–68. New Delhi: Kali for Women.

Mansfield, John. (1993) "The Personal Laws or Uniform Civil Code?" In Robert Baird (ed.), *Religion and Law in Independent India*. Delhi: Manohar.

Manto, Saddat Hasan. (1955) *Thanda Gosht*. Lahore: Maktab e she'r o Adab.

Marchand, Marianne H. (1995) "Latin American Women Speak on Development: Are We Listening Yet?" In Marianne H. Marchand and Jane Parpart (eds.), *Feminism, Postmodernism and Development*, 56–72. London: Routledge.

———, and Jane Parpart (eds.). (1995) *Feminism, Postmodernism and Development*. London: Routledge.

Mazumdar, Sucheta. (1992) "Women, Culture and Politics: Engendering the Hindu Nation." *South Asia Bulletin* 12, 2: 1–24.

———. (1995) "Women on the March: Right-wing Mobilization in Contemporary India." *Feminist Review* 49: 1–28.

McCarthy, Florence. (1993) "Development from Within: Forms of Resistance to Development Processes among Rural Bangladeshi Women." In Alice Clark (ed.), *Gender and Political Economy: Explorations of South Asian Systems*, 322–53. Delhi: Oxford University Press.

McGilvray, Dennis B. (1982) "Sexual Power and Fertility in Sri Lanka: Batticaloa Tamils and Moors." In Carol MacCormack (ed.), *Ethnography of Fertility and Birth*, 25–73. London: Academic Press.

Menon, Ritu, and Kamla Bhasin. (1993) "Recovery, Rupture, Resistance: Three Perspectives on the Recovery Operation in Post-Partition India." *Economic and Political Weekly*, 28, 17. Review of Women's Studies: WS 2–11.

———. (1996) "Abducted Women, the State and Questions of Honour: Three

Perspectives on the Recovery Operation in Post-Partition India." In Kumari Jayawardena and Malathi de Alwis (eds.), *Embodied Violence: Communalising Women's Sexuality in South Asia*, 1–31. New Delhi: Kali for Women.

Mernissi, Fatima. (1975a) *The Fundamentalist Obsession with Women*. Lahore: Simorgh.

———. (1975b) *Beyond the Veil: Male Female Dynamics in a Modern Muslim Society*. Cambridge, Mass.: Schenkman.

Metcalf, Barbara D. (1982) *Islamic Revival in British India: Deoband,1860–1900*. Princeton: Princeton University Press.

———. (1987) "Islamic Arguments in Contemporary Pakistan." In William R. Roff and Dale F. Eickelman (eds.), *Islam and the Political Economy of Meaning: Comparative Studies of Muslim Discourse*. London and Berkeley: University of California Press.

———. (1993) "Living Hadith in the Tablīghī Jama'at." *Journal of Asian Studies* 52, 3: 584–608.

———. (1994a) "'Remaking Ourselves': Islamic Self-Fashioning in a Global Movement of Spiritual Renewal." In Martin Marty and Scott Appleby (eds.), *Accounting for Fundamentalisms*. Chicago: University of Chicago Press.

———. (1994b) "Reading and Writing about Muslim Women in British India." In Zoya Hasan (ed.), *Forging Identities: Gender, Communities and the State*, 1–21. New Delhi: Kali for Women.

——— (ed. and trans.). (1990) *Perfecting Women: Maulana Ashraf 'Ali Thanawi's Bihishtı Zewar*. Berkeley: University of California Press.

Mies, Maria, and Vandana Shiva. (1993) *Ecofeminism*. London: Zed Books.

Miller, Daniel. (1995) "Introduction: Anthropology, Modernity and Consumption." In Daniel Miller (ed.), *Worlds Apart: Modernity through the Prism of the Local*, 1–22. London: Routledge.

Minault, Gail. (1986) *Voices of Silence*, Delhi: Chanakya.

———. (1993) The School for Wives: The Ideal Woman as Educated Muslim. Aziz Ahmad Lecture, Centre for South Asian Studies, University of Toronto.

———. (1994) "Other Voices, Other Rooms: The View from the Zenana." In Nita Kumar (ed.), *Women as Subjects: South Asian Histories*, 108–24. Calcutta: Stree; Chalottesville: University of Virginia Press.

——— (ed.). (1980) *The Extended Family: Women and Political Participation in India and Pakistan*. Delhi: Chanakya.

Moghadam, Valentine M. (1991) "Islamist Movements and Women's Responses in the Middle East." *Gender and History*. 3, 3: 268–86.

———. (1994) "Introduction: Women and Identity Politics in Theoretical and Comparative Perspective." In Valentine M. Moghadam (ed.), *Identity Politics and Women: Cultural Reassertions and Feminisms in International Perspective*, 3–26. Boulder: Westview Press.

——— (ed.). (1994a) *Identity Politics and Women: Cultural Reassertions and Feminisms in International Perspective*. Boulder: Westview Press.

———— (ed.). (1994b) *Gender and National Identity: Women and Politics in Muslim Societies.* London: Zed Books.

Mohanty, Chandra. (1988) "Under Western Eyes: Feminist Scholarship and Colonial Discourses." *Feminist Review* 30: 61–88.

————, Ann Russo, and Lourdes Torres (eds.). (1991) *Third World Women and the Politics of Feminism.* Bloomington: Indiana University Press.

Molyneux, Maxine. (1985) "Mobilization without Emancipation? Women's Interests, State and Revolution in Nicaragua." *Feminist Studies* 11: 227–54.

Moser, Caroline. (1993) *Gender Planning and Development: Theory, Practice and Training.* London: Routledge.

Muhammad 'Isa Firozpuri, Miyanji. (n. d.) *Tabligh ka maqami kam* (The local work of Tabligh). Delhi: Rabbani Buk Depo.

Muhammad Sani Hasani. (n. d.) *Sawanih-i Hazrat Maulana Muhammad Yusuf Kandhalawi* (The life of Hazrat Maulana Muhammad Yusuf Kandhalawi). Lucknow: Nadwatu'l-'ulama.

Muhammad Talib. (1990) Construction and Reconstruction of the World in Tablighi Ideology: Reflections on the Experiences of Selected Cases from Indian Society. Typescript.

Muhammad Zakariyya Kandhalawi, Maulana. (n. d.) *Teachings of Islam.* New Delhi: Ishaat-e-Islam. [English translation of Urdu *Faza'il-i A'mal* (The Merits of Action), issued in sections between 1928 and 1940, available in multiple editions, some of which are entitled *Tablighi Nisab* (The Tabligh Curriculum)].

Mukherjee, Nilmoni. (1975) *A Bengal Zamindar: Jayakrishna Mukherjee of Uttarpara and His Times, 1808–1888.* Calcutta: Firma K. L. Mukhopadhyay.

Mukhopadhyay, Carol C., and Susan Seymour (eds.). (1994) *Women, Education and Family Structure in India.* Boulder: Westview Press.

Mukhopadhyay, Maitrayee. (1994) "Between Community and State: The Question of Women's Rights and Personal Laws." In Zoya Hasan (ed.), *Forging Identities: Gender, Communities and the State*, 108–29. New Delhi: Kali for Women.

Mumtaz, Khawar. (1988) "Women in the Informal Sector in Pakistan: Productivity, Employment, and Potential for Change—Two Case Studies of Lahore." Islamabad: Development Research and Management Services.

————. (1991) "Khawateen Mahaz-e-Amal and the Sindhiani Tehrik: Two Responses to Political Development in Pakistan." *South Asia Bulletin* 11: 1–2: 101–9.

————. (1994) "Identity Politics and Women: 'Fundamentalism' and Women in Pakistan." In Valentine M. Moghadam (ed.), *Identity Politics and Women: Cultural Reassertions and Feminisms in International Perspective*, 228–42. Boulder: Westview Press.

————, and Farida Shaheed. (1987) *Women of Pakistan: Two Steps Forward, One Step Back?* London: Zed Books.

Nadwi, S. Abul Hasan Ali. (1983 [1948]) *Life and Mission of Maulana Mohammad Ilyas.* Lucknow: Academy of Islamic Research and Publications.

Nanda, Meera. (1991) "Is Modern Science a Western Patriarchal Myth? A Critique of Populist Orthodoxy." *South Asia Bulletin* 11, 1–2: 32–61.

Nandy, Ashish. (1983) *The Intimate Enemy: Loss and Recovery of Self Under Colonialism.* Delhi: Oxford University Press.

———. (1990) "The Politics of Secularism and the Recovery of Religious Tolerance." In Veena Das (ed.), *Mirrors of Violence: Communities, Riots and Survivors in South Asia*, 69–93. Delhi: Oxford University Press.

Narayana, G., and John F. Kantner. (1992) *Doing the Needful: The Dilemma of India's Population Policy.* Boulder: Westview Press.

Nasr, Seyyed Vali Reza. (1994) *The Vanguard of the Islamic Revolution: The Jama'at-i Islami of Pakistan.* Berkeley: University of California Press.

Nasrin, Taslima. (1993) *Lajja* (Shame). Translated Tutul Gupta. New Delhi: Penguin Books.

Nicholson, Linda J. (ed.). (1990) *Feminism/Postmodernism.* London: Routledge.

Obeyesekere, Gananath. (1984) *The Cult of the Goddess Pattini.* Chicago: University of Chicago Press.

O'Hanlon, Rosalind. (1985) *Caste, Conflict and Ideology: Mahatma Jotirao Phule and Low Caste Protest in Nineteenth Century Western India.* Cambridge: Cambridge University Press.

———. (1991) "Issues of Widowhood: Gender and Resistance in Colonial Western India." In Douglas Haynes and Gyan Prakash (eds.), *Contesting Power: Resistance and Everyday Social Relations in South Asia*, 62–108. Delhi: Oxford University Press.

Oldenberg, Veena. (1991) "Lifestyle as Resistance: The Case of the Courtesans of Lucknow." In Douglas Haynes and Gyan Prakash (eds.), *Contesting Power: Resistance and Everyday Social Relations in South Asia*, 23–61. Delhi: Oxford University Press.

Omvedt, Gail. (1980) *We Will Smash This Prison: Indian Women in Struggle.* London: Zed Press.

———. (1993) *Reinventing Revolution: New Social Movements and the Socialist Tradition in India.* Armonk, NY, and London: M. E. Sharpe.

———. (1994) *Dalits and the Democratic Revolution.* New Delhi: Sage.

Osmany, Shireen H. (1992) *Bangladesh Nationalism: History of Dialectics and Dimensions.* Dhaka: University Press.

Owens, Roger. (1985) *Migrant Workers in the Gulf.* Minority Rights Group Report No. 68. London: Minority Rights Group.

Pakistan Institute of Labour Education and Research and Shirkat Gah. (1993) Female Participation in the Formal Labour Force. Unpublished report of study.

Palriwala, Rajni, and Indu Agnihotri. (1996) "Tradition, the Family, and the State: Politics of the Contemporary Women's Movement." In T. V. Sathyamurthy (ed.), *Region, Religion, Caste, Gender and Culture in Contemporary India*, 503–32. Delhi: Oxford University Press.

Pandey, Gyanendra. (1990) *The Construction of Communalism in Colonial North India.* Delhi: Oxford University Press.

———. (1991) "In Defence of the Fragment: Writing about Hindu-Muslim Riots in India Today." *Economic and Political Weekly* 26, 11–12: 559–72.

——— (ed.). (1993) *Hindus and Others: The Question of Identity in India Today.* Delhi: Viking.

Papanek, Hanna. (1973) "Purdah: Separate Worlds and Symbolic Shelter." *Comparative Studies in Society and History* 15: 289–325.

———. (1979) "Family Status Production: The 'Work' and 'Non-work' of Women." *Signs* 4, 4: 775–81.

———. (1994) "The Ideal Woman and the Ideal Society: Control and Autonomy in the Construction of Identity." In Valentine M. Moghadam (ed.), *Identity Politics and Women: Cultural Reassertions and Feminisms in International Perspective,* 42–75. Boulder: Westview Press.

Parashar, Archana. (1992) *Women and Family Law Reform in India: Uniform Civil Code and Gender Equality.* New Delhi: Sage.

Parker, Andrew, M. Russo, D. Sommer, and P. Yaeger (eds.). (1992) *Nationalisms and Sexualities.* London: Routledge.

Parpart, Jane L. (1995) "Deconstructing the Development 'Expert': Gender, Development and the 'Vulnerable Groups.' " In Marianne H. Marchand and Jane Parpart (eds.), *Feminism, Postmodernism and Development,* 221–43. London: Routledge.

Patel, Vibhuti. (1994). "Women and Structural Adjustment in India." *Social Scientist,* 22, 3–4: 1–12.

Pateman, Carol. (1989) *The Disorder of Women.* Cambridge: Polity Press.

Pathak, Zakia, and Rajeshwari Sunder Rajan. (1989) "Shahbano." *Signs* 14, 3: 558–82.

Peach, Ceri. (1990) "Estimating the Growth of the Bangladeshi Population of Great Britain." *New Community* 16, 4: 481–91.

Phillips, Anne. (1987) *Divided Loyalties: Dilemmas of Sex and Class.* London: Virago.

Poddar, Hanuman Prasad. (1992) *Nari Siksha.* Gorakhpur: Gita Press.

Qadeer, Imrana, and Zoya Hasan. (1987) "Deadly Politics of the State and Its Apologists." *Economic and Political Weekly* 22, 46: 1946–49.

Qurashi, M. M. (1989) "The Tabligh Movement: Some Observations." *Islamic Studies* 28, 3: 237–48.

Raheja, Gloria G., and Ann Gold. (1994) *Listen to the Heron's Words: Reimagining Gender and Kinship in North India.* Berkeley: University of California Press.

Rajan, Rajeshwar S. (1993) *Real and Imagined Women: Gender, Culture and Postcolonialism.* London: Routledge.

Ramanamma, Asha, and Bhambawala, Usha. (1980) "The Mania for Sons." *Social Science and Medicine* 14B: 107–10.

Ramsukhdas, Swami. (1992a) *How to Lead a Householder's Life.* Gorakhpur: Gita Press.

———. (1992b) *Disgrace of Mother's Prowess,* Gorakhpur: Gita Press.

Ramzanoglu, Caroline. (1989) *Feminism and the Contradictions of Oppression*. London: Routledge.

Rashid, Abbas. (1985) "Pakistan: The Ideological Dimension." In Mohammad Asghar Khan (ed.), *Islam, Politics and the State: The Pakistan Experience*, 69–94. London: Zed Books.

————. (1994) "Pakistan: The Politics of 'Fundamentalism.'" In Kumar Rupesinghe and Khawar Mumtaz (eds.), *International Conflicts in South Asia*, 55–80. London: Sage.

————, and Farida Shaheed. (1993a) Ethnic and Sectarian Violence in Pakistan. Paper presented at the seminar Violence in Society, Goethe Institute, Karachi.

————. (1993b) Pakistan: Ethno-politics and Contending Elites. Prepared as part of the U.N.R.I.S.D. Project on Ethnic Conflict and Development.

Rashiduzzaman, M. (1994) "The Liberals and the Religious Right in Bangladesh." *Asian Survey* 34, 11: 974–90.

Ray, Raka. (1988) "The Contested Terrain of Reproduction: Class and Gender in Schooling in India." *British Journal of Sociology of Education* 9, 4: 387–401.

Razack, Sherene. (1991) *Canadian Feminism and the Law: The Women's Legal Education and Action Fund and the Pursuit of Equality*. Toronto: Second Story Press.

————. (1994) "What Is to Be Gained by Looking People in the Eye? Culture, Race and Gender in Cases of Sexual Violence." *Signs* 19, 4: 894–921.

Rex, John. (1986) *Race and Ethnicity*. Milton Keynes: Open University Press.

Rose, Kalima. (1992) *Where Women Are Leaders: The SEWA Movement in India*. New Delhi: Vistaar Publications; London: Zed Books.

Rouse, Shahnaz. (1986) "Women's Movement in Pakistan: State Class and Gender." *South Asia Bulletin* 5, 1: 30–37.

————. (1988) Agrarian Transformation in a Punjabi Village: Structural Change and Its Consequences. Ph.D. diss., University of Wisconsin, Madison.

————. (1993) "Discourse on Gender in Pakistan: Convergence and Contradiction." In Douglas Allen (ed.), *Religion and Political Conflict in South Asia*, 87–112. Delhi: Oxford University Press; Westport: Greenwood Press.

Roy, Asim. (1982) "The *pī mār* Tradition: A Case Study in Islamic Syncretism in Traditional Bengal." In F. Clothey (ed.), *Images of Man: Religious and Historical Processes in South Asia*, 112–41. Madras: New Era.

————. (1983) *The Islamic Syncretic Tradition in Bengal*. Princeton: Princeton University Press.

Rushdie, Salman. (1991) *Imaginary Homelands*. London: Granta Books.

Saberwal, Satish, and Mushirul Hasan. (1984) "Moradabad Riots 1980: Causes and Meanings." *Economic and Political Weekly* 19, 3: 208–27.

Said, Edward W. (1978) *Orientalism: Western Conceptions of the Orient*. New York: Pantheon.

————. (1993) *Culture and Imperialism*. London: Chatto & Windus.

Saigol, Rubina. (1994) "Boundaries of Consciousness: The Interface Between the Curriculum, Gender and Nationalism." In Nighat Said Khan, Rubina Saigol, and Afiya Shehrbano Zia (eds.), *Locating the Self: Perspectives on Women and Multiple Identities*, 41–76. Lahore: ASR.

Sangari, Kumkum. (1996) "Consent, Agency and the Rhetorics of Incitement." In T. V. Sathyamurthy (ed.), *Region, Religion, Caste, Gender and Culture in Contemporary India*, 463–502. Delhi: Oxford University Press.

———, and Sudesh Vaid. (1996) "Institutions, Beliefs and Ideologies: Widow Immolation in Contemporary Rajasthan." In Kumari Jayawardena and Malathi de Alwis (eds.), *Embodied Violence: Communalising Women's Sexuality in South Asia*, 240–96. New Delhi: Kali for Women.

——— (eds.). (1989) *Recasting Women: Essays in Colonial History*. New Delhi: Kali for Women.

Sarkar, Sumit. (1989) *Modern India, 1885–1947*. London: Macmillan.

———. (1993) "The Fascism of the Sangh Parivar." *Economic and Political Weekly* 28, 5: 163–67.

Sarkar, Tanika. (1991) "The Woman as Communal Subject: Rashtrasevika Samiti and Ram Janmabhoomi Movement." *Economic and Political Weekly* 26, 35: 2057–65.

———. (1992) "The Hindu Wife and the Hindu Nation: Domesticity and Nationalism in nineteenth Century Bengal." *Studies in History* 8, 2: 213–37.

———. (1993) "Rhetoric Against the Age of Consent: Resisting Colonial Reason and the Death of a Child Wife." *Economic and Political Weekly* 28, 36: 1869–78.

———. (1995) "Heroic Women, Mother Goddesses: Family and Organisation in Hindutva Politics." In Tanika Sarkar and Urvashi Butalia (eds.), *Women and the Hindu Right*, 181–215. London: Zed Books; New Delhi: Kali for Women.

———. (1996) "Educating the Children of the Hindu Rashtra." In Praful Bidwai, Harbans Mukhia, and Achin Vanaik (eds.), *Religion, Religiosity and Communalism*, 237–48. Delhi: Manohar.

———, and Urvashi Butalia (eds.). (1995) *Women and the Hindu Right*. London: Zed Books; New Delhi: Kali for Women.

Sathyamurthy, T. V. (ed.). (1996) *Region, Religion, Caste, Gender and Culture in Contemporary India*. Delhi: Oxford University Press.

Schirmer, Jennifer G. (1989) "Those Who Die for Life Cannot Be Called Dead: Women and Human Rights Protest in Latin America." *Feminist Review* 32: 3–29.

———. (1993) "The Seeking of Truth and the Gendering of Consciousness: The CoMadres of El Salvador and the CONAVIGUA Widows of Guatemala." In Sarah Radcliffe and Sally Westwood (eds.), *VIVA: Women and Popular Protest in Latin America*, 30–64. London and New York: Routledge.

Scott, James. (1985) *Weapons of the Weak: Everyday Forms of Peasant Resistance*. New Haven: Yale University Press.

Segal, Lynne. (1987) *Is the Future Female? Troubled Thoughts on Contemporary Feminism*. London: Virago.

Sen, Amartya. (1990) "Gender and Co-operative Conflicts." In Irene Tinker

(ed.), *Persistent Inequalities: Women and World Development*, 123–49. New York: Oxford University Press.

Sen, Gita, and Caren Grown. (1987) *Development, Crises and Alternative Visions.* London: Earthscan, for Development Alternatives with Women for a New Era (DAWN).

Sen, Ilina. (1990) *A Space within the Struggle: Women's Participation in People's Movements.* New Delhi: Kali for Women.

Sen, Rangalal. (1986) *Political Elites in Bangladesh.* Dhaka: University Press.

Shah, Kalpana, Smita Shah, and Neha Shah. (1993) "The Nightmare of Surat." *Manushi* 74–75: 50–58.

Shaheed, Farida. (1990) "The Pathan-Muhajir Conflicts, 1985–6: A National Perspective." In Veena Das (ed.), *Mirrors of Violence: Communities, Riots and Survivors in South Asia*, 194–214. Delhi: Oxford University Press.

———. (1994) "Controlled or Autonomous: Identity and the Experience of the Network of Women Living under Muslim Laws." *Signs*, 19, 4: 997–1019.

———, and Khawar Mumtaz. (1990) "The Rise of the Religious Right and its Impact on Women." *South Asia Bulletin* 10, 2: 9–17.

———. (1992) "Islamization and Women: The Experience of Pakistan." *Special Bulletin on Fundamentalism and Secularism in South Asia.* Lahore: Shirkat Gah and Women Living Under Muslim Laws.

Sharma, Ursula. (1978) "Segregation and its Consequences in India." In Pat Caplan and Janet Bujra (eds.), *Women United, Women Divided.* London: Tavistock.

———. (1980) *Women, Work and Property in North West India.* London: Tavistock.

———. (1986) *Women's Work, Class and the Urban Household.* London: Tavistock.

Shastri, Amita. (1993) "Women in Development and Politics: The Changing Situation in Sri Lanka." In Alice Clark (ed.), *Gender and Political Economy: Explorations of South Asian Systems*, 246–72. Delhi: Oxford University Press.

Shirkat Gah and Women Living Under Muslim Laws. (1994) *Handbook on Family Laws in Pakistan.* Lahore: Shirkat Gah and Women Living Under Muslim Laws.

———. (1995a) *Handbook on Customary Practices.* Lahore: Shirkat Gah.

———. (1995b) *Women's Laws, Initiatives in the Muslim World.* Lahore: Shirkat Gah and Women Living Under Muslim Laws.

Shiva, Vandana. (1988) *Staying Alive: Women, Ecology and Development.* London: Zed Books.

Showstack Sassoon, Anne (ed.). (1987) *Women and the State: The Shifting Boundaries of Public and Private.* London: Hutchison.

Sobhan, Rehman. (1980) "Growth and Contradictions within the Bangladesh Bourgeoisie." *Journal of Social Studies* 9: 1–27.

———, and Muzaffer Ahmed. (1981) *Public Enterprise in an Intermediate*

Regime: A Study in the Political Economy of Bangladesh. Dacca: Bangladesh Institute of Development Studies.

Sobhan, S. (1994) "National Identity, Fundamentalism and the Women's Movement in Bangladesh." In Valentine M. Moghadam (ed.), *Gender and National Identity: Women and Politics in Muslim Societies,* 63–80. London: Zed Books.

Som, Reba. (1994) "Jawaharlal Nehru and the Hindu Code: A Victory of Symbol over Substance?" *Modern Asian Studies* 28, 1: 165–94.

Spencer, Jonathan. (1990) "Collective Violence and Everyday Practice in Sri Lanka." *Modern Asian Studies* 24, 3: 603–23.

———. (1992) "Problems in the Analysis of Communal Violence." *Contributions to Indian Sociology,* n.s., 26, 2: 261–79.

Stree Shakti Sanghatana. (1987) *We Were Making History: Life Stories of Women in Telangana People's Struggle.* New Delhi: Kali for Women.

Tax, Meredith. (1993) "Taslima Nasrin: A Background Paper." *Bulletin of Concerned Asian Scholars* 25, 4: 72–74.

Thapar, Suruchi. (1993) "Women as Activists, Women as Symbols: A Study of the Indian Nationalist Movement." *Feminist Review* 44: 81–96.

Thompson, Catharine S. (1985) "The Power to Pollute and the Power to Preserve: Perceptions of Female Power in a Hindu Village." *Social Science and Medicine* 26: 701–11.

Toprak, Binnaz. (1994) "Women and Fundamentalism: The Case of Turkey." In Valentine M. Moghadam (ed.), *Identity Politics and Women: Cultural Reassertions and Feminisms in International Perspective,* 293–306. Boulder: Westview Press.

Troll, Christian W. (1985) "Five Letters of Maulana Ilyas (1885–1944), the Founder of the Tablighi Jama'at, Translated, Annotated, and Introduced." In Christian W. Troll, *Islam in India: Studies and Commentaries,* vol. two: *Religion and Religious Education,* 136–76. Delhi: Vikas.

United Nations. (1979) *Convention on the Elimination of Discrimination against Women.*

———. (1993) *Declaration on the Elimination of Violence against Women (Vienna Declaration).*

USAID. (1991) *Democracy and Governance.* Washington, D.C.: USAID Directorate for Policy.

van der Veer, Peter. (1993) "The Foreign Hand: Orientalist Discourse in Sociology and Communalism." In Carol A. Breckenridge and Peter van der Veer (eds.), *Orientalism and the Postcolonial Predicament,* 23–44. Philadelphia: University of Pennsylvania Press.

Vanaik, Achin. (1990) *The Painful Transition: Bourgeois Democracy in India.* London: Verso Books.

Visaria, Leela. (1985) "Infant Mortality in India: Levels, Trends and Determinants." *Economic and Political Weekly* 20, 34: 1352–59; 35: 1399–1405; 36: 1447–50.

Visram, R. (1986) *Ayahs, Lascars and Princes: The Story of Indians in Britain, 1700–1947.* London: Pluto Press.

Wadley, Susan. (1977) "Women and the Hindu Tradition." *Signs* 3, 1: 113–25.

———. (1994) *Struggling with Destiny in Karimpur, 1925–1984.* Berkeley: University of California Press.

Waheeduzzafar. (1971) "Muslim Socio-Religious Movements." In S. T. Lokhandwala (ed.), *India and Contemporary Islam: Proceedings of a Seminar,* 138–42. Simla: Indian Institute for Advanced Studies.

Wahiduddin Khan. (1986) *Tabligh Movement.* New Delhi: Maktaba Al-Risala.

Weiss, Anita. (1992) *Walls within Walls: Life Histories of Working Women in the Old City of Lahore.* Boulder, San Francisco, and Oxford: Westview Press.

White, Sarah. (1992) *Arguing with the Crocodile: Gender and Class in Bangladesh.* London: Zed Books.

Willis, Paul. (1977) *Learning to Labour.* Westmead: Saxon House.

Working Group on Women's Rights. (1996) "Reversing the Option: Civil Codes and Personal Laws." *Economic and Political Weekly* 31, 20: 1180–83.

World Bank. (1994a) *Governance: The World Bank's Experience.* Washington, D.C.: World Bank.

———. (1994b) *The World Bank and Participation: Report of the Learning Group on Participatory Development.* Washington, D.C.: Operations Policy Department, World Bank.

Zartman, I. William. (1992) "Democracy and Islam: The Cultural Dialectic." *Annals* 525: 181–91.

Zia, Afiya Sherbano. (1994) *Sex Crime in the Islamic Context: Rape, Class and Gender in Pakistan.* Lahore: ASR.

Zia, Shahla. (1994) Some Experiences of the Women's Movement—Strategies for Success. Working paper, The Women and Law Country Project, Pakistan.

Contributors

Amrita Basu is Professor of Political Science and Women's and Gender Studies at Amherst College. She is author of *Two Faces of Protest: Contrasting Modes of Women's Activism in India* (1992); editor of *The Challenge of Local Feminisms: Women's Movements in Global Perspective* (1995); and co-editor of *Community Conflicts and the State in India* (forthcoming, 1997). She has written extensively on Hindu nationalism in contemporary India.

Malathi de Alwis is a doctoral candidate in the Department of Anthropology at the University of Chicago. She is co-editor of *Embodied Violence: Communalising Women's Sexuality in South Asia* (1996).

Shelley Feldman is Associate Professor of Development Sociology and Director of the South Asia Program at Cornell University. She is co-editor of *Unequal Burden: Economic Crises, Persistent Poverty, and Women's Work* (1982) and of numerous articles on fundamentalist practices, non-governmental organizations, and informal economic networks in Bangladesh. One of her current research projects examines the partition of Bengal and another explores patterns of rural industrialization in Bangladesh.

Katy Gardner is a lecturer in social anthropology at the University of Sussex. Her publications include *Global Migrants, Local Lives: Travel and Transformation in Rural Bangladesh* (1995); *Anthropology, Development and the Post-Modern Challenge* (1996) and *Songs at the River's Edge: Stories from a Bangladeshi Village* (1997). She has recently completed fieldwork among Bengali elders in London.

Zoya Hasan is a Professor of Political Science at the Jawaharlal Nehru University in New Delhi. She is the author of *Dominance and Mobilization: Rural Politics in Uttar Pradesh* (1989); *Quest for Power: Oppositional Movements* and *Post-Congress Politics in Uttar Pradesh* (forthcoming); editor of *Forging Identities: Gender, Community and the State* (1994); and co-editor of *The State, Political Processes and Identity: Reflections on Modern India* (1989).

Patricia Jeffery is Professor of Sociology at the University of Edinburgh. She has conducted fieldwork among women at a Muslim shrine in Delhi (1975–76) and among Hindu and Muslim families in Bijnor District, U.P. (1982–83; 1985; 1990–91). Her publications include *Frogs in a Well: Indian Women in Purdah* (1979); (with Roger Jeffery) *Labour Pains and Labour Power: Women and Childbearing in Rural North India* (1989), and *Don't Marry Me to a Plowman* (1996).

Roger Jeffery is Professor of Sociology of South Asia at the University of Edinburgh. He has studied medical policy-making in India (1975–76) and conducted social demographic research in Bijnor district, UP (1982–83 and 1990–91). He is the author of *The Politics of Health in India* (1988); (with Patricia Jeffery) *Population, Gender and Politics* (1997); and co-editor of *Girls' Schooling, Women's Autonomy and Fertility Change in South Asia* (1996).

Barbara D. Metcalf is Professor of History and Dean of the Division of Social Sciences, College of Letters and Sciences, University of California, Davis. She is the author of Islamic Revival in British India: Deoband, 1860–1900 (1982); translator and commentator on *Perfecting Women: Maulana Ashraf 'Ali Thanawi's Bihishti Zewar* (1990); and editor and contributor to two books: *Moral Conduct and Authority: The Place of Adab in South Asian Islam* (1984) and *Making Muslim Space in North America and Europe* (1996).

Ritu Menon is co-founder of Kali for Women, Asia's first feminist press. She is co-editor of *Against All Odds: Essays on Women, Religion and Development from India and Pakistan* (1994) and co-author of *Witness to Freedom: How Women Experienced the Partition of India* (forthcoming).

Shahnaz Rouse is a member of the Sociology Faculty at Sarah Lawrence College in New York. She has written on class and gender Lawrence College in New York. She has written on class and gender in the context of social movements, agrarian transformation, and religious politics, and is presently engaged in a comparative study of Gender and Nationalism in pre-revolutionary Egypt and pre-independence India.

Tanika Sarkar teaches History at Saint Stephen's College, University of Delhi. She is the author of *Bengal, 1928–1934: The Politics of Protest* (1987), co-author of *Khaki Shorts and Saffron Flags: A Critique of the Hindu Right*, and co-editor of *Women and the Hindu Right*. She has published extensively on nationalist, peasant, tribal and working class politics in colonial India, gender issues in nineteenth century Bengal, and movements of the Hindu Right in contemporary India.

Farida Shaheed, a Sociologist by training, is senior coordinator of Shirkat Gah Women's Resource Centre (Lahore and Karachi), a rounding member of Women's Action Forum, and the Asia Coordinator of Women Living Under Muslim Laws. Her publications include the co-authored *Two Steps Forward, One Step Back? Women of Pakistan* (1987) and several articles on women and Islam.

Index

KING ALFRED'S COLLEGE
LIBRARY